THE ADVENTUROUS LIFE
OF A VERSATILE ARTIST

H O U D I N I

The Book of Houdini

By Harry Houdini & Nevetz Azraz

Published By Galgalim Press

THE ADVENTUROUS LIFE OF A VERSATILE ARTIST HOUDINI

THE ADVENTUROUS LIFE OF A VERSATILE ARTIST

HOUDINI

THE WORLD FAMOUS SELF-LIBERATOR

HOUDINI,

Presenting the Greatest Performance of his Strenuous Career, liberating himself after being Locked in a

WATER TORTURE CELL

(Houdini's own Invention) whilst Standing on his Head, his Ankles Clamped and Locked above in the centre of the Massive Cover.

A FEAT WHICH BORDERS ON THE SUPERNATURAL

$1,000

HOUDINI offers this sum to any one proving that it is possible to obtain air in the upside-down position in which he releases himself from this

Water Filled Torture Cell.

Six Million of these Books in circulation since 1900, in various Forms, Editions and Languages.

HOUDINI
THE ADVENTUROUS LIFE OF A VERSATILE ARTIST.

(Revised 2017).

HARRY HOUDINI, "the World's Handcuff King and amazing Prison Breaker," a title universally and unanimously bestowed upon him, has had a career as adventurous and romantic as the most imaginative writer could possibly conjure.

Indeed, this wonderful genius, with a science concerning bolts, bars, locks, and chains that will yet revolutionize the world's methods of safeguarding itself against "the men that prowl in the night," confirms the truth of the ancient adage that "truth is stranger than fiction."

Just remember for a moment that he is the man to whom the shrewdest police, the sharpest detectives, and the most watchful jail wardens look with awe and anxiety.

And they are eminently right in this attitude of disquiet, because they know that buried in the brain of Houdini lies the secret of an unknown power he alone possesses that makes their prisons as powerless as Japanese screens, and renders their multiple-locking handcuffs, leg irons, and all the other prison paraphernalia, no more binding than store twine.

Suppose the innate and inherent integrity of character that Houdini possesses, in common with most men brought up within the circle of a mother's sweet influence, were to be swept aside by the desire for riches not his own. There are many men of many millions to-day whose money is not their own. Suppose he should be captured by a band of desperate men determined to wrest from Houdini this secret worth millions. Suppose a great hypnotist were to obtain dominance over this mystery-enveloped genius and use his baneful powers for evil designs. What then?

A slight knowledge of the marvels Houdini has accomplished mixed with a little imagination would create as many more suppositions of this kind as this book could contain.

But, to be brief, admitting the possibility of the happening of any of these suppositious instances, and you will gain a clear idea of the extraordinary character and quality of Houdini's powers. It is often the best way to see the full scope of a cause by carefully ascertaining its effect. This analytical method is equally applicable to Houdini, and recognizing the harm he would receive were his secrets confided to unworthy hands, you gain an adequately impressive idea of the enormity of responsibility that rests upon him.

Time and time again Houdini has encountered such perils, and in every case he owes his life and the preservation of his secret to his extraordinary acuteness of perception, to his marvelous knowledge of human nature, to his physical prowess that is far greater than appears from a merely superficial inspection, and, last and greatest of all, to the fact that the majority of people witnessing his wonders attribute a quasi supernatural power.

His press clipping books teems with stories proving the truth of one and all of these assertions. To glance over its pages enchains the reader's attention more closely that if he were absorbing an exciting romance. Accounts of thrilling jail-breaking feats are pasted beside stirring chronicling of handcuff escapes. Columns upon columns of laudatory press criticisms crowd colored cartoons and caricatures that connect Houdini and the great men of Europe in the great political crisis of the last few years.

It being true "that genius is but the capacity for hard work," then it is only a proper introductory tribute to Houdini to state that he is not a mushroomgrowth, sprouting and decaying in a night.

In the development and perfection of his astounding powers over metallic components Houdini has labored as tirelessly as Galileo constructing his astronomical theory, as Stephenson building the first locomotive, as Edison bringing to view the telephone, as Marconi revealing the wireless telegraph.

"How does he do it?" is the universal query.

Of course, he does not, he dare not tell what exertions of power, natural or supernatural, he makes in freeing himself from handcuffs, and in escaping from the dungeons that have held felons until the grave finally hid them forever.

Guesses are multiplied many, many times by all sorts and conditions of men and women. As many theories have been propounded as there are stars in the firmament. Some say he slips out of handcuffs like an eel slipping through an amateur fisherman's fingers. Others say he manipulates cell locks by muscular magnetism. A third class declares that he squeezes himself through bars of cells. Still more say spirits aid him in his escapes. And so, ad infitum.

Suffice it is to say that Houdini actually does all that the newspapers credit him doing.

He was born March 24th, 1874, in Budapest, Hungary, and a little calculation will show that he is still far from the meridian of life. From the beginning, he showed an insight into mechanics and mechanism that may be compared with the early endeavors of other men who have wrought wonders in the name of science. He showed a tendency toward travel, too, and in his ninth year had a brief experience with Jack Hoefler's "five cent" circus in his home town. Then came an apprenticeship as a mechanic, and after an uneventful term with "the tools of trade" Houdini resolved to see the great world with his own eager eyes. So he ran away from home, as so many others have done that in later years attributed their greatness to their early contact with the corrugated side of life. He joined a small circus, and, being exceptionally bright, he soon learned to conduct the Punch and Judy show, to do a ventriloquial act, and also to play clown on the bars. It may be, too, that "he doubled in brass" or played in the band, though he has never said so.

Here began the experiences that quickly ripened Houdini into the World's Handcuff King and Prison Breaker, which he is, has been and always will be. In exploring his wits for exploits to amuse and entertain the audiences, Houdini hit upon the feat of escaping from ropes tied round him in every conceivable way. He became so expert that he eventually offered a challenge of $25 to any one who could tie him so that he could not escape. And he never has lost a cent of the proffered money.

Then came the full turning-point in his career when he looked for greater worlds to conquer, and began the mastery of handcuffs, leg irons, shackles, etc. Of course, proficiency came with practice in secret, and then the public was permitted to witness the efforts of the young wizard.

Houdini went to England without an engagement. He went to Mr. Slater, manager of the Alhambra, London, gave several trial shows, got a contract for two weeks, then one for six months at £60 a week.

1877   3½ YEARS OF AGE   8 YEARS OF AGE

AGE 15

15 YEARS OF AGE   19 YEARS OF AGE

HOUDINI AT DIFFERENT AGES OF HIS CAREER

Since then he has been a top-of-the-bill star everywhere. He has made enormous salaries on the continent, where he is tremendously popular. He has broken records for paid admissions all over Continental Europe. In the week he performed before the Grand Duke of Russia he earned in public and private performances over £400, an enormous salary in those days.

In 1905, he returned to America for a brief tour, and he became at once the sensation in every city. Jails have fallen before his power like cities in the olden time before the armies of Caesar. The police of America join the gendarmerie of Europe in declaring, "Nothing on earth can hold him a prisoner." All the strongest cells and prisons in the United States have succumbed to the mysteriously potent force he exerts. Perhaps his most historic feat was his escape in January, 1906, from Cell 2, Condemned Murderers' Row, in the United States Jail at Washington, D. C., the very cell in which Guiteau, the assassin of President Garfield was confined until he was led forth to be hanged. Another great work was his escape from double confinements in the Boston Tombs at Boston, Mass. March 20, 1906.

Since 1908 Houdini has dropped handcuffs, and has made his performance replete with new mysteries, introducing his original invention—escaping out of an air-tight galvanized iron can filled with water, after it has been locked into an iron -bound chest, and the intricate inexplicable escape from the Water Torture Cell, and releasing himself from a regulation strait jacket in full view of the audience, and during the week accepting various challenges.

Any reader of this who wishes to challenge Houdini, or has any novel method of securing Houdini, must write to publicly advertise address and name of Challenger or Challengers. No Challenge can be accepted for same date on which it is sent.

-

Instead of remaining in America six months as his original contract stipulated, he was the sensation of show business from his opening 1905, until his departure for Germany, August 1908.

NEW YORK
THE GREAT WHITE WAY

His leap from the Frederichstrasse Bridge, in Berlin, Germany, heavily manacled, September 5th, 1908; his daring plunge into the Weser, Bremen, having to break through ice, Paris, from the roof of the gruesome Morgue, April 7th, 1909, brought record houses at the Circus Busch, Berlin, and Alhambra Theatre, Paris, causing his imitators to try and duplicate his feats. Two were fortunately saved from a watery grave, Alburtus, in Atlantic City, being saved by the life-saving guard, Menkis was brought up in an unconscious state, and Ricardo jumped handcuffed from the Luippold Bridge, Landshut, Bavaria, April 14th, 1909, and was drowned.

Cold waters have no terrors for Houdini, as he dived manacled into the Mersey River, Liverpool, December 7th, 1908, also in the Egbaston Reservoir, Birmingham, December 15th, 1908. In all dives, Houdini makes use of the regulation police handcuffs, chains, and leg irons.

Houdini returned to America again in 1914, just before the World War, toured the country, appearing for two seasons at the World's biggest Theatre, the New York Hippodrome, the first season presenting his inventions, The Vanishing Elephant, in which he caused an elephant named "Jennie" to vanish, who weighed over ten thousand pounds, and said to be a daughter of the beloved Barnum's "Jumbo," and in the second half of the Hippodrome show, performing the Submarine Box feat, escaping from same whilst under water, and the box being entirely filled with water.

Second season, introducing the Escape from Strait Jacket, suspended sixty feet in mid-air, hanging by his ankles, and presenting for the first time on any stage another of his inventions, The Whirlwind of Colors, in which he produced hundreds of yards of silks, giant flags, and for a finish the only tame American Eagle of this decade. It is known that Old Abe was a tame eagle, used by the Union soldiers as a mascot, but this Young Abe, trained by Houdini is the only one known that any one could handle.

Houdini gave his services to the Government, giving performances in the camps, for two consecutive years, not accepting engagements, and is proud of the fact of having sold over two million dollars worth of liberty bonds.

The years of 1918, 1920 and 1921 he became a Cinema star, recognizing the fact that Dame Nature would demand her due, and that the future generations would not believe that any man could perform the feats with which he is credited. So, he originally went into a company to produce a 15 episode serial, "The Master Mystery," making such a sensational success that Mr. Jesse L. Lasky engaged him for a feature picture, "The Grim Game," and before this was released, Mr. Lasky re-engaged Houdini for a second picture, "Terror Island." Both features were the sensations of the year.

To fulfill contracts made eight years before, Houdini, in January, 1920, returned to England for a tour of the principal music halls. So great was his success that even his former triumphs were eclipsed. Throngs followed him whenever he appeared on the streets of the provincial towns of Great Britain. He broke house record after house record, drawing such box office returns that the Moss Empires management waived its right to hold him to the figure named in the eight-year-old contract and voluntarily doubled his salary.

Upon his return to America Houdini organized his own film producing company of which more will be told in subsequent pages.

OFFICIAL POLICE NEWS FROM GERMANY!
HARRY HOUDINI, THE AMERICAN HANDCUFF KING, SUES THE COLOGNE POLICE FOR LIBEL, AND WINS!!!

A Condensed History of the Lawsuit Against the Cologne Police!

The police of Germany are very strict in matters of false billing or misrepresenting exhibitions to the public, and the case of the well-known Dr. Slade, also a well-known American "thaumaturgic" performer, as also an equally familiar "magnetic" woman, and several others who have clashed with the German police will probably also call in mind the latest case of the flower medium, Mrs. Rothe, who was sentenced to two years in prison and 500 marks fine.

What for? Well, she deceived the public in telling them that she could obtain communications from the spirit world.

This the police claim was obtaining money under false pretense, and there you are.

The Cologne police claimed that Houdini was also traveling about misrepresenting, and that all he did was "swindle." The chief one was Schutzmann Werner Graff, who openly published a false story in the *Rheinische Zeitung*, which put Houdini in a very bad light, and, as a man of honor, Houdini could not overlook the insult.

He claimed that he had been slandered, and asked an apology, also a retraction of the false stories, which all the press of Germany had copied; but was simply laughed at for his trouble.

Engaging the best lawyer of Cologne, Herr Rechtsantwalt Dr. Schreiber, Louisenstrasse 17, this able lawyer defended Houdini in all three instances.

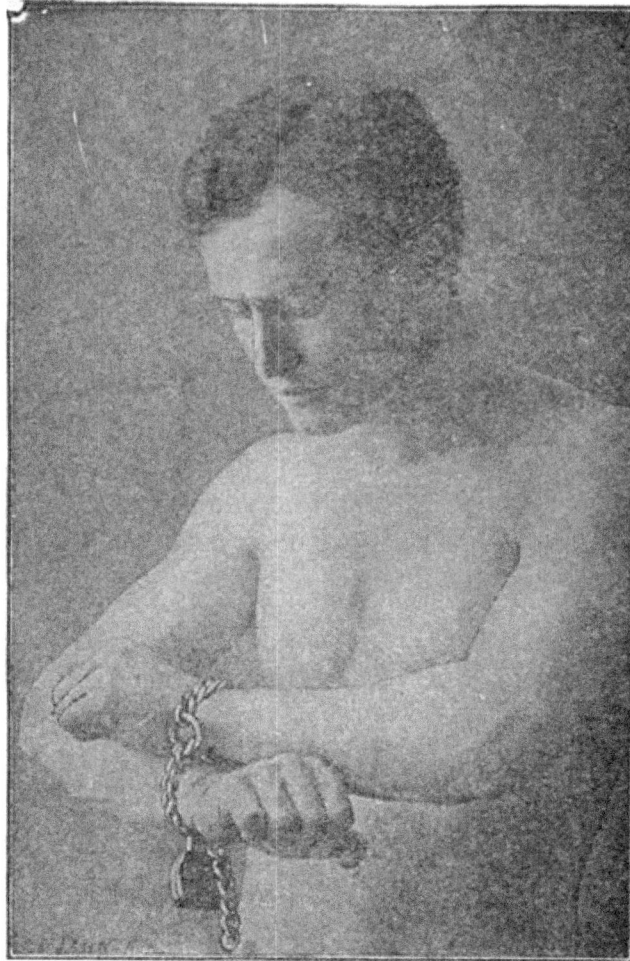

Houdini, as Chained and Handcuffed Before the Judges in the First Trial of His Action Against the Royal Police of Cologne.

The first trial occurred in Cologne, Feb. 19, 1902; in this trial Houdini charged the Schutzman Werner Graff for publicly slandering him, whereupon, as answer, Herr Graff told the judge and jury that he was willing to prove that Houdini was misrepresenting, that he could chain Houdini so that he could not release himself. Houdini permitted himself to be chained by Herr Transport Police Lott, and to show how easy it was he wilfully showed to the judge and jury how he opened the chain and lock.

After a four days' trial, Houdini won the lawsuit, and the Cologne police were fined, and were to publicly apologize to Houdini, "In the Name of the Kaiser."

Instead of so doing, they took it to the higher court, "Strafkammer." At this trial they had specially manufactured a lock, which was made by Master Mechanic Kroch, a lock that when once locked nothing would open it; even the key could not open the lock.

The police asked that Houdini should show his ability by opening this lock after it had once been locked.

-

The following is a translation of what the press had to say at the second trial.

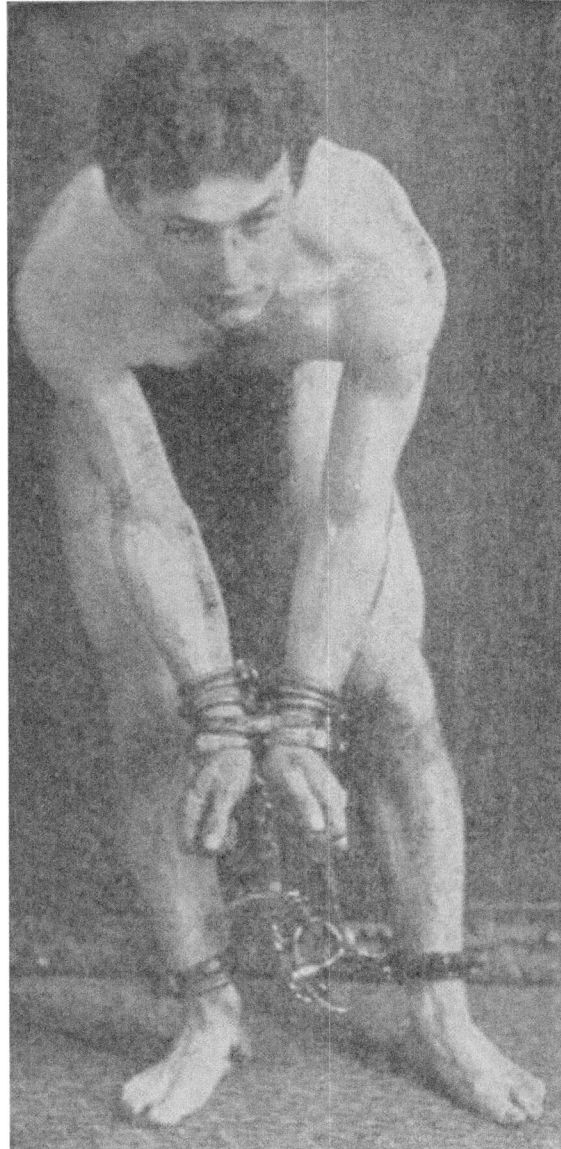

Houdini as Handcuffed and Manacled by the San Francisco Police, July, 1899.

In the highest court (Strafkammer zu Köln Yuli 26, 1902) Police Officer Werner Graff was found guilty of slandering Harry Houdini, heavily fined, he must pay all costs, and insert an advertisement in all of the Cologne newspapers, proclaiming his punishment, at the same time, "IN THE NAME OF THE KING," openly apologize to Houdini for insulting him.

This open apology is the severest punishment that can be given to a royal official, and as the lawsuit has been running over a year, the costs will run into the *thousands of marks*.

The case was first tried in the Schöffengericht Köln, Feb. 19, 1902, and Werner Graff was found guilty, but he took it to the highest court, and again Houdini won.

The Cologne police claimed that all Houdini advertised to do was misrepresentation (this was the cause of the lawsuit); for the trial they had a *special lock made that, after it was once locked, no key would open it.*

This lock they challenged Houdini to open, to prove that he was not misrepresenting.

Houdini accepts the challenge, walks into the room selected by the jury where he could work unhindered. In four minutes, with a quiet smile, reenters the court room, and hands the judges the prepared lock opened.

Among the thirty police officials that testified against Houdini were some of the highest officials of Cologne, but Houdini won; in fact, he was "one" too many for them.

Houdini as Handcuffed and Manacled by the Dresden (Germany) Police, September, 1900.

Houdini as Handcuffed, Elbow-ironed, and Thumbscrewed by the Berlin Police, October, 1900.

It being a disgrace for Schutzman Werner Graff to have this punishment on him, with the assistance of the police, he took it to the highest court in Germany, "Oberlandesgericht," and there the learned judges again gave Houdini the verdict from which there is no appeal.

Below is a free translation of the apology as printed in the German papers:

IN THE NAME OF THE KING

BE it known that the artiste, known as HARRY HOUDINI, of America, New York City, against the Cologne Police Schutzman Werner Graff, for slandering (insulting).

The Demonstration Before the German Judiciary.

[Text in illustration: The Imperial Police of Cologne slanderously libeled HARRY HOUDINI, stating his advertised tricks were swindles!

HOUDINI answered them by sueing for "An Honorary Public Apology". The Police lost the Case in the three highest Courts, as they were unable to fetter or Chain HOUDINI in an unescapeable manner. He was even successful in opening a special lock that they had constructed which after it had once been locked could not be opened!

First Trial "Königliches Schöffengericht" in Köln. Feb. 26 1902

Second Trial "Königliche Strafkammer" in Köln. July 26 1902

Third Trial "Königliches Oberlandesgericht". Sept. 26, 1902

Having lost the case in all three trials the Police were ultimately compelled to publicly advertise "An Honorary Apology" and pay all costs of the trials.

By command of Kaiser WILHELM II. Emperor of Germany.

The Royal Schöffengericht, the third "Ferienstrafkammer," found Werner Graff guilty of slandering Houdini, and the Oberlandesgericht Court also find that the Royal Schöffengericht was justified in finding Graff guilty of the charges. Werner Graff is guilty of "Openly Slandering" Houdini, for being the chief instigator of the article which he caused to be inserted in the *Rheinische Zeitung* July 25, 1901, number of edition 170, and the headlines which read "Houdini, the world-famous Handcuff Releaser." Being found guilty of the above charge, Werner Graff is fined 30 marks in money, and should he fail to pay the sum fine, he will serve a day in prison for every 5 marks; and is also fined to pay all costs of the three trials.

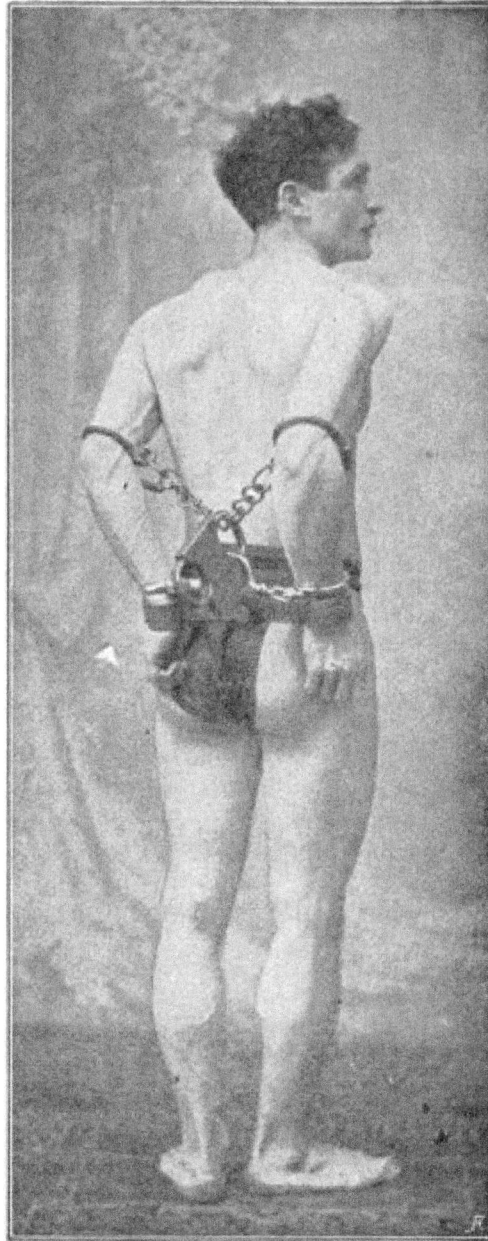

Houdini, as Handcuffed by the Vienna Police, March, 1902.

Houdini has the right to publish the verdict one time in the Cologne newspapers at the cost of Schutzman Werner Graff.

For the rightful writing of this verdict, we sign as responsibilities, Coln, Oct. 24, 1902. Stock Sekretar.

Gerichtsschreiber des Kgl. Amtsgericht Abtlg VI.—9.

Signed for Houdini,

Rechtsanwalt Dr. Schreiber Köln.

-

It will be of interest to note that Houdini has escaped out of prisons and cells in the following cities:

New York, W. 125th Street Police Station, W. 68th Street Police Station, and W. 37th Street; Brooklyn, N. Y.; Newark, N. J.; Salem, Mass.; Lowell, Mass.; Rochester, N. Y.; Baltimore; Washington (3 different places); Detroit, Mich.; Philadelphia, Pa.; Providence, R. I.; Kansas City; Buffalo, N. Y.; and Chicago, Ill.; Amsterdam, Hague; Dordrecht, Holland; Moscow, Russia; Halifax; Bradford; Leicester; Burnley; Leeds; Newcastle-upon-Tyne; Sheffield; Liverpool; South Shields; Salford; Huddersfield; Manchester; St. Helens; Stockton-on-Tees; Eastbourne; Newport, Mon.

Space prohibits the publication of all certificates from the various chiefs of police, but a few are selected, which follow:

Chief Constable's Office,

Sheffield, Jan. 19, 1904.

This is to certify that Mr. Harry Houdini was this day stripped stark naked and locked in the cell which once contained Charles Peace. The cell was searched and triple-locked, but Mr. Houdini released himself and redressed in five minutes, having also opened the iron gate of the corridor.

Charles J. Scott, Commander (R.N.)

Chief Constable, Sheffield.

Witness to the foregoing feat,

George H. Barker, Deputy Chief Constable.

An exceedingly rare photograph of Charles Peace, shrewdest, most dangerous and notorious criminal in the annals of Crime in Great Britain. Peace broke jail a number of times but failed to escape from this cell in Sheffield. He was hanged at the Armley jail. Houdini escaped from this cell, as Chief Constable Scott's certificate shows.

May 10, 1903.

Harry Houdini was made to disrobe, and in a nude condition was locked into the Moscow transportation cell or carette, and in less than 20 minutes he had managed to make his escape. The searching Houdini had to submit to in the hands of the secret Russian police was the severest he has ever had to undergo. Never in the history of the Russian police has any one been able to escape out of this or any other transportation carette. This feat was accomplished in the presence of Chief of the Secret Police Cos, Lebadeff.

Houdini was booked for one month in Moscow, but after this feat he was prolonged for four months, and proved the greatest sensation that ever visited Russia.

-

From the German police Houdini possesses certificates from the cities of Berlin, Dresden, Dusseldorf, Essen Ruhr, Barmen, Bremen, Dortmund, Leipzig, Frankfort A/M, Hanover, etc.; but the following is the principal one:

ROYAL POLICE PRESIDIUM,

BERLIN, Sept. 20, 1900.

Harry Houdini, the American, was handcuffed and leg-ironed with the irons used here, in the presence of a large number of the highest police officials of Germany. Houdini managed to free himself from everything, by mysteriously opening the locks, in a manner which is unexplainable to us. The cuffs were uninjured.

(Signed) VON HULLESSEM, Royal Police Director, Berlin.

VON WINDHEIM, The Royal Police President, Berlin.

-

Von Windheim was the highest police official in all Germany. The Kaiser's signature was the only name that stood higher in Germany.

The Preparation for Incarceration in the Siberian Transport Carette.

[Text in illustration: Chief of the Secret Russian Police LEBEDOEFF has HARRY HOUDINI stripped stark naked and searched then locked up in the Siberian Transport Cell or Carette, May 10/1903 in Moscow and in 28 minutes HOUDINI had made his escape to the unspeakable astonishment of the Russian Police.]

The Daily Illustrated Mirror, March 18th, 1904.

HOW HE PICKED THE "MIRROR" HANDCUFFS IN ONE HOUR AND TEN MINUTES.

Not a seat was vacant in the mighty Hippodrome, yesterday afternoon, when Harry Houdini, the "Handcuff King," stepped into the arena, and received an ovation worthy of a monarch.

For days past all London has been aware that on Saturday night last a representative of the *Mirror* had stepped into the arena, in response to Houdini's challenge to anybody to come forward and successfully manacle him, and had there and then made a match with America's Mysteriarch for Thursday afternoon.

In his travels the journalist had encountered a Birmingham blacksmith who had spent five years of his life in devising a lock, which, he alleged, "no mortal man could pick." Promptly seeing he was in touch with a good thing, the press man had at once put an offer upon the handcuff containing this lock, and brought it back to London with him.

It was submitted to London's best locksmiths, who were unanimous in their admiration of it, asserting that in all their experience they had never before seen such wonderful mechanism.

As a result, the editors of the *Mirror* determined to put the lock to the severest test possible by challenging Mr. Houdini to be manacled with the cuffs.

Like a true sportsman, Mr. Houdini accepted our challenge in the spirit in which it was given, although, on his own confession, he did not like the look of the lock.

MIGHTY AUDIENCE.

Mr. Houdini's call was for three o'clock yesterday, but so intense was the excitement that the 4,000 spectators present could scarcely restrain their impatience whilst the six excellent turns which preceded him, cheered to the echo on other occasions, got through their "business."

Waiting quietly and unnoticed by the arena steps, the *Mirror* representative watched Mr. Houdini's entrance, and joined in giving his opponent-to-be in the lists one of the finest ovations mortal man has ever received.

"I am ready," said Houdini, concluding his address to the audience, "to be manacled by the *Mirror* representative, if he be present."

A hearty burst of applause greeted the journalist as he stepped into the arena and shook hands with the "Handcuff King."

Then, in the fewest possible words, the press man called for volunteers from the audience to act upon a committee to see fair play, and Mr. Houdini asked his friends also to step into the arena and watch his interests.

HOUDINI HANDCUFFED.

This done, the journalist placed the handcuffs on Mr. Houdini's wrists and snapped them. Then, with an effort, he turned the key six times, thus securing the bolt as firmly as possible.

The committee being satisfied as to the security of the handcuff, Mr. Houdini said:—

"*Ladies and Gentlemen:*—I am now locked up in a handcuff that has taken a British mechanic five years to make. I do not know whether I am going to get out of it or not, but I can assure you I am going to do my best."

Applauded to the echo, the Mysteriarch then retired within the cabinet that contains so many of his secrets.

All correct chronometers chronicled 3.15.

In a long line in front of the stage stood the committee. Before them, in the center of the arena, stood the little cabinet Houdini loves to call his "ghost house." Restlessly pacing to and fro, the *Mirror* representative kept an anxious eye on it.

FALSE HOPE OVERTHROWN.

Those who have never stood in the position of a challenger can scarcely realize the sense of responsibility felt by one who has openly thrown down the gauntlet to a man who is popular with the public.

The *Mirror* had placed its reliance on the work of a British mechanic, and if Houdini succeeded in escaping in the first few minutes, it was felt that the proceedings would develop into a mere farce.

But time went by; 5, 10, 15, 20 minutes sped. Still the band played on. Then, at 22 minutes, Mr. Houdini put his head out of the "ghost house," and this was the signal for a great outburst of cheering.

"He is free! He is free!" shouted several; and universal disappointment was felt when it was ascertained that he had only put his head outside the cabinet in order to get a good look at the lock in strong electric light.

From a Photo of the Famous Scene in the London, England, Hippodrome, when Houdini was Handcuffed by the London Illustrated Mirror Representative.

The band broke into a dreamy waltz as Houdini once more disappeared within the canopy. The disappointed spectators looked at their watches, murmured "What a shame!" gave Houdini an encouraging clap, and the journalist resumed his stride.

At 35 minutes, Mr. Houdini again emerged. His collar was broken, water trickled in great channels down his face, and he looked generally warm and uncomfortable.

"My knees hurt," he explained to the audience. "I am not done yet."

The "house" went frantic with delight at their favorite's resolve, and this suggested an idea to the *Mirror* representative.

He spoke rapidly to Mr. Parker, the Hippodrome manager, who was at the side of the stalls. That gentleman looked thoughtful for a moment, then nodded his head and whispered something to an attendant.

A WELCOME CONCESSION.

Presently the man appeared bearing a large cushion.

"The *Mirror* has no desire to submit Mr. Houdini to a torture test," said the representative; "and if Mr. Houdini will permit me, I shall have great pleasure in offering him the use of this cushion."

The "Handcuff King" was glad evidently of the rest for his knees, for he pulled it through into the "ghost house."

Ladies trembled with suppressed excitement, and, despite the weary wait, not a yawn was noticed throughout the vast audience. For 20 minutes more the band played on, and then Houdini was seen to emerge once more from the cabinet.

Still handcuffed!

Almost a moan broke over the vast assemblage as this was noticed. He looked in pitiable plight from his exertions and much exhausted.

He looked about for a moment, and then advanced to where his challenger stood.

"Will you remove the handcuffs for a moment," he said, "in order that I may take my coat off?"

For a few seconds the journalist considered. Then he replied: "I am indeed. Sorry to disoblige you, Mr. Houdini, but I cannot unlock those cuffs unless you admit you are defeated."

The reason was obvious. Mr. Houdini had seen the cuffs locked, but he had never seen them unlocked. Consequently, the press man thought there might be more in the request than appeared on the surface.

FROCK COAT SACRIFICED.

Houdini evidently does not stick at trifles. He maneuvered until he got a penknife from his waistcoat pocket. This he opened with his teeth, and then, turning his coat inside out over his head, calmly proceeded to cut it to pieces.

The novelty of the proceeding delighted the audience, who yelled themselves frantic. The *Mirror* representative had rather a warm five minutes of it at this juncture. Many of the audience did not see the reason of his refusal, and expressed their disapproval of his action loudly.

Grimly, however, he looked on and watched Mr. Houdini once more reenter the cabinet. Time sped on, and presently somebody recorded the fact that the Mysteriarch had been manacled just one hour. Ten minutes more of anxious waiting, and then a surprise was in store for everybody.

VICTORY.

The band was just finishing a stirring march when, with a great shout of victory, Houdini bounded from the cabinet, holding the shining handcuffs in his hand—free!

A mighty roar of gladness went up. Men waved their hats, shook hands one with the other. Ladies waved their handkerchiefs, and the committee, rushing forward as one man, shouldered Houdini, and bore him in triumph round the arena.

But the strain had been too much for the "Handcuff King," and he sobbed as though his heart would break.

With a mighty effort, however, he regained his composure, and received the congratulations of the *Mirror* in the true sportsmanlike spirit he has shown throughout the contest.

PRESENTATION MODEL

The journalist intimated to the audience that a beautiful solid silver model of the handcuffs would be made, and asked Mr. Houdini's permission to present this to him at no distant date.

A SPORTSMAN'S TELEGRAM.

Late last night Mr. Houdini sent us the following telegram:

Editor "Mirror," 2, Carmelite Street, London. E. C.

"Allow me to thank you for the open and upright manner in which your representative treated me in to-day's contest. I must say that it was one of the hardest, but at the same time one of the fairest tests I ever had."

"HARRY HOUDINI."

HOUDINI, manacled and chained, Diving head first off Queen's Bridge, into the Yarra River, Melbourne, Australia, Feb. 18th, 1910.

Australia's Coast is infested with Man-eating Sharks, luckily for Houdini, none happened to be around when he dived.

––––––––––

AN EPISODE IN HOUDINI'S LIFE.

Star, Blackburn, England, Saturday, Oct. 25, 1902.

MANACLED BY A STRONG MAN.

TRUSSED TILL MIDNIGHT.

Unparalleled Scenes at the Palace Theatre.

Never in the history of Blackburn or music hall life has there been witnessed so remarkable a scene as occurred last night. Houdini, the Handcuff King, and Mr. Hodgson, principal of the School of Physical Culture, provided a big sensation for the patrons of the Palace Theatre, Blackburn.

Houdini, who has been appearing at the Palace during the week, claims to be able to release himself from any of the regulation shackles or irons used by the police of Europe or America, and offered nightly to forfeit £25 if he failed to prove his claim.

Mr. Hodgson, of the Physical Culture School, took up the challenge, stipulating that he was to use his own irons and fix them himself. Houdini consented, and deposited the £25 with the editor of the *Daily Star.*

The trial of skill and strength was fixed to take place last night, and the crowd which came together to witness it crammed the theatre literally from floor to ceiling—even standing room being ultimately unobtainable.

Shortly after ten o'clock the parties to the challenge faced each other, and excitement at once became intense.

Mr. Hodgson produced 6 pairs of heavy irons, furnished with clanking chains and swinging padlocks. These were carefully examined by Houdini, who raised some disappointment and much sympathetic cheering by stating that his claim was that he could escape from "regulation" irons. The "cuffs" brought by Mr. Hodgson, he said, had been tampered with— the iron being wrapped round with string, the locks altered, and various other expedients adopted to render escape more difficult.

Mr. Hodgson's answer, given dramatically from the stage, was that he stipulated that he should bring his own irons.

Houdini again protested that Mr. Hodgson was going beyond the challenge, but added that he was quite willing to go on, if only the audience would give him a little time in which to deal with the extra difficulties.

This announcement was greeted with great cheering, and the work of pinioning proceeded.

First, Mr. Hodgson, with the aid of a companion, fixed a pair of irons over Houdini's upper arm, passing the chain behind his back and pulling it tight, and fixing the elbows close to the sides.

To make assurance doubly sure, he fixed another pair in the same way, and padlocked both behind.

Then, starting with the wrists, he fixed a pair of chained "cuffs" so that the arms, already pulled stiffly behind, were now pulled forward. The pulling and tugging at this stage was so severe—the strong man exercising his strength to some purpose—that Houdini protested that it was no part of the challenge that his arms should be broken.

He also reminded Mr. Hodgson that he was to fix the irons himself.

This led to Mr. Hodgson's assistant retiring.

Proceeding, Mr. Hodgson fixed a second pair of "cuffs" on the wrists and padlocked both securely, Houdini's arms being then trussed to his side so securely that escape seemed absolutely impossible.

Still, Mr. Hodgson was not finished with him.

Getting Houdini to kneel down, he passed the chain of a pair of heavy leg irons through the chains which bound the arms together at the back. These were fixed to the ankles, and after a second pair had been added, both were locked, and Houdini now seemed absolutely helpless.

A canopy being placed over Houdini in the middle of the stage, the waiting began, and excitement grew visibly every minute.

Meanwhile Mr. Hodgson and others kept strict watch on the movements of Houdini's wife and brother (Hardeen), who were both on the stage.

At the end of about 15 minutes, the canopy was lifted and Houdini was revealed lying on his side, still securely bound. It was at first thought he had fainted, but he soon made it known that all he wished was to be lifted up. This Mr. Hodgson refused to do, at which the now madly excited audience hissed and "booed" him for his unfair treatment, and Hardeen lifted his brother to his knees. The curtain of the cabinet was again closed.

Another 20 minutes passed, and again the curtain was lifted. This time Houdini said his arms were bloodless and numb owing to the pressure of the irons, and asked to have them unlocked for a minute so that the circulation could be restored.

Mr. Hodgson's reply, given amidst howls, was: "This is a contest, not a love match. If you are beaten, give in."

Great shouting and excited calling followed, which was renewed when Dr. Bradley, after examining Houdini, said his arms were blue, and it was cruelty to keep him chained up as he was any longer.

Still Mr. Hodgson was obdurate, and the struggle proceeded, Houdini again appealing for time.

Fifteen minutes more: Houdini appeared and announced that one hand was free.

This was the signal for terrific cheering, which was continued after the canopy was dropped.

At intervals Houdini now appeared, and announced further progress in his escape; and when, shortly after midnight, he came out with torn clothing and bleeding arms, and threw the last of the shackles on the stage, the vast audience stood up and cheered and cheered, and yelled themselves hoarse to give vent to their overwrought feelings. Men and women hugged each other in mad excitement. Hats, coats, and umbrellas were thrown up into the air, and pandemonium reigned supreme for 15 minutes.

Houdini, when quietness had been restored, said he had been doing the handcuff trick now for 14 years, but never had he been subjected to such brutality as that to which his bleeding arms and wrists gave witness.

When Houdini again obtained a hearing, it was to state that, not only had the irons been altered, but the locks had been plugged.

It was well after midnight when the huge audience left the theatre, and broke up into excited, gesticulating groups.

———————

Condemned Murderers Released by Houdini.

The Washington Post, Sunday, Jan. 7, 1906.

OUT OF GUITEAU CELL.

HOUDINI MIXES THINGS UP AT THE UNITED STATES JAIL.
PRISONERS CHANGED IN CELLS.

Consternation Accompanies Feats of the Expert Lock-picker, Who Gets Laurels from the American Police Chairman After His Third Exploit in Washington—Crowds Are Transfixed.

Two condemned murderers, four others under indictment, and two noted criminals were released from the United States jail yesterday and for a brief time tasted a counterfeit liberty.

Harry Houdini, the international Prison Breaker and Handcuff King, as he is styled, was the hero of a sensational exploit. On the invitation of Warden Harris and the jail authorities he ravaged bolts and locks.

Houdini escaped from the cell in which Charles J. Guiteau, the assassin of President Garfield, was confined, released all the other inmates of the murderers' row cells, and transferred each into some other cell than the one to which he was originally committed.

-

For several days—in fact, since Houdini's remarkable escape from the Tenth precinct—Warden Harris, of the cathedral-like prison along the Eastern Branch of the Potomac, has been endeavoring to secure Houdini for a cell-breaking exploit, as the warden had full faith in the efficiency of his lock system. He wished to have this faith justified by an attempt at escape of Houdini, and his failure would induce that state of mind.

JAMES A. GARFIELD
the Martyred President

Copyright and Published by J. F. RYDER, Cleveland, O.
The sitting for this portrait was made June 10th, 1880

Until yesterday Houdini has been so occupied with his other invitations to break out of the police cells and the other penal institutions that he had abandoned the idea of an adventure at the jail. Not wishing to seem discourteous, he concluded about noon yesterday to present his compliments to Warden Harris and assure him that he would be pleased to test the jail.

CROWD QUICKLY GATHERS

The news of his presence traveled the length of the offices on the inside of the big structure, and here there gathered in the warden's office the following officials and visitors: Deputy Warden W. Grayson Urner, Capt. Ed. S. Randell, Guards John C. Campbell, George C. Gumm, James Corrigan, and John P. Hickey, Jail Physician Dr. D. Kerfoot Shute, Dr. H. I. Sout, Dr. T. Sullivan, Clerk J. Fred Harris, and Messrs. Robert R. Mahorney, Theo Judd, Frank Jones, David M. Proctor, and John T. Ward.

Houdini was invited to examine the cell arrangement and was shown first to Murderers' Row, which is in the south wing and comprises seventeen cells, containing Walter H. Hamilton, sentenced to be hanged last November, but now living through stayed proceedings; Richard Chase, sentenced to twelve years for manslaughter; Thomas S. Whitney, John Mercer, Edward Ferguson, Jeremiah Donovan, and Henry Gaskins—these having been indicted for murder, their alleged crimes being still fresh in the public mind; also James A. Backus, the alleged money-order raiser, and Clarence Howlett, sentenced for housebreaking.

GUITEAU, the assassin of President Garfield. Houdini escaped from the murderer's cell in which this assassin was secured.

Houdini was chiefly interested in cell No. 2, the one occupied by Guiteau, and presumably the safest of the lot, although it was from the outside of this cell that "Avenger" Jones shot into it in his effort to kill the assassin. It now holds Hamilton, who is alleged to have smothered his wife to death and then sat all night beside the body of his victim, indulging in a drunken orgy. The officials say that he is one of the most orderly prisoners ever out there. Howard Schneider, who murdered his wife and her brother, and Shæfer, the murderer hanged a short time ago, also occupied this cell.

PONDEROUS BARRED DOORS.

All these cells are brick structures with their doors sunk into the walls fully three feet from the face of the outer corridor wall. When the heavily barred door is closed, an armlike bar runs out to the corridor wall and then angles to the right and slips over a steel catch which sets a spring that fastens the lock. The latter is only opened by a key, and there are no less than five tumblers in the lock. One key opens all the doors in the corridor.

With Houdini there, it was very natural that everybody should express the ardent desire to have him then and there go into a cell and see if he could release himself, and Houdini, with his accustomed courtesy, yielded a ready acquiescence. He insisted, however, that he preferred to try cell No. 2, for the reason that it is the hardest one there to get out of alive, as he expressed it, and because of the notorious murderers who have spent their last moments on earth within its whitewashed walls.

This was agreed upon, and then he was stripped to the skin and locked into No. 2 with Hamilton, the negro, who crouched in the far corner of the cell, presumably laboring under the belief that one of the arch-fiends was already there to get him for a red-hot furnace. In two minutes Houdini was out of that cell, free, the lock holding him hardly longer than it took him to get into the place and get his bearings. Then, without the knowledge of the waiting officials who had retired from view, Houdini quickly ran to the cells of Chase, Whitney, Mercer, Ferguson, Donovan, Gaskins, Backus, and Howlett. To each occupant the unclad cell-breaker seemed like an apparition from some other world, and the astonishment he created when he commanded each to come out and follow him can be better imagined than described.

PRISONERS ARE DUMBFOUNDED

Chase gave a gasp of fear, and then cried, "Have you come to let me out? What are you doing without clothes?" He supposed then that Houdini was an escaping fellow-prisoner. He followed at Houdini's heels and the cell-breaker dashed with him down to the end of the corridor, where he opened the cell containing Clarence Howlett.

"What are you doing here?" said Houdini to the astonished Howlett. "What are you in for?"

"I'm a housebreaker," said the prisoner, as though making his last confession.

"You're a bad one," said Houdini, "or you could get out of here. Come along." Howlett followed his strange captor, and Houdini then thrust Chase into the cell and rushed Howlett up to Chase's cell.

This scene, strange and strenuous, was repeated again and again, until every desperate man was changed into another cell than his own. All were in a tumult. Twenty-one minutes after Houdini had been locked in the cell he had done all the quick changing and stood before his free audience in the main hall, clothed as in every-day manner.

When the officials found what he had done with their prisoners, their amazement passed all bounds. They took the slight change Houdini made in their plans with the utmost good nature, and soon had everything straightened out, and each of the men back in his cell. At the conclusion, Warden Harris gave the cell-breaker a certificate, of which the following is a copy:

"This is to certify that Mr. Harry Houdini, at the United States jail to-day, was stripped stark naked, thoroughly searched, and locked up in cell No. 2 of the south wing, the cell in which Charles J. Guiteau was confined from the date of his commitment, July 2, 1881, until the day on which he was executed, June 30, 1882. Mr. Houdini, in about 2 minutes, managed to escape from that cell, and then broke into the cell in which his clothing was locked up. He then proceeded to release from their cells all the prisoners on the ground floor. There was positively no chance for any collusion or confederacy. Mr. Houdini accomplished all of the above-mentioned feats, in addition to putting on all his clothing, in 21 minutes.

"J. H. HARRIS.

"Warden United States Jail, D. C."

Major Sylvester yesterday prepared for Houdini the following statement:

TO WHOM IT MAY CONCERN: No individual should be disinclined to profit by the abilities displayed by others, and, in order that defective means of restraint might be discovered in the holding of prisoners in this jurisdiction, and with a view to remedying any insecurity which might exist, Mr. Houdini, the expert man with locks, was permitted to examine a modern cell lock and attachment, and then placed in an entirely different cell from the one he examined. He was searched, and in a nude condition placed behind the bars, and, as supposed, secured. This was in the presence of the Engineer Officer of the District of Columbia, myself, and several officers. In 26 minutes he emerged from the cell and corridor fully attired.

"The experiment was a very valuable one in that the department has been instructed as to the adoption of further security which will protect any lock from being opened or interfered with. The act was interesting and profitable, and worthy of study.

"Mr. Houdini impressed his audience as a gentleman and an artist who does not profess to do the impossible.

"RICHARD SYLVESTER,

"Major and Superintendent."

SOME OF THE GREAT FEATS ACCOMPLISHED BY HOUDINI.

Broke out of the Siberian Prison Van in Moscow, Russia, in May, 1903.

Leaped, heavily handcuffed, in zero weather, from Belle Island Bridge, in Detroit, Mich., in December 2nd, 1906, and released himself under the icy water.

Leaped into San Francisco Bay, San Francisco, Calif., on August 26th, 1907, handcuffed with hands behind his back, with more than 75 pounds of ball and chain locked to his body.

Escaped from a plate glass box made by the Pittsburg Plate Glass Co., and did not even scratch the glass. Boston Mass., Jan. 20th 1907.

After being rivetted into a large hot water boiler by the employees of the Marine Boiler Works, of Toledo, on March 15th, 1907, Houdini escaped without leaving any traces of his exit.

The biggest-little mystery feat—the East Indian needle masterpiece, wherein Houdini swallows 100 needles, 20 yards of thread, and brings up the needles threaded.

Escaped from paper bags, zinc lined piano boxes, packing cases, padded cells, straight-jackets, insane cribs, willow hampers, iron cages, a U.S. Mail Pouch furnished with a rotary lock belonging to the U.S. Government, a large Football, made by Reach Company, of

Philadelphia, a large Derby Desk, with secret locks, Burglar-proof safes, etc., etc. Handcuffed nailed into a packing case, 200 lbs. of iron weights chained to the box and was then thrown overboard into New York Bay.

Houdini has escaped from cells in almost every city in America, the most notable one being from the Murderers' Cell in U.S. Jail at Washington, D.C., which confined Guiteau, the murderer of President Garfield.

Houdini presents the largest, the smallest and most perplexing mystery in the world and history of magic.

The smallest. The East Indian Needle Mystery, in which he swallows 50 to 100 needles, 20 yards of thread, and brings them all up threaded, after his mouth and throat have been examined by a committee of Surgeons. In Boston, at Keith's Theatre, 1906, at special morning performance, he performed this feat before sixteen hundred physicians, and not one could give a correct solution as to his method.

The largest and one of his original inventions being the complete vanishing of a Ten-Thousand-pound Elephant, in full glare of the light and right over the tank of a Quarter of a Million Gallons of Water on the stage of New York Hippodrome, 1916-1917. He performed this the entire season, creating the greatest amount of talk ever caused by any Illusionist with any vanishing mystery.

The greatest mystery ever presented, original inventions of Houdini, one of the Chinese Torture Cell, and the Escape from a Packing Case which being weighted with 300 lbs. of pig iron is thrown overboard into the ocean, and from which he releases himself in less than two minutes.

-

KANSAS CITY, MO., April 11, 1900.

TO WHOM IT MAY CONCERN: We, the undersigned, do hereby certify that we saw Harry Houdini stripped nude, thoroughly searched from head to foot, and his mouth sealed up, making it an utter impossibility for him to have anything concealed on his person. We saw him handcuffed and leg-ironed with five different cuffs, and his hands locked to his feet.

He was led into a cell, which was also securely locked with what is known as the three-bond lock, guaranteed by the makers to be burglar proof. Nevertheless, Houdini succeeded in making his escape out of all the irons, also from the cell, in less than 8 minutes. There was no possible chance of confederacy.

Signed and sealed by JOHN HAYES, Chief of Police.

John Halpin, Inspector of Detectives.

J. C. Snavly, Jailer.

THE DISAPPEARING ELEPHANT
The largest vanish the world has ever known, as invented and presented by Houdini
at the New York Hippodrome.

Daily Express, London, Feb. 3, 1904.

WIZARD IN GAOL.

OPENS CELLS AND IS TAKEN FOR THE DEVIL.

HIS 61st ESCAPE.

I certify that today, Mr. Harry Houdini showed his abilities in releasing himself from restraint.

He had three pairs of handcuffs, one a very close-fitting pair, placed round his wrists, and he was placed in a nude state in a cell which had been previously searched. Within 6 minutes he was free from the handcuffs, had opened the cell door, and had opened the doors of all the other cells in the corridor, had changed a prisoner from one cell to another, and had so securely locked him in that he had to be asked to unlock the door.

(Signed) LEONARD DUNNING,

Head Constable, Liverpool.

Feb. 2, 1902.

Mr. Dunning has since been knighted and is now head of the Police Constabulary, being located in London, his official title being His Majesty's Inspector of Constabulary, London, England.

-

For him it is literally true that—

Stone walls do not a prison make,

    Nor iron bars a cage.

Were he a criminal—his clear, straightforward eyes negative the suggestion—he would be a nightmare to the police of Britain, for he would walk out of gaol as coolly and smilingly as he did twice out of Liverpool Bridewell yesterday.

It was an eventful day at the sinister-looking building that stands off busy Dale Street.

High police officials, clever detectives, leading city business men who hold office on the watch committee, all sustained a severe shock by their loss of faith in what they had regarded as an inviolable stronghold.

No one has been known previously to escape from the bolts and bars behind which Liverpool quarters its criminals.

SURRENDERS TO POLICE.

In the afternoon, Houdini had a pleasant interview with Head Constable Dunning.

"Want to try our locks? Certainly. You're welcome; but, of course, we will take some precautions."

"I want you to do so," replied Houdini. "I will strip naked. You can then handcuff me and put me in your strongest cell, and after you have searched me and the cell you leave me, locking the door. I will join you in a minute or two."

Houdini was as good as his word. Not only did he escape, but he had torn from his hands and arms three pairs of handcuffs, which had been put on him by officers with absolute belief in their restraining power.

Even these feats were not enough for this man, who does things that would have made Jack Sheppard die of envy. He felt sure there was nothing in Bridewell to baffle him.

Running along the corridor, he opened the doors of other cells, which he had thought were all empty. When he reached No. 14 and flung open the door, he confronted a prisoner.

"I don't know which of us was the more surprised," said Houdini to an *Express* representative.

STARTLED PRISONER

Here was I, standing absolutely nude before a terrified, miserable object.

Poor fellow! what a shock it was for him. He was an Irishman just recovering from a drunken bout.

"'Arrah!' he said, when he had recovered; 'I thought it was the divil.'"

The shivering prison-breaker hurried the wretched prisoner out of cell No. 14 into No. 15 and locked him in. Then he ran along the passage to greet the head constable and the other officials.

Only 6 minutes had elapsed since he had been locked in the cell naked and handcuffed. The cell door was inspected and found uninjured.

Then one of the gaolers, walking along the corridor, espied door No. 14 open and a prisoner gone.

"That's all right," said the irrepressible Houdini. "I've had him out and locked him up in No. 15." Hearty laughter followed the narration of this achievement, and the officials went to No. 15.

So securely had the Irishman been locked up that it was necessary to call upon Houdini to unfasten the door. The Irishman was found in a somewhat bewildered state, but he probably "sobered" quicker than he would have done in less eventful circumstances.

Houdini left the bridewell the proud possessor of the certificate which is reproduced at the head of this article.

ANOTHER EXPERIMENT

In the evening Houdini, accompanied by an Express representative, again walked into the bridewell to settle a point which had been raised since his feat in the afternoon.

Was the door which had been fastened against him single, double, or triple locked?

The matter could easily be settled. Houdini would just do the trick again. Only this time he would do it with his clothes on, as time was pressing.

Liverpool's bridewell is as an unsightly a place as a bridewell can be. No one would mistake it for a spa hotel or a convalescent home.

Beneath a dark arch you pass, and in the great door which you find opposite is a little window which is unlocked when you knock, and through which you are viewed before you are permitted even to stand upon the threshold.

Houdini and his companion were admitted.

"More lock-breaking?

"Yes; I am ready for more—as many as you like."

Accompanied by a gaoler, Houdini and the **Express** representative ascended a flight of stone steps and passed along dimly lighted corridors, whose atmosphere seemed to reek with crime and mystery.

Passing through a gate, a row of cells was reached, upon any one of which Houdini might operate.

Here was one marked with a strange device. Houdini would try this one.

It was a felon's cell—stronger than some of the others, though it could not have been darker or more forbidding.

Houdini entered. He was backed in by the **Express** representative. He was inside, safe and sound.

SECOND ESCAPE

There could be no doubt about that. At the first turn of the key the lock went forward twice; at the second, once. Houdini was behind a triple lock in the dark, dreary cell.

The **Express** representative and the gaoler left him there, and retired beyond an iron gate which bars the passage.

"The gate is a greater test than the cell," said the gaoler.

"It's locked before it's locked, if you understand. Shut it, and it's locked, and then you can lock it again."

The gaoler hand only secured it when Houdini presented himself.

"That's as quick as I've ever done it," said he. And then he tackled the gate.

A moment's hesitation. The gaoler shook his head, and a smile was just overspreading his features, when lo! Houdini flung open wide the gate.

He agreed that the gate was "tougher," as he expressed it, than the cell.

Houdini is an American. Only his strong arms and his supple, yet powerful hands give the slightest clue of his prison-breaking capacity.

He does not look a gaolbird, but the escape he made for the benefit of **Express** readers was his 61st.

Bright-eyed, smart, active, and a good talker, he has traveled far and wide, and has broken out of the prisons of many countries.

"I have never failed," said Houdini, "but I don't say there is no cell I cannot break out of. As to handcuffs, the hardest job I ever had was with a pair made at Krupp's. It took me 40 minutes to get out of them, but I did it."

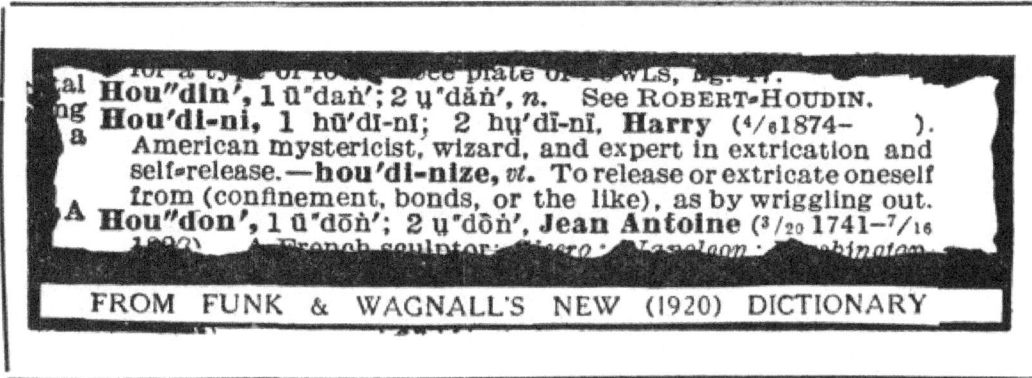

Hou'di-ni, 1 hū'dī-nī; 2 hu'dï-nï, Harry (4/6 1874-   ). American mystericist, wizard, and expert in extrication and self-release.—hou'di-nize, *vt.* To release or extricate oneself from (confinement, bonds, or the like), as by wriggling out.

FROM FUNK & WAGNALL'S NEW (1920) DICTIONARY

———————

Houdini Outwits Fiji Islander Swimming Champion.

Houdini, the man of mystery, who is now appearing in our midst, is certainly a peculiar species of a human being. From all accounts, the energy, the work and feats of this man will, sometime in the future, be the finish of this now wonderful and famous performer.

The restless striving to do something better than another human being has brought him to the highest pinnacle of fame, has earned for him princely salaries, and when one considers the risks he has taken, no one can begrudge him the prime minister's salary, which he is earning.

To show the restless craving of this man for excelling in things where it is impossible to be of any value to him in any way or form, an incident regarding this man is well worth relating. He was returning from Australia, and the steamer, after leaving Brisbane touched Suva, on the Fiji Islands, a place infested with the most voracious man-eating sharks, known in the world's history. It is stated that they will not touch a black man, and perhaps, that is why the Fiji Islanders stand in no fear of being devoured by sharks, and whenever a shark enters the harbour, it is one of the sights of the country, same as it is in Colombo or Port Said. The Natives dive for coins that the passengers throw overboard. One big fellow seemed to be a most wonderful diver and would always come up with the coin in his mouth, pretending to the average spectator that he had cought the coin in his mouth.

Houdini, being an observant spectator, claimed that the man caught the coins in his hand, that is, picked the coin in the water with his hand and placed it in his mouth. This was disputed. Houdini, being offered to wager that if the man's hands were tied behind his back, which would not impede him in making his dive, that he could not catch the coin in his mouth, and Houdini agreed that he would allow himself to be handcuffed, with his hands behind his back, and that he would come up with the coin in his mouth.

An interpreter was called and the Black agreed to undergo the test. The dive was to be made off the steamer, and the Captain warned Houdini that he stood in grave danger of the sharks.

Undaunted, Houdini went below, donned a bathing suit, had a pair of regulation handcuffs locked behind his back; the Black had his hands tied behind him with a cord—he refused to have the handcuffs placed on him, and he said they were too heavy—two coins were thrown overboard, two splashes were simultaneously heard.

Quick as a tiger's spring the Fiji Islander, with his sleek, glossy body, hurled himself through the air and was beneath the surface of the water even while Houdini was perched for his spring. But the jumps were so quickly made, one after the other, that unless you saw the men as they entered the water, you would have thought that it was one prolonged splash. Thirty seconds passed; neither one of the two men appeared. One minute passed, and the black head of the Fiji Islander came up, almost livid for want of air. Fifteen seconds passed by, and, feet first, up came Houdini.

The Fiji Islander did not have his coin, and it seems that Houdini had gathered both of them and had them in his mouth.

He was drawn up with exciting hurry, for the fins of the sharks were seen moving about with rapidity, and, being hauled on deck, Houdini was declared to have won the wager.

The Black's hands were released, were cut apart, the handcuffs were unlocked from Houdini's wrists, and instead of keeping the money, Houdini made it a present to the Black.

In a private interview, on being asked how he defeated the Black, Houdini said with a good-natured smile, "You can pick up a coin in a glass tank with your hands tied behind your back, because you can use your mouth, teeth and tongue to manipulate the coin, but when you are in an ocean and the coin is falling downwards it is almost next to impossible to catch a coin and bring it up in your mouth."

"You ask me how I did it? I will let you in the secret—I didn't do it at all. When I was under the water I released one of my hands which gave me the use of both of them; I caught my coin and I noticed that the Black was unable to get his coin. I swam after him until he had given up trying to get it, and we had gone down to such a distance that my ears rang, my head was splitting, and all I could see was the white shining piece of money—it was an English two-shilling piece. Eventually I grabbed the coin, put it in my mouth and came up. As I came up, I happened to have my hands free and as I could not stop myself with the force I had sent myself up with my hands I turned around and came up feet first, and this allowed me to put my hands behind my back and the regulation handcuff, as you know, being a snap lock, I locked my hands together and to all intents and purposes my hands were locked during the entire feat. That is why I gave the Fiji Islander the entire amount at stake."

"Was I afraid of the sharks?"

"Yes and No! Being able to see under water, I kept a sharp look-out, and as soon as I would have seen anything that looked like a shark I would have done a record swim to the boat."

"No, I would not care to do it again; it was not for the money, it was simply to show that I was as good a swimmer as some of those Fiji Islanders."

-

HISTORICAL LOCK PICKERS.

It used to be the fashion among inventors to challenge the trade and other persons, to pick them.

In some cases, even rewards were offered to any one who could do so.

It is believed that Mr. Joseph Bramah was the first to do this and in 1801, he displayed in his shop window in Piccadily, London, a board to which was attached a padlock, manufactured by himself, and which bore the following inscription:—

"The artist who can make an instrument that will pick or open this lock shall receive 200 guineas the moment it is produced."

In 1832, a Wolverhampton locksmith, having claimed to having picked 18 Chubb locks, Mr. Chubb challenged him to open one of his locks under certain conditions.

Mr. Hart tried and failed, giving the explanation that it was not the regular commercial Chubb lock, but one that had a special bridge ward.

Mr. Chubb replied that Mr. Hart did not pick any lock, but made false keys by a process of cutting blanks.

In America the great lock of Dr. Andrews, in 1841, being heralded as an unpickable lock, with two sets of tumblers, was produced, the inventor offering 500 dollars to any one who could pick this.

It was picked by Pettitt and Hall, of Boston, with what is known as the smoke process.

1851. HOBBS PICKS BRAMAH AND CHUBB LOCK.

In 1851 Mr. A. C. Hobbs arrived from America, picked a Chubb lock before a committee, and picked the Bramah lock, winning thereby the 200 guineas that for 50 years no one was able to claim.

Mr. Hobbs offered 200 guineas to anyone who would pick his lock. An engineer named Garbutt, known as an expert, took up the challenge, and failed after trying thirty days.

1855.—YALE PICKS HOBBS' LOCK.

As an additional element to this controversy, in 1855, Linnius Yale, Jr., discovered how to pick the then celebrated Day and Newell Parautoptic Bank Lock.

It was of American origin, and was known in England as Hobbs Lock, but was the invention of a Mr. Pyle.

Yale also discovered that he could pick the best Bank Lock—the Double Treasury, which he himself had designed.

And eventually demonstrated that any lock having a key hole could be opened by any expert with the necessary skill and time at his disposal.

Accordingly Mr. Yale proceeded to develop the combination or Dial Lock.

1870.—SARGENT PICKS YALE LOCK.

The general use of this lock led to the controversy in the United States in 1870; and the Yale lock was picked by James Sargent, of the firm of Sargent and Greenleaf, a lock inventor, a leading maker of Bank Locks, and the inventor of the Time Lock.

1905.—HOUDINI PICKS SARGENT LOCK.

Houdini bearded the lion in his den by escaping from a Police Cell in Rochester, N. Y., which was securely locked with one of the Sargent and Greenleaf Locks, placing himself on record as one of the great lock pickers of the world.

Of the thousands of locks he has picked all over the world, the following police certificates places him among the historical lock pickers, in fact, second to none.

POLICE HEADQUARTERS, ROCHESTER, N. Y.
U. S. OF AMERICA.

We, the undersigned, certify that we saw Harry Houdini, the bearer of this note, stripped naked, searched, locked in one of the cells at Police Headquarters, and handcuffed with three pairs of cuffs, also strapped with a strap extending from pair of cuffs and buckled at the back.

He removed the cuffs, unlocked the cell, got into an adjoining cell and returned with his clothes on.

After unlocking the cell in which he was first placed, he had to unlock the cell in which his clothing was left.

This was witnessed by the following persons, at Police Headquarters, this city, December 4th, 1905.

J. C. HAYDEN, Chief of Police.

Mr. James Sargent personally complimented Houdini on his rare skill. They became friends and spent hours together exchanging lock opening secrets.

NOTE.—We beg to acknowledge our indebtedness to the following publications for data used in this article—Price's Book on "Locks and Keys" 1856; New International Encyclopedia 2nd Edition; (Dodd Mead and Co., New York); and Encyclopedia Americana, J. M. Stoddart, 1886.

-

POLICE HEADQUARTERS, CHICAGO, ILL., U. S. OF AMERICA.

This is to certify that the undersigned saw Harry Houdini stripped stark naked, searched from head to foot, and shackled with handcuffs around the wrists and leg irons around his ankles.

He was then placed in a cell which required TWO LARGE keys of different makes and patterns to open the lock. The keys are of such a nature that it would have been positively impossible for him to have concealed them on his body.

We searched the cell and thoroughly searched Houdini from head to foot, also between his toes and the soles of his feet. Nevertheless, in fifteen minutes he managed to release himself from the manacles and make his escape from the cell.

There was positively no chance for outside assistance.

(Signed), ANDREW ROHAN,

Chief of Detectives. Nov. 24, 1906.

_____

The Only Paper in the City that Dares Print the News

Los Angeles Record

21st Year. WED. DEC. 1, 1915. No. 6485

2,000 HISS J. WILLARD.

CHAMPION DRIVEN FROM THEATER BY HOOTS AND CALLS

Boxing has been given its worst black eye here to-day by none other than Jess Willard, heavy-weight champion who was so badly worsted to a wordy clash with Harry Houdini, a performer at the Orpheum Theater, last night, that the audience hissed him from the house.

Nearly 2,000 persons were present at the dramatic scene and seemed unanimous in groaning, hooting and booing Willard.

The trouble was precipitated by Willard's gruff refusal to comply with a friendly request made by Houdini that he act on a committee to watch the performer's act from the stage.

It was not known that Willard was present until Houdini came before the footlights and requested any "gentleman" in the audience to step on the stage and guard those present from any possible deception.

After about 10 men had stepped on the platform, Houdini stepped forward and said, smiling:

"Now I need three more gentlemen on this stage and there is a man here to-night who doesn't know I am aware of his presence. He will be enough for three ordinary gentlemen if he will serve on this committee."

"He is Jess Willard, our champion."

Taken by surprise, the audience was silent for a moment and then broke into tumultous hand-clapping. Cheers and shrieks resounding throughout the house.

Houdini looked up on the balcony, where Willard was seated, and said:

"I will leave it to the audience, Mr. Willard. You see they want to see you."

A fresh outburst occurred, even more violent than before.

"Aw, g'wan with your act," came Willard's rough reply as the audience stilled itself. "I paid for my seat here."

"But, Mr. Willard," expostulated Houdini, "I—

"Give me the same wages you pay those other fellows and I'll come down," rumbled Willard's deep voice.

The audience, scenting something unusual, was very quiet.

"Sir, I will gladly do so," returned Houdini, heatedly. "Come on down—I pay these men nothing."

"Aw' g'wan with the show," roared Willard, growling something that sounded like "four-flusher" and "faker."

Willard's boorish replies evidently displeased those present, for a few scattering hisses came about this time.

Houdini stepped to the footlights and held up his hand for silence.

It was readily granted.

"Jess Willard, I have just paid you a compliment," said Houdini dramatically. "Now I want to tell you something else.

"I will be Harry Houdini, Jess Willard, when you are NOT the heavyweight champion of the world."

A roar of applause shook the house. Men and women alike joined in the clapping and cheering.

A deep rumble from the balcony indicated that Willard was trying to make some retort, and the cheers veered suddenly to hoots and groans.

"I made a mistake," said Houdini, addressing the audience. "I asked GENTLEMEN to step on this stage and GENTLEMEN only."

A renewed outburst occurred, during which Willard evidently left the theater. He was not to be found after the next act had started.

THE PICTURE SHOW. Mar. 20th, 1920

Half-an-hour with Houdini,
THE EXPERT OF EXTRICATION

"Danger does not mean anything to me; I was just born without the ingredient of fear. Apart from the many risks I have taken in the course of my professional career, I have saved lives any number of times, and I have simply taken it all as a matter of course. People talk of being afraid to die; on the contrary, I am so well prepared for such an emergency that not only is my will drawn up, but I have a bronze memorial bust all ready, because I thought it better to have one that was really like me!"

THE HANDCUFF KING

Thus spoke Houdini, the "handcuff king," the great magician and genius of escape, on a certain sunny morning a few weeks ago. He sat with his back to the light, but though his face was in shadow the compelling blue grey eyes, and strong, bronzed features glowed with an intensity and vitality such as one rarely meets.

"Tell me," I begged, "are the feats you do on the screen different to those you do enact before the footlights?"

"Entirely different," was the reply.

"In fact, some of the biggest critics have said that I am more wonderful on the screen than on the stage. That, I consider, is one of the greatest compliments ever paid me. But it has taken years of training to produce the tricks, or problems, I do in my films."

Houdini has made, to date, three pictures. The first of these, "The Master Mystery," a serial, is now enjoying enormous popularity all over the country. The remaining two, "The Grim Game," and "Terror Island," are feature pictures, and are still unreleased by Paramount Artcraft though this year will see the first-named on our screens. In the making of "The Master Mystery," Houdini sustained seven black eyes and a broken wrist. He also broke his wrist whilst making "The Grim Game."

A TENSE MOMENT

"During the screening of this picture I thought at one time in the course of the action, that my end had come," he told me. "I was 3,000 feet up in an aeroplane, circling over another machine. The plan was for me to drop from my 'plane into the cockpit of the other by means of a rope. I was dangling from the rope-end ready for the leap. Suddenly a strong wind turned the lower plane upwards, the two machines crashed together—nearly amputating my limbs—the propellers locked in a deadly embrace, and we were spun round and round and round." Houdini pronounced the latter words with a peculiarly apt "whirring" intonation, graphically illustrating them by the circular action of the arms. "But," he continued, "by a miracle, the 'planes were righted into a half-glide, and, though they were smashed into splinters by their terrific impact, I managed to escape unhurt. As usual, Houdini became undone!" concluded the narrator with a laugh.

HIS GREATEST STUNT

"What do you consider the greatest stunt you have done for the screen?" I asked, when I had recovered my breath.

"Another incident in the same picture," answered Houdini. "I stood in the archway of a prison, thus——" Here he took up a crouching position in the corner of the room, and enacted the whole thing for my benefit. "A heavily loaded lorry, going at twenty-two or four miles an hour rolled by me. I threw myself on the ground, completely rolling over between the fast revolving fore and hind wheels, over and over, till I caught the transmission bar, and hung there for very dear life! Thus was I carried to the aid of the heroine. Though my words may not convey very much, this was my greatest stunt. It allowed for no rehearsals—I said to the camera-man, 'Get this now or never!' And had I made the slightest false move I should have been crippled for life, if not killed."

In spite of the risks he has taken before the camera, Houdini has a profound love and admiration for the "movies."

"I think the film profession is the greatest," he told me "and that the moving picture is the most wonderful thing in the world. One reason why I love the screen is because it has use for the derelicts of life, and gives employment to the old as well as the young. I entered the profession myself because I knew I should eventually be losing my strength, and before that happened I wanted to perpetuate my feats, and by so doing everyone, in all parts of the world, can see them. Pictures have increased my drawing power two-hundredfold."

Houdini, as related at the commencement of this chat, had one of his greatest compliments paid him by critics of his film work, but before I left him he confessed that what he considers the very greatest tribute ever made to his unique achievements is recorded in a dictionary! Turn to Funk and Wagnall's Standard Dictionary, and there you will find it:

"HOU'DI-NI. 1, hu'di-ni;

2, hu'di-ni, HARRY (4-6, 1874). American mystericist, wizard, and expert in extrication and self-release HOU'DI-NIZĒ vt. To release or extricate oneself from (confinement, bonds, or the like), as by wriggling out."

So, taking Houdini all in all, I may consider the fact that this wonder-man, this "expert in extrication," made no effort to escape from at least one thing this interview!

MAY HERSCHEL CLARKE.

———

Sat.]   ROCHESTER EVENING TIMES   [Nov. 4
1916

Minister uses Houdini's name for Sermon

His Art of Getting Out of Things as Topic of Sermon

The name of Houdini, who has been a headliner at a local theater this week will figure in the sermon at the Genesee Street Baptist Church, to-morrow morning, where the pastor, Rev. Clark, will talk on "Houdini and the Art of Getting Out of Things." The pastor, however, insures that he will reveal none of the vital points of the art, but declares that the sermon will be entirely spiritual.

THE SUN

Pittsburg Monday, Nov. 6th, 1916

20,000 People see Houdini Thrilling Air Struggle.

WIZARD TIED IN JACKET IS FREE IN 3 MINUTES.

STRAPPED TIGHTLY BY GUARDS FROM MAYVIEW HE HANGS HEAD DOWN WARD.

SUN BUILDING IS SCENE. WHILE SPINNING DIZZILY FIFTY FEET ABOVE PAVEMENT HE ESCAPES FROM BONDS.

Swaying, head downwards, like a grotesque human pendulum, 50 feet above the pavement in front of The Sun Building, Harry Houdini, "handcuff king," defier of locks, bars and bonds, freed himself from the grip of a canvas, leather-reinforced straight-jacket, in a fraction more than three minutes, shortly after 12.40 o'clock this afternoon.

The waving of his free hands and arms, that a crowd estimated at 20,000 has seen bound by two attendants from the Mayview (old Marshalsea) Hospital for the Insane, told the watchers that Houdini had achieved one of the most unique feats in his strange career. As he was lowered swiftly to the ground, a great cheer arose, followed by another and another as he stood upright and bowed to the throng which not only packed the streets but filled every window and roof top within view of the scene.

WIZARD IS ON TIME

Urbane, smiling, the elusive Houdini appeared in the office of "The Sun" at 12 o'clock. R. D. Polling and H. Guthrie, the two attendants from Mayview detailed to truss him up, awaited him, and with them the straight-jacket, in a satchel.

Houdini shook hands with both men, speaking humorously of his position as substitute for the deranged persons the two Attendants ordinarily handle. The two men, clad in the white uniforms used by them when on duty, surveyed their voluntary victim noted his short, stocky form, his powerful arms and shoulders, his steady, bright eyes.

Both have had long experience in binding frenzied men. Both were determined, they told Houdini, to use the full resource of that experience in binding him. They knew the prowess of the man they had to deal with. They did not comment upon the outcome of the test.

They were there, they said, to do their work as best they knew how.

Houdini urged speed of action, and absolute surety in fastening the innumerable straps of the straight-jacket.

"Treat me," he advised, smiling, "as you would the most dangerous of the criminal insane."

EVERY MOVE IS WATCHED

The strait-jacket was taken out of the satchel. The handcuff king examined it carefully, while a group of persons looked on. Not a move he made was lost. He dropped the piece of canvas and leather carelessly, smiled again, and said:

"Very good. Are we ready?"

It was almost 12.30 o'clock. Houdini glanced out the window, and again his characteristic, quiet smile came to his face as he saw Wood street and Liberty avenue congested from wall to wall with closely packed, restless humanity.

Then a white-clad attendant on each side, he went downstairs to the street to be bound.

A suppressed shout came from the crowd as he appeared in the doorway of The Sun building. It increased in volume as with the attendants and two members of "The Sun" at 12 o'clock. R. D. Polling wagon that had been pulled up on the pavement, and that was serving as a stage.

Above him, like a gallows, a single beam projected from a window at the top story of the building, and a rope swung clear, coiling in sinister fashion at his feet.

Houdini had removed the outer clothing from the upper part of his body.

"Ready," he said.

STRAPS ARE FASTENED

The two attendants pressed close. His arms were inserted in the long, closed sleeves of the straitjacket. One of the attendants clasped him about the body, as if fearing he would make some mad effort to escape. The other standing behind him, fastened strap after strap, with a steady deftness that made both for security and speed, and revealed long practice.

"Make it tight," came the quiet word from the prisoner.

The man's knees went up for purchase in the small of Houdini's back. Using apparently every ounce of strength in his broad-shouldered six-foot body, the attendant drew the big strap through the buckle until it would not yield even a sixteenth of an inch more. He caught it there and made it fast.

Then the arms of the prisoner were crossed over his body, and the ends of those closed sleeves were brought around in back. Again the knee was brought into use. Again the strap was pulled to its highest tension.

The crowd watched, stirred with a constant murmur and movement.

Then Houdini's ankles were fastened to the rope, by a special appliance that prevented injury, but insured safety.

A word was spoken. The two attendants seized the bound man's body. Workmen drew the rope steadily through the pulleys. Houdini's feet went up, and as his body cleared the platform, it was released.

HANGS IN MID-AIR

The handcuff king dangled head downward. Each moment he was drawn higher, swaying slightly, spinning dizzily. Up-up, past the windows in the fifth story of the Sun building. Houdini was drawn.

Then he hung still.

Only for a second. While watchers gleamed in the crowd below, the handcuff king was seen to struggle, not frantically, but with a steady, systematic swelling and contracting of muscles, and almost imperceptible lithe, wrigglings of the torso.

The struggle went on. One minute—two—then three——

Would he do it? Hundreds in the crowd undoubtedly were asking that question. From above came an inarticulate shout. The muffled arms writhed one after another over Houdini's head. His hand, still encased in the sleeves of the strait-jacket, fumbled quickly and effectively with the buckles at his back. Another contortion and the strait-jacket slipped down over his chest, over his head, and was flung from his arms to the street, in a crumpled heap.

Houdini was free.

The arms waved. Houdini had triumphed—as he always triumphs.

Less than a minute later, while the crowd's cheers still rang against the grey walls of surrounding buildings, he slipped down the face of the building to the platform. The attendants received him in a twinkling, and he stood erect, unconsciously throwing back his broad shoulders.

The little man with the touch of grey at his temples bowed quietly, still with that imperturbable smile. And the crowd cheered him again, before it began slowly to dissolve.

Houdini duplicated this feat at the Boston Post, Boston, Mass., December 22, 1921, drawing the biggest crowd that ever crushed into Tremont Street.

Trophy won by Houdini.

The accompanying illustration is the prize offered by the Australian Aerial League for the first successful flight on a heavier than air machine. Won by Houdini March 16, 1910, Digger's Rest, near Melbourne Australia. Houdini piloted his own machine—a Voision Biplane equipped with a E.N.V. 60.80 H.P. Motor. During his Australian Tour Houdini made 18 successful flights.

———————

LONDON, ENGLAND

HOLBORN EMPIRE BESIEGED BY CROWD INSIDE AND OUTSIDE—UNPARALLELED
SCENES WITNESSED IN HIGH HOLBORN—POLICE RESERVES CALLED OUT

A packed house, to show its disapproval of the management's action, remains at the Holborn Empire, from 2:00 to 9:00 P. M., waiting for Houdini's appearance as advertised. Police forces were called out as the matinee crowd, refusing to leave the theatre, the evening crowd blockaded traffic, being unable to gain admittance. Unparalleled scenes witnessed in High Holborn.

"THE PERFORMER" LONDON ENGLAND, DECEMBER 15, 1910.

A STAND FOR JUSTICE
Houdini's Protest

"For some mysterious reason, surprisingly little attention has been given in the daily papers to a remarkable 'scene' at the Holborn Empire last Thursday, when Houdini made a plucky and public-spirited protest against prevailing matinee methods. We must, we suppose, attribute to the present obsession of politics the scant attention given to a very unusual incident, of interest alike to the public and the profession.

"Having received an intimation from the management that, although he was topping the week's bill, his services would not be required at the Thursday matinee, 'owing to the length of the programme,' Houdini expressed himself perfectly agreeable to this arrangement, subject to the condition that due intimation should be given to the public that he would not be appearing.

"This condition not being complied with, he took an opportunity of going on to the stage at the conclusion of one of the matinee turns in order to quietly explain the reason for his non-appearance and to show that it was not his fault that he was breaking faith with the public. He did not urge the audience, as was stated in some reports, to stay until he appeared, but said that he assumed some at least had come to see him perform and that it seemed to him such were certainly to have their money back if they did not see him.

"The performance went on quietly until 'God Save the King,' when the audience took the matter into its own hands and refused to disperse, calling for Houdini to appear. After a scene of considerable excitement, 150 persons ultimately accepted the management's offer of vouchers for another performance and left the building, but the great bulk of the audience remained until after the conclusion of Houdini's performance at the first evening house, when they trooped out, leaving the place only a quarter full.

"The queues which formed up for the first house had in the main to be accommodated at the second house, and great difficulty was experienced in controlling the further arrivals for the second performance.

"The audience's just appreciation of Houdini's protest was voiced in the remarks of a Labor leader who helped to beguile the interval between the afternoon and evening houses by making a speech. He said that he had frequently attended such matinees, and had always attributed the frequent failure of some one or more well-known artists to appear to his (or her) personal indifference or indolence, but that now they knew the real reason why the public were disappointed.

"In view of a managerial allegation to the afternoon audience that Houdini was not allowed to appear because he had broken his contract, we quote from a further considered protest with which Houdini prefaced his performance at the first house in the evening. He said:

"'Before proceeding with my performance this evening, I believe that there is an explanation due to a great many who are assembled here as to the cause of my non-appearance here this afternoon, and if it would interest you to hear, I will explain. I wish to inform you that it is positively no fault of mine, because I was here in the building, ready to work, but the management refused to allow me to go on. I will read a number of letters that I have here, which thoroughly explain the case, and I wish to inform you that I have played a good many weeks on this tour, and never knew exactly where I was going until a few days ahead. I was billed to appear at the Holborn a short time ago, and, without any notification whatever, I was sent to Woolwich, and the public received no explanation why I did not appear here.

"'Very likely a great many thought that I had broken faith with the public, and last night I received a letter—dated the 6th—after the second performance (about 11 o'clock) which was 33 hours later than dated, notifying me that my services were not required for the matinee performance.'

"Having quoted this letter and his reply stating the condition on which he was agreeable to the arrangement, Houdini continued:

"'Now, ladies and gentlemen, I wanted to keep faith with the public, and informed the management that I would give the salary that I was earning at the matinee to the V. A. B. F. if they would only allow me to appear, as I knew my reputation was at stake. Being billed, and not appearing, what would the public think? Despite this, I was not allowed to appear, and I trust that those who are assembled here this evening will see my motive in allowing the public to know the real cause of my non-appearance, and that it was positively not my fault.'

"The first result of this dignified protest was that Houdini's services were, notwithstanding notice to the contrary, requisitioned for the Saturday matinee."

-

Houdini, in his speech to the audience that evening, was forcible and to the point, informing them that it was the greatest compliment that had ever been paid him—an audience waiting seven hours in a theatre for him—and that he would never forget it—and he never will.

———————

Boston Daily Globe, March 19, 1906.

HOUDINI ESCAPES FROM CITY PRISON

Handcuffed, Ironed, and Locked in Cell, He takes only 16 Minutes to Get Out and over the Wall

Harry Houdini, the young man who, apparently, cannot be held in restraint by steel bars, handcuffs, prison locks, or other restraining measures, gave the Boston Police Department a terrific jolt this forenoon when he escaped from double confinement in the city prison, commonly known as the Tombs, a prison which the heads of the police department had confidently believed to be escape proof.

SUPT. WILLIAM H. PIERCE, WHO LOCKED CELL DOORS

Superintendent of Police William H. Pierce personally superintended the confinement of Houdini, himself locked the wizard into a cell on the second tier of the prison, after he had clamped handcuffs on his wrists and leg irons about his ankles, and the superintendent's face wore a smile of confidence and assurance after he had locked the cell doors and went down into the office of the prison to await results.

The superintendent's smile didn't wholly come off when, a few minutes later, he learned that Houdini not only had escaped from his cell, but that he had escaped from the prison, and was nearly a half-mile away; but the smile was faded and frayed at the edges, and no questioning could get the superintendent to say what he thought of the wonderful performance. All that could be gotten out of him was, "I have nothing to say."

Heretofore the police have believed that no one locked in a cell at the Tombs could possibly get out; but Houdini not only got out, but he opened door after door after he had removed the handcuffs and leg irons, and walked from one part of the prison to another with apparently as much freedom as though he wasn't met every few feet with a lock that had been considered impregnable.

CLOSELY SEARCHED FOR KEYS.

Briefly, here is just what happened: Houdini had secured permission from Superintendent Pierce to make an effort to escape from the city prison, and this forenoon, in the presence of about 30 men, the superintendent let Houdini into cell No. 77 on the ground floor of the Tombs, where Houdini, in the presence of the witnesses of the test, removed every stitch of his clothing, which he left lying on the bunk in the cell. When he came out, Capt. Clarence A. Swan, the keeper of the prison, locked the cell door upon Houdini's clothing, and then the young man was taken to the second floor of the block of cells, where Superintendent Pierce and a number of the men witnessing the test searched his hair for possible concealed keys or other instruments. Not a thing was found, and Houdini even asked to have his feet examined so there would be no question of his having a key concealed between his toes, and this was done.

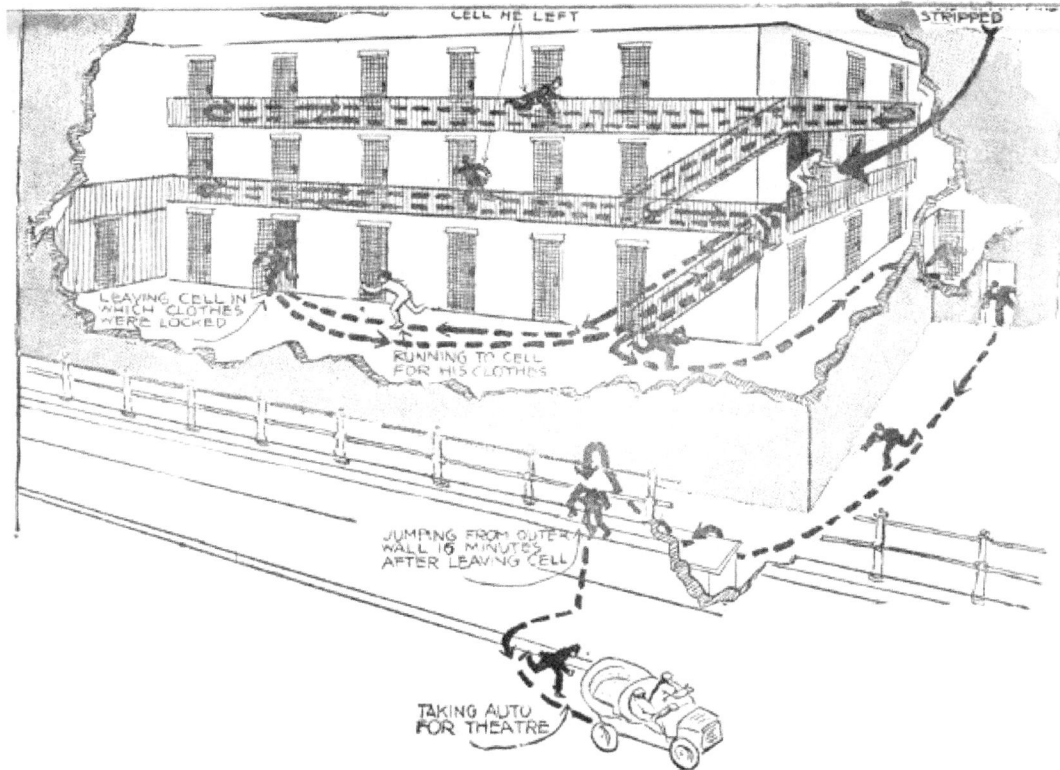

Labels in the illustration:
CELL HE LEFT
STRIPPED
LEAVING CELL IN WHICH CLOTHES WERE LOCKED
RUNNING TO CELL FOR HIS CLOTHES
JUMPING FROM OUTER WALL 16 MINUTES AFTER LEAVING CELL
TAKING AUTO FOR THEATRE
Cut by permission of The Boston Journal

Boston Journal, Tuesday, March 20, 1906.

**SHACKLED AND LOCKED IN, HOUDINI BREAKS JAIL.
CENTRAL FIGURES IN WIZARD HOUDINI'S MYSTIFYING JAIL ESCAPE AND DIAGRAM OF HIS MOVEMENTS.**

Cut by permission of The Boston Journal.

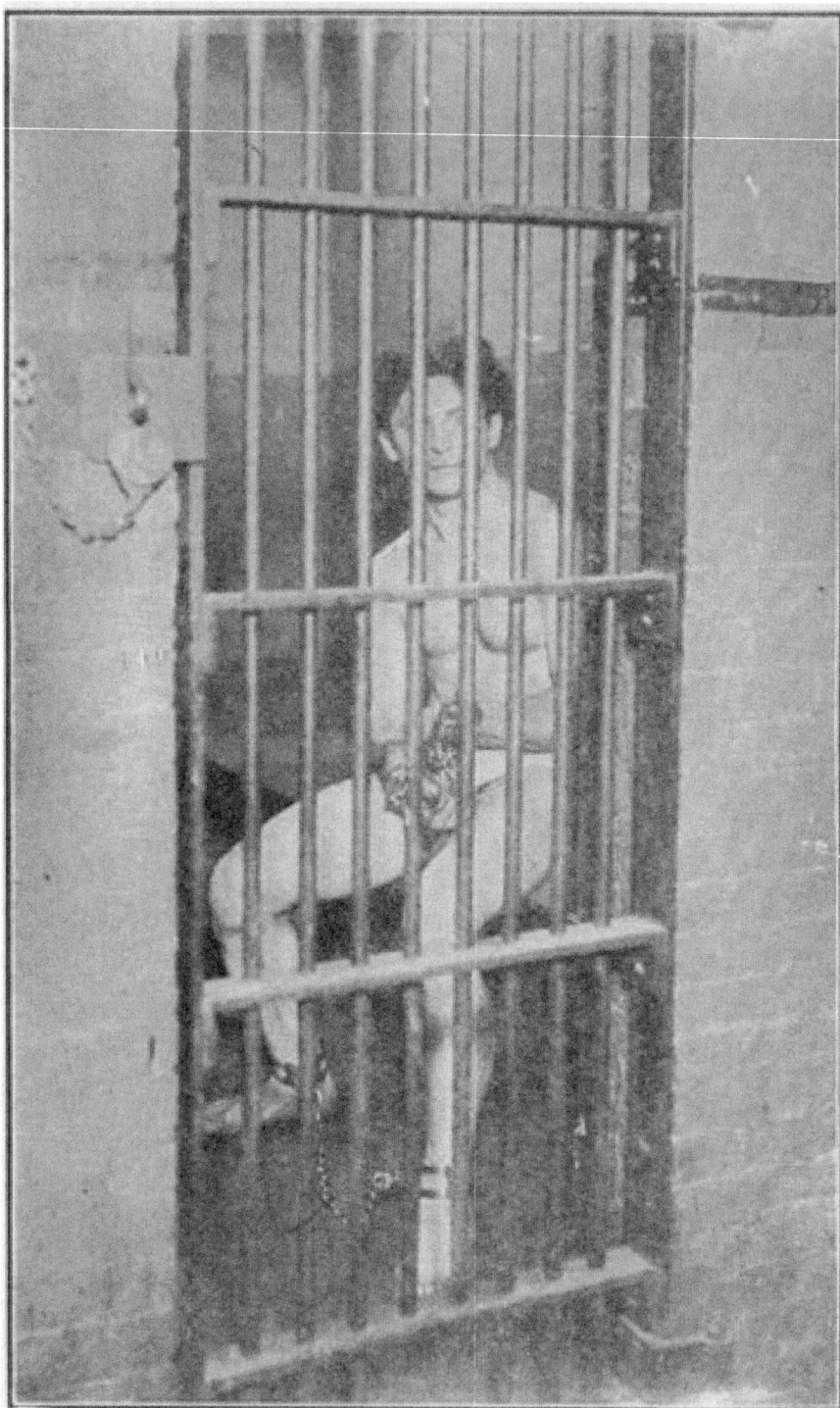

Inside the Cell at the City Tombs, Boston, Mass.

SUP'T. PIERCE LEFT HIM SHACKLED AND HANDCUFFED IN CELL No. 60

SUP'T. PIERCE SAT CHUCKLING IN THE CAPTAIN'S OFFICE WAITING FOR HOUDINI TO WHISTLE FOR HIM.

IN SIXTEEN MINUTES AFTER BEING LOCKED UP HE ESCAPED OVER THE WALL.

THE SUP'T. FOUND THE SHACKLES AND HANDCUFFS—BUT NO HOUDINI.

Caricatures by permission of Boston Post.

Then Superintendent Pierce took a pair of the most approved handcuffs used in the police department and fastened them securely about Houdini's wrists, and on his bare ankles he clamped a pair of tested steel leg irons so tightly that the iron sank into the flesh. After that Houdini was locked in cell No. 60, and Superintendent Pierce and the witnesses went downstairs and out into the office, expecting Houdini would go there, providing he got out of his cell, and the police officials who were present seemed to feel pretty confident that he couldn't do that. This feeling was shared by some of the outsiders present, who could not bring themselves to believe that it could be done.

Over the Wall at the City Tombs, Boston, Mass.

Photo with permission of the Boston Globe.

The only condition Houdini attached to his performance was that no one should be allowed to go into the part of the prison where he was confined to watch him escape, and the superintendent and the witnesses respected that condition, and most of them stayed in the captain's office. A few of the witnesses, however, went out into Somerset Street to wait and watch; for, knowing Houdini, they were prepared to see him come out anywhere.

These confident ones were rewarded for their trust, for 16 minutes after Houdini had been locked, naked, handcuffed, and ironed by the legs, into cell 60, he was seen running, fully dressed, except that he had not put on his collar and tie, across the prison yard, to climb up the wall leading into Somerset Street, to vault the iron railing at the top, and then to leg it like a scared rabbit over the hill in the direction of Keith's Theatre.

THE LITERARY HOUDINI

As is the case with many great men, the gift of being able to do many things, and to do each thing well, is Houdini's, who besides his achievements as a mystifier has also won wide recognition as an author. That he has found time to write a great deal is attested by his list of books, namely: "Miracle Mongers and Their Methods," "The Unmasking of Robert Houdin," "The Sane Side of Spiritualism," "The Right Way to do Wrong," "Magic Made Easy," "My Training and my Tricks," "Paper Prestidigitation," "Handcuff Secrets," "Magical Rope Ties and Escapes," "Good Night Stories for Children," "Dan Cupid the Magician" (a series) and "Magicians' Romances." Numerous magazine articles and stories swell his literary output to greater proportions. Editor for two years on standard work of magic, "The Conjurors Magazine."

In addition he has also written the stories for the feature films in which he was starred, namely, "The Man From Beyond" and "Haldane of the Secret Service," which were picturized by his own producing organization, Houdini Picture Corporation; "The Grim Game" and "Terror Island," written in collaboration with Arthur B. Reeve and John W. Grey, produced by Famous Players-Lasky Corporation.

HOUDINI PICTURE CORPORATION

In 1921, upon returning from his triumphant tour of Great Britain, Houdini organized his own film producing company for the purpose of making special feature pictures. The company, incorporated as Houdini Picture Corporation, capitalized at $500,000, began operations in the spring.

At the time of this writing two features have been completed—"The Man from Beyond" and "Haldane of the Secret Service." The first is characterized by those who have seen it at private pre-release showings as the most unusual picture ever screened, containing, as it does, originality of thought, novelty of treatment, and a thrilling finish that encompasses any thrilling situation yet produced for motion pictures.

The second picture, with interlocking scenes taken abroad, tells a mystery story and likewise demonstrates the ingenuity and resourcefulness of Houdini as producer, author and star.

Both pictures will soon be released to the public.

———————

Scenes from Photoplays

JESSE L. LASKY

Presents

HOUDINI

IN

"The Grim Game"

A Paramount-Artcraft
Picture

This picture contains the only airplane collision in the clouds ever photographed.

$1,000 reward to anyone proving the collision in the clouds is not genuine.

Starring Houdini

JESSE L. LASKY
Presents

HOUDINI

IN

"TERROR ISLAND"

A Paramount-Artcraft
Picture

The most amazing under water scenes ever enacted were recorded by the camera for "Terror Island."

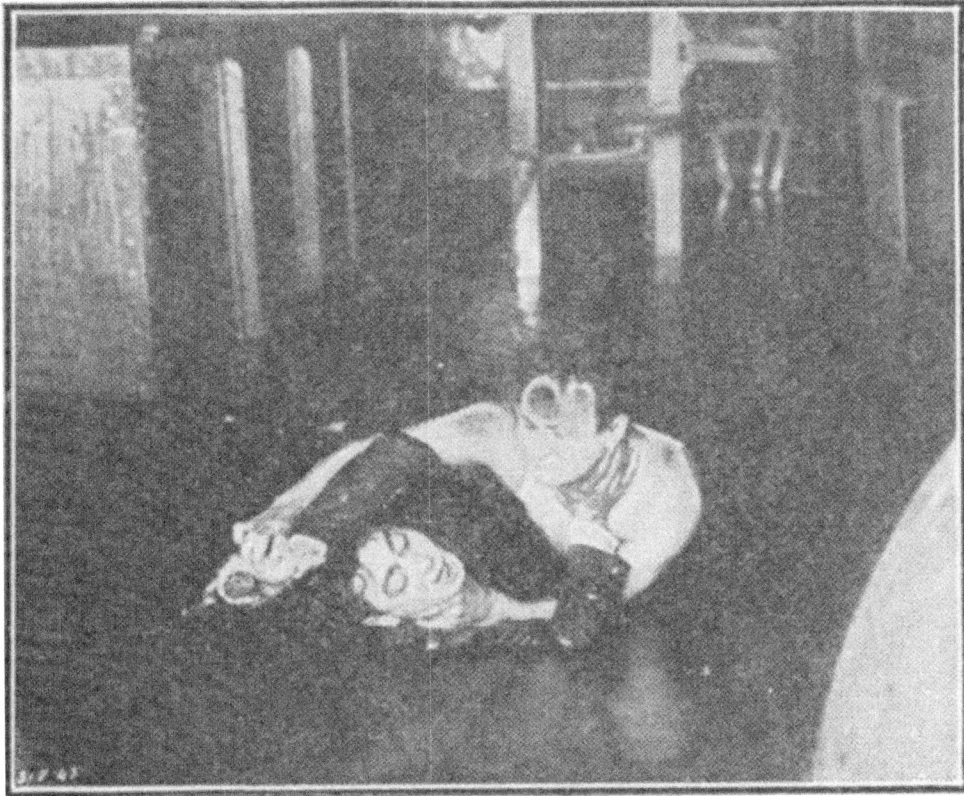

Scenes from Photoplays

HOUDINI PICTURE
CORP.
Presents

HOUDINI

in

"The
Man

From
Beyond"

Shortly to be
Released

Starring Houdini

HOUDINI PICTURE
CORP.
Presents

HOUDINI

in

"Haldane

of the

Secret
Service"

*An International
Mystery Drama
shortly to be released.*

Picture Plays, Confessions Album.
No. 14.—MR. HARRY HOUDINI

1. What is your favorite theater?

All the world is a theater to me.

2. Which is your favorite hobby?

Browsing in old bookstalls, seeking old dramatic items for my library.

3. Which is your favorite pastime?

Out door athletics and long distance swims.

4. Which is your favorite song?

"Auld Lang Syne."

5. Which is your favorite sweetmeat?

Candied fruits.

Mrs. HARRY HOUDINI

6. What is your idea of comfort?

Seated in a large arm chair in library and hearing Mrs. Houdini call up: "Young man your lunch is ready."

7. Which is your unlucky day?

Haven't any; an unfortunate incident at any time simply builds a foundation for something better.

8. What is your favorite motto?

"And this, too—shall pass away."

9. When have you felt at your worst?

Once when sailing round the world, at a longitude of 80°, we had two Tuesdays in one week and no Wednesday, which meant losing a Christmas, and I was seasick at the time. It will be an awful thing to eclipse my painful anguish.

10. What is your pet aversion?

The bald-headed man who says: "Ah, I remember you when I was a boy."

MY MOTHER

11. What is your greatest ambition?

To live a life and die being worthy of the mother who bore me.

12. What is your favorite holiday resort?

Hollywood, California.

13. Who is your favorite author?

My dad.

14. What is your idea of misery?

Arriving in a town at midnight on a drizzly wet, foggy night, and finding all the hotels full up.

Snap shot photograph of packing case containing six hundred pounds of iron weights and Houdini, as it was dropped into New York Bay. Houdini escaped from the box at the bottom of the bay in two minutes and fifty-five seconds.

DR. WILLIAMS ENGINEERING THE "THREAD THE NEEDLES TRICK"

HOUDINI ABOUT TO DISAPPEAR

WELL, GOODBYE

The National Casket Company challenged Houdini to escape from one of their heavy hickory coffins after they had fastened the cover down with six inch screws. Houdini accepted the test, which took place before members of the Boston Athletic Association, Boston, Mass. He escaped, the coffin was intact, showing no means of egress.

MR. PHIL SEARS

MR. COTTON

INTERESTED SPECTATORS IN THE FRONT ROW.

A LITTLE MORE AIR FOR MR. HOUDINI

THE HAGGARD HOUDINI REAPPEARS

HOPE I GET OUT OF MINE AS QUICKLY

How does he do it?

JAMES W. HARRIS,
WARDEN.

W. CRAYTON UNGER,
DEPUTY WARDEN.

United States Jail,

Washington, D. C., January 6th, 1906

This is to certify that Mr. Harry Houdini, at the United States
Jail today, was stripped stark naked, thoroughly searched, and locked
up in cell No. 2 of the South Wing,--the cell in which Charles J.
Guiteau, the assassinator of President Garfield, was confined during his incarceration, from the date of his commitment, July 2nd,
1881, until the day on which he was executed, June 30th, 1882.
Mr. Houdini, in about two minutes, managed to escape from that cell,
and then broke into the cell in which his clothing was locked-up.
He then proceeded to release from their cells all the prisoners on
the ground floor. There was positively no chance for any confederacy or collusion.

Mr. Houdini accomplished all of the above-mentioned facts, in
addition to putting on all his clothing, in twenty-one minutes.

J. W. Harris

Warden United States Jail, D. C.

AUDUBON PRINTERS
MITCHEL SQUARE
NEW YORK

How does he do it?

JAMES   H.   HARRIS,
 WARDEN,

W. GRAYSON URNER,

DEPUTY WARDEN,

United States Jail,

Washington, D.C., January 6th, *1906*

This is to certify that Mr. Harry Houdini, at the United States Jail today, was stripped stark naked, thoroughly searched, and locked up in cell No. 2 of the South Wing,—the cell in which Charles J. Guiteau, the assassinator of President Garfield, was confined during his incarceration, from the date of his commitment, July 2nd, 1881, until the day on which he was executed, June 30th, 1882. Mr. Houdini, in about two minutes, managed to escape from that cell, and then broke into the cell in which his clothing was locked up. He then proceeded to release from their cells all the prisoners on the ground floor. There was positively no chance for any confederacy or collusion.

Mr. Houdini accomplished all of the above-mentioned facts, in addition to putting on all his clothing, in twenty-one minutes.

J. H. Harris

Warden United States Jail, D. C.

AUDUBON PRINTERS
MITCHEL SQUARE
NEW YORK

_____

THE UNMASKING
of
ROBERT-HOUDIN

BY HARRY HOUDINI

Harry Houdini

99

Table of Contents

The Unmasking of Robert Houdin by Harry Houdini

THE UNMASKING

OF

ROBERT-HOUDIN

BY

HARRY HOUDINI

NEW YORK
THE PUBLISHERS PRINTING CO.
1908

Composition, Electrotyping and Printing by
The Publishers Printing Company
New York, N.Y., U.S.A.

INTRODUCTION

THIS book is the natural result of the moulding, dominating influence which the spirit and writings of Robert-Houdin have exerted over my professional career. My interest in conjuring and magic and my enthusiasm for Robert-Houdin came into existence simultaneously. From the moment that I began to study the art, he became my guide and hero. I accepted his writings as my text-book and my gospel. What Blackstone is to the struggling lawyer, Hardee's "Tactics" to the would-be officer, or Bismarck's life and writings to the coming statesman, Robert-Houdin's books were to me.

To my unsophisticated mind, his "Memoirs" gave to the profession a dignity worth attaining at the cost of earnest, life-long effort. When it became necessary for me to take a stage-name, and a fellow-player, possessing a veneer of culture, told me that if I would add the letter "i" to Houdin's name, it would mean, in the French language, "like Houdin," I adopted the suggestion with enthusiasm. I asked nothing more of life than to become in my profession "like Robert-Houdin."

By this time I had re-read his works until I could recite passage after passage from memory. Then, when Fate turned kind and the golden pathway of success led me into broader avenues of work, I determined that my first tour abroad should be dedicated to adding new laurels to the fame of Robert-Houdin. By research and study I would unearth history yet unwritten, and record unsung triumphs of this great inventor and artiste. The pen of his most devoted student and follower would awaken new interest in his history.

Robert-Houdin in his prime, immediately after his retirement. From the Harry Houdini Collection.

Alas for my golden dreams! My investigations brought forth only bitterest disappointment and saddest of disillusionment. Stripped of his self-woven veil of romance, Robert-Houdin stood forth, in the uncompromising light of cold historical facts, a mere pretender, a man who waxed great on the brainwork of others, a mechanician who had boldly filched the inventions of the master craftsmen among his predecessors.

"Memoirs of Robert-Houdin, Ambassador, Author and Conjurer, Written by Himself," proved to have been the penwork of a brilliant Parisian journalist, employed by Robert-Houdin to write his so-called autobiography. In the course of his "Memoirs," Robert-Houdin, over his own signature, claimed credit for the invention of many tricks and automata which may be said to have marked the golden age in magic. My investigations disproved each claim in order. He had announced himself as the first magician to appear in regulation evening clothes, discarding flowing sleeves and heavily draped stage apparatus. The credit for this revolution in conjuring belonged to Wiljalba Frikell. Robert-Houdin's explanation of tricks performed by other magicians and not included in his repertoire, proved so incorrect and inaccurate as to brand him an ignoramus in certain lines of conjuring. Yet to the great charm of his diction and the romantic development of his personal reminiscences later writers have yielded unquestioningly and have built upon the historically weak foundations of his statements all the later so-called histories of magic.

For a time, the disappointment killed all creative power. With no laurel wreath to carve, my tools lay idle. The spirit of investigation languished. Then came the reaction. There was work to be done. Those who had wrought honestly deserved the credit that had been taken from them. In justice to the living as well as the dead the history of the magic must be revised. The book, accepted for more than half a century as an authority on our craft, must stand forth for what it is, a clever romance, a well-written volume of fiction.

That is why to-day I offer to the profession of magic, to the world of laymen readers to whom its history has always appealed, and to the literary savants who dip into it as a recreation, the results of my investigations. These, I believe, will show Robert-Houdin's true place in the history of magic and give to his predecessors, in a profession which in each generation becomes more serious and more dignified, the credit they deserve.

**Frontispiece of "Hocus Pocus," Second Edition, 1635, one
of the earliest works on magic. From the Harry Houdini Collection.**

My investigations cover nearly twenty years of a busy professional career. Every hour which I could spare from my professional work was given over to study in libraries, to interviews with retired magicians and collectors, and to browsing in old bookstores and antique shops where rare collections of programs, newspapers, and prints might be found.

John Baptist Porta, the Neapolitan writer on magic. From an old woodcut in the Harry Houdini Collection.

In order to conduct my researches intelligently, I was compelled to pick up a smattering of the language of each country in which I played. The average collector or proprietor of an old bookshop is a canny, suspicious individual who must accept you as a friend before he will uncover his choicest treasures.

As authorities, books on magic and kindred arts are practically worthless. The earliest books, like the magician stories written by Sir John Mandeville in 1356, read like prototypes of to-day's dime novels. They are thrilling tales of travellers who witnessed magical performances, but they are not authentic records of performers and their work.

One of the oldest books in my collection is "Natural and Unnatural Magic" by Gantziony, dated 1489. It is the author's script, exquisite in its German chirography, artistic in its illuminated illustrations, but worthless as an historical record, though many of the writer's descriptions and explanations of old-time tricks are most interesting.

Early in the seventeenth century appeared "Hocus Pocus," the most widely copied book in the literature of magic. The second edition, dated 1635, I have in my library. I have never been able to find a copy of the first edition or to ascertain the date at which it was published.

A few years later, in 1658, came a very important contribution to the history of magic in "Natural Magick in XX. Bookes," by John Baptist Porta, a Neapolitan. This has been translated into nearly every language. It was the first really important and exhaustive work on the subject, but, unfortunately, it gives the explanation of tricks, rather than an authentic record of their invention.

In 1682, Simon Witgeest of Amsterdam, Holland, wrote an admirable work, whose title reads "Book of Natural Magic." This work was translated into German, ran through many an edition, and had an enormous sale in both Holland and Germany.

Frontispiece from Simon Witgeest's "Book of Natural Magic" (1682), showing the early Dutch conception of conjuring. From the Harry Houdini Collection.

In 1715, John White, an Englishman, published a work entitled "Art's Treasury and Hocus Pocus; or a Rich Cabinet of Legerdemain Curiosities." This is fully as reliable a book as the earlier "Hocus Pocus" books, but it is not so generally known.

Richard Neve, who was a popular English conjurer just before the time of Fawkes, published a book on somewhat similar lines in 1715.

Germany contributed the next notable works on magic. First came Johann Samuel Halle's "Magic or the Magical Power of Nature," printed in Berlin, in 1784. One of his compatriots, Johann Christian Wiegleb, wrote eighteen books on "The Natural Magic" and while I shall always contend that the German books are the most complete, yet they cannot be accepted as authorities save that, in describing early tricks, they prove the existence of inventions and working methods claimed later as original by men like Robert-Houdin.

English books on magic were not accepted seriously until the early part of the nineteenth century. In Vol. III. of John Beckmann's "History of Inventions and Discoveries," published in 1797, will be found a chapter on "Jugglers" which presents interesting matter regarding magicians and mysterious entertainers. I quote from this book in disproving Robert-Houdin's claims to the invention of automata and second-sight.

About 1840, J. H. Anderson, a popular magician, brought out a series of inexpensive, paper-bound volumes, entitled "A Shilling's Worth of Magic," "Parlor Magic," etc., which are valuable only as giving a glimpse of the tricks contemporary with his personal successes. In 1859 came Robert-Houdin's "Memoirs," magic's classic. Signor Blitz, in 1872, published his reminiscences, "Fifty Years in the Magic Circle," but here again we have a purely local and personal history, without general value.

JOHN WHITE, Author of ART's Treasury, and Hocus Pocus; or a Rich Cabinet of Legerdemain Curiosities.

John White, an English writer on magic and kindred arts in the early part of the eighteenth century.

Only portrait in existence and published for the first time since his book was issued in 1715.

From the Harry Houdini Collection.

Thomas Frost wrote three books relating to the history of magic, commencing about 1870. This list included "Circus Life and Circus Celebrities," "The Old Showmen and the Old London Fairs," and "Lives of the Conjurers." These were the best books of their kind up to the time of their publication, but they are marked by glaring errors, showing that Frost compiled rather than investigated, or, more properly speaking, that his investigations never went much further than Morley's "Memoirs of Bartholomew Fair."

Charles Bertram who wrote "Isn't it Wonderful?" closed the nineteenth-century list of English writers on magic, but his work is marred by mis-statements which even the humblest of magicians could refute, and, like Frost, he drew heavily on writers who preceded him.

So far, in the twentieth century, the most notable contribution to the literature of magic is Henry Ridgely Evans' "The Old and the New Magic," but Mr. Evans falls into the error of his predecessors in accepting as authoritative the history of magic and magicians furnished by Robert-Houdin. He has made no effort whatever to verify or refute the statements made by Robert-Houdin, but has merely compiled and re-written them to suit his twentieth-century readers.

Frontispiece from Richard Neve's work on magic, showing him performing the egg and bag trick about 1715.
Photographed from the original in the British Museum by the author.

Signor Antonio Blitz, author of "Fifty Years in the Magic Circle" (1872). Original negative of this photograph is in the Harry Houdini Collection.

The true historian does not compile. He delves for facts and proofs, and having found these he arrays his indisputable facts, his uncontrovertible proofs, to refute the statements of those who have merely compiled. That is what I have done to prove my case against Robert-Houdin. I have not borrowed from the books of other writers on magic. I have gone to the very fountain head of information, records of contemporary literature, newspapers, programmes and advertisements of magicians who preceded Robert-Houdin, sometimes by a century. It would cost fully a million dollars to forge the collection of evidence now in my hands. Men who lived a hundred years before Robert-Houdin was born did not invent posters or write advertisements in order to refute the claims of those who were to follow in the profession of magic. These programmes, advertisements, newspaper notices, and crude cuts trace the true history of magic as no romancer, no historian of a single generation possibly could. They are the ghosts of dead and gone magicians, rising in this century of research and progress to claim the credit due them.

Philip Astley, Esq., an historical circus director, a famous character of Bartholomew Fair days, and author of "Natural Magic" (1784). From the Harry Houdini Collection.

Charles Bertram (James Bassett), the English author and conjurer, who wrote "Isn't it Wonderful?" Born 1853, died Feb. 28th, 1907. From the Harry Houdini Collection.

Often when the bookshops and auction sales did not yield fruit worth plucking, I had the good fortune to meet a private collector or a retired performer whose assistance proved invaluable, and the histories of these meetings read almost like romances, so skilfully did the Fates seem to juggle with my efforts to secure credible proof.

To the late Henry Evans Evanion I am indebted for many of the most important additions to my collection of conjuring curios and my library of magic, recognized by fellow-artistes and litterateurs as the most complete in the world.

Evanion was an Englishman, by profession a parlor magician, by choice and habit a collector and savant. He was an entertainer from 1849 to the year of his death. For fifty years he spent every spare hour at the British Museum collecting data bearing on his marvellous collection, and his interest in the history of magic was shared by his excellent wife who conducted a "sweet shop" near one of London's public schools.

While playing at the London Hippodrome in 1904 I was confined to my room by orders of my physician. During this illness I was interviewed by a reporter who, noticing the clippings and bills with which my room was strewn, made some reference to my collection in the course of his article. The very day on which this interview appeared, I received from Henry Evanion a mere scrawl stating that he, too, collected programmes, bills, etc., in which I might be interested.

I wrote at once asking him to call at one o'clock the next afternoon, but as the hour passed and he did not appear, I decided that, like many others who asked for interviews, he had felt but a passing whim. That afternoon about four o'clock my physician suggested that, as the day was mild, I walk once around the block. As I stepped from the lift, the hotel porter informed me that since one o'clock an old man had been waiting to see me, but so shabby was his appearance, they had not dared send him up to my room. He pointed to a bent figure, clad in rusty raiment. When I approached the old man he rose and informed me that he had brought some clippings, bills, etc., for me to see. I asked him to be as expeditious as possible, for I was too weak to stand long and my head was a-whirl from the effects of la grippe.

Last photograph of Henry Evans Evanion, conjurer and collector, taken especially for this book in which he was deeply interested. Died June 17th, 1905. From the Harry Houdini Collection.

With some hesitancy of speech but the loving touch of a collector he opened his parcel.

"I have brought you, sir, only a few of my treasures, sir, but if you will call—"

I heard no more. I remember only raising my hands before my eyes, as if I had been dazzled by a sudden shower of diamonds. In his trembling hands lay priceless treasures for which I had sought in vain—original programmes and bills of Robert-Houdin, Phillippe, Anderson, Breslaw, Pinetti, Katterfelto, Boaz, in fact all the conjuring celebrities of the eighteenth century, together with lithographs long considered unobtainable, and newspapers to be found only in the files of national libraries. I felt as if the King of England stood before me and I must do him homage.

Physician or no physician, I made an engagement with him for the next morning, when I was bundled into a cab and went as fast as the driver could urge his horse to Evanion's home, a musty room in the basement of No. 12 Methley Street, Kennington Park Road, S.E.

Very rare and extraordinarily fine lithograph of Robert-Houdin, which he gave only to his friends. It depicts him among his so-called inventions. His son, Emile, doing second sight, is behind him. The writing and drawing figure is on his left. On his right under the clockwork is a drawing which, on close examination of the original, shows the suspension trick. From the Harry Houdini Collection.

In the presence of his collection I lost all track of time. Occasionally we paused in our work to drink tea which he made for us on his pathetically small stove. The drops of the first tea which we drank together can yet be found on certain papers in my collection. His wife, a most sympathetic soul, did not offer to disturb us, and it was 3:30 the next morning, or very nearly twenty-four hours after my arrival at his home, when my brother, Theodore Weiss (Hardeen), and a thoroughly disgusted physician appeared on the scene and dragged me, an unwilling victim, back to my hotel and medical care.

Such was the beginning of my friendship with Evanion. In time I learned that some of his collection had been left to him by James Savren, an English barber, who was so interested in magic that at frequent intervals he dropped his trade to work without pay for famous magicians, including Döbler, Anderson, Compars Herrmann, De Liska, Wellington Young, Cornillot, and Gyngell. From these men he had secured a marvellous collection, which was the envy of his friendly rival, Evanion. Savren bequeathed his collection to Evanion, and bit by bit I bought it from the latter, now poverty stricken, too old to work and physically failing. These purchases I made at intervals whenever I played in London, and on June 7th, 1905, while playing at Wigan, I received word that Evanion was dying at Lambeth Infirmary.

After the show, I jumped to London, only to find that cancer of the throat made it almost impossible for him to speak intelligibly. I soon discovered, however, that his chief anxiety was for the future of his wife and then for his own decent burial. When these sad offices had been provided for, he became more peaceful, and when I rose to leave him, knowing that we had met probably for the last time, he drew forth his chiefest treasure, a superb book of Robert-Houdin's programmes, his one legacy, which is now the central jewel in my collection. Evanion died ten days later, June 17th, and within a short time his good wife followed him into the Great Unknown.

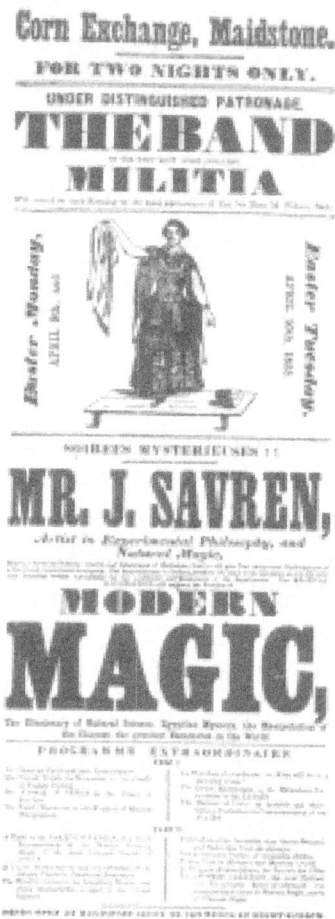

Poster used by James Savren. From the Harry Houdini Collection.

Even more dramatic was my meeting with the widow of Frikell, the great German conjurer.

I had heard that Frikell and not Robert-Houdin was the first magician to discard cumbersome, draped stage apparatus, and to don evening clothes, and I was most anxious to verify this rumor, as well as to interview him regarding equally important data bearing on the history of magic. Having heard that he lived in Kötchenbroda, a suburb of Dresden, I wrote to him from Cologne, asking for an interview. I received in reply a curt note: "Herr verreist," meaning "The master is on tour." This, I knew, from his age, could not be true, so I took a week off for personal investigation. I arrived at Kötchenbroda on the morning of April 8th, 1903, at 4 o'clock, and was directed to his home, known as "Villa Frikell." Having found my bearings and studied well the exterior of the house, I returned to the depot to await daylight. At 8:30 I reappeared at his door, and was told by his wife that Herr Frikell had gone away.

I then sought the police department from which I secured the following information: "Dr." Wiljalba Frikell was indeed the retired magician whom I was so anxious to meet. He was eighty-seven years old, and in 1884 had celebrated his golden anniversary as a conjurer. Living in the same town was an adopted daughter, but she could not or would not assist me. The venerable magician had suffered from domestic disappointments and had made a vow that he would see no one. In fact, he was leading a hermit-like life.

Armed with this information, I employed a photographer, giving him instructions to post himself opposite the house and make a snap shot of the magician, should he appear in the doorway. But I had counted without my host. All morning the photographer lounged across the street and all morning I stood bareheaded before the door of Herr Frikell, pleading with his wife who leaned from the window overhead. With that peculiar fervency which comes only when the heart's desire is at stake, I begged that the past master of magic would lend a helping hand to one ready to sit at his feet and learn. I urged the debt which he owed to the literature of magic and which he could pay by giving me such direct information as I needed for my book.

The Author standing in front of Villa Frikell at Kötchenbroda, Germany, where the master magician, Wiljalba Frikell, spent the last years of his life. From the Harry Houdini Collection.

Frau Frikell heard my pleadings with tears running down her cheeks, and later I learned that Herr Frikell also listened to them, lying grimly on the other side of the shuttered window.

At length, yielding to physical exhaustion, I went away, but I was still undaunted. I continued to bombard Herr Frikell with letters, press clippings regarding my work, etc., and finally in Russia I received a letter from him. I might send him a package containing a certain brand of Russian tea of which he was particularly fond. You may be sure I lost no time in shipping the little gift, and shortly I was rewarded by the letter for which I longed. Having decided that I cared more for him than did some of his relatives, he would receive me when next I played near Kötchenbroda.

With this interview in prospect, I made the earliest engagement obtainable in Dresden, intending to give every possible moment to my hardly-won acquaintance. But Fate interfered. One business problem after another arose, concerning my forthcoming engagement in England, and I had to postpone my visit to Herr Frikell until the latter part of the week. In the mean time, he had agreed to visit a Dresden photographer, as I wanted an up-to-date photograph of him and he had only pictures taken in his more youthful days. On the day when he came to Dresden for his sitting, he called at the theatre, but the attachés, without informing me, refused to give him the name of the hotel where I was stopping.

Last photograph of Herr and Frau Frikell, taken especially for this work. Frikell died Oct. 8th, 1903, the day after this photograph was taken. From the Harry Houdini Collection.

After the performance, I dropped into the König Kaffe and was much annoyed by the staring and gesticulations of an elderly couple at a distant table. It was Frikell with his wife, but I did not recognize them and, not being certain on his side, he failed to make himself known. That was mid-week, and for Saturday, which fell on October 8th, 1903, I had an engagement to call at the Villa Frikell. On Thursday, the Central Theatre being sold out to Cleo de Merode, who was playing special engagements in Germany with her own company, I made a flying business trip to Berlin, and on my return I passed through Kötchenbroda. As the train pulled into the station I hesitated. Should I drop off and see Herr Frikell, or wait for my appointment on the morrow? Fate turned the wheel by a mere thread and I went on to Dresden. So does she often dash our fondest hopes!

My appointment for Saturday was at 2 P.M., and as my train landed me in Kötchenbroda a trifle too early I walked slowly from the depot to the Villa Frikell, not wishing to disturb my aged host by arriving ahead of time.

I rang the bell. It echoed through the house with peculiar shrillness. The air seemed charged with a quality which I presumed was the intense pleasure of realizing my long cherished hope of meeting the great magician. A lady opened the door and greeted me with the words: "You are being waited for."

I entered. He was waiting for me indeed, this man who had consented to meet me, after vowing that he would never again look into the face of a stranger. And Fate had forced him to keep that vow. Wiljalba Frikell was dead. The body, clad in the best his wardrobe afforded, all of which had been donned in honor of his expected guest, was not yet cold. Heart failure had come suddenly and unannounced. The day before he had cleaned up his souvenirs in readiness for my coming and arranged a quantity of data for me. On the wall above the silent form were all of his gold medals, photographs taken at various stages of his life, orders presented to him by royalty— all the outward and visible signs of a vigorous, active, and successful life, the life of which he would have told me, had I arrived ahead of Death. And when all these were arranged, he had forgotten his morbid dislike of strangers. The old instincts of hospitality tugged at his heart strings, and his wife said he was almost young and happy once more, when suddenly he grasped at his heart, crying, "My heart! What is the matter with my heart? O——" That was all!

There we stood together, the woman who had loved the dear old wizard for years and the young magician who would have been so willing to love him had he been allowed to know him. His face was still wet from the cologne she had thrown over him in vain hope of reviving the fading soul. On the floor lay the cloths, used so ineffectually to bathe the pulseless face, and now laughing mockingly at one who saw himself defeated after weary months of writing and pleading for the much-desired meeting.

I feel sure that the personal note struck in these reminiscences will be forgiven. In no other way could I prove the authoritativeness of my collection, the thoroughness of my research, and the incontrovertibility of the facts which I desire to set forth in this volume.

THE UNMASKING OF
ROBERT-HOUDIN

CHAPTER I

SIGNIFICANT EVENTS IN THE LIFE OF ROBERT-HOUDIN

ROBERT-HOUDIN was born in Blois, France, December 6th, 1805. His real name was Jean-Eugene Robert, and his father was Prosper Robert, a watchmaker in moderate circumstances. His mother's maiden name was Marie Catherine Guillon. His first wife was Josephe Cecile Eglantine Houdin, whose family name he assumed for business reasons. He was married the second time to Françoise Marguerite Olympe Naconnier. His death, caused by pneumonia, occurred at St. Gervais, France, on June 13th, 1871.

Jean-Eugene Robert-Houdin. Photograph taken—about 1868. From the Harry Houdini Collection.

Barring the above facts, which were gleaned from the register of the civil authorities of St. Gervais, all information regarding his life previous to his first public appearance in 1844 must be drawn from his own works, particularly from his autobiography, published in the form of "Memoirs." Because of his supreme egotism, his obvious desire to make his autobiography picturesque and interesting rather than historically correct, and his utter indifference to dates, exact names of places, theatres, books, etc., it is extremely hard to present logical and consistent statements regarding his life. Such discrepancies arise as the mention of three children in one chapter and four in another, while he does not give the names of either wife, though he admits his obligation to both good women.

According to his autobiography, Jean-Eugene Robert was sent to college at Orleans at the tender age of eleven, and remained there until he was eighteen. He was then placed in a notary's office to study law, but his mechanical tastes led him back to his father's trade, watchmaking. While working for his cousin at Blois, he visited a bookshop in search of

Berthoud's "Treatise on Clockmaking," but by mistake he was given several volumes of an old encyclopædia, one of which contained a dissertation on "Scientific Amusements," or an exposition of magic. This simple incident, he asserts, changed the entire current of his life. At eighteen, he first turned his attention to magic. At forty, he made his first appearance as an independent magician or public performer.

On page 44 of his "Memoirs," American edition, Robert-Houdin refers to this book as an encyclopædia, but several times later he calls it "White Magic." In all probability it was the famous work by Henri Decremps in five volumes, known as "La Magie Banche Dévoilée," or "White Magic Exposed." This was written by Decremps to injure Pinetti, and it exposed all the latter's tricks, including the orange tree, the vaulting trapeze automaton, and in fact the majority of the tricks later claimed by Robert-Houdin as his own inventions.

In 1828, while working for M. Noriet, a watchmaker in Tours, Jean-Eugene Robert was poisoned by improperly prepared food, and in his delirium started for his old home in Blois. He was picked up on the roadside by Torrini, a travelling magician, who nursed him back to health in his portable theatre. Just as young Jean recovered Torrini was injured in an accident, and his erstwhile patient remained to nurse his benefactor and later to help Torrini's assistant present the programme of magic by which they made their living. His first public appearance as the representative of Torrini was made at Aubusson.

The only Robert-Houdin poster showing his complete stage setting. This lithograph was made in France. From the Harry Houdini Collection.

To-day, Thursday, July 3, 1845,

First Representation

OF

The Fantastic Soirees

OF

Robert-Houdin,

Automata, Sleight-of-Hand, Magic.

The Performance will be composed of entirely
novel Experiments invented by

M. Robert-Houdin,

Among them being:

The Cabalistic Clock   Obedient Cards
Auriol and Deburean   The Miraculous Fish
The Orange-Tree   The Fascinating Owl
The Mysterious Boquet   The Pastrycook of the
Pierrot in the Egg   Palais Royal

To Commence at Eight o'clock.

Box office open at half past Seven.

*Price of Places: Upper Boxes, 1 fr. 50 c.; Stalls, 3 fr.;
Boxes, 4 fr.; Dress Circle, 5 fr.*

Programme for the opening of Robert-Houdin's theatre in Paris. Reproduced from the American edition of his "Memoirs."

Robert-Houdin's favorite lithograph for advertising purposes. Used on the majority of his posters and in the original edition of his "Memoirs." From the Harry Houdini Collection.

Torrini was an Italian whose real name was Count Edmond de Grisy. He was a contemporary of Pinetti. In all probability, during the long summer of their intimate companionship, Torrini not only initiated his fascinated young guest into his own methods of performingtricks, but also into the secrets of Pinetti's tricks. In his "Memoirs," Robert-Houdin makes no secret of the fact that both Comus and Pinetti, together with their tricks, were topics of conversation between himself and Torrini.

A very rare, and possibly the only, programme in existence, chronicling Robert-Houdin's first appearance before Queen Victoria, July 19th, 1848. The original, now in the Harry Houdini Collection, was presented to James Savren by Robert-Houdin.

Poster used by Robert-Houdin during an Easter engagement at the St. James Theatre, London. From the Harry Houdini Collection.

When Torrini was able to resume his performances, Jean-Eugene returned to his family in Blois. During the next few years he mixed amateur acting with his daily labor, leaning more and more toward the profession of public entertainer. But his ambitions along this line were nipped in the bud by marriage. Mademoiselle Houdin, whose father was a celebrated watchmaker in Paris, visited old friends in Blois, their native town, and became the fiancée of young Robert. As the new son-in-law was to share the elder Houdin's business and naturally wished to secure such benefits as might accrue from so celebrated a family of watch and clock makers, he applied to the council of state and secured the right to annex "Houdin" to his name, Jean-Eugene Robert, and thereafter was known only as Robert-Houdin.

His life between 1838 and 1844 was divided between reading every work obtainable on magic, and his duties in his father-in-law's shop, where he not only made and repaired clocks, but built and repaired automata of various sorts. His family shared with him many financial vicissitudes, and about 1842-43 his first wife died, leaving him with three young children to raise. Earlier in his "Memoirs" he speaks of having four children, so it is more than likely that one died before his wife. He married again soon, and though he gives his second wife great credit as a helpmate he does not state her name.

Robert-Houdin as he appeared to the English critics. Reproduced from the Illustrated London News, December 23d, 1848.

ROBERT HOUDIN'S SOIREES FANTASTIQUES Poster used in 1848 in London by Robert-Houdin. From the Harry Houdini Collection.

By this time he had acquired more than passing fame as a repairer of automata, and in 1844 he mended Vaucanson's marvellous duck, one of the most remarkable automata ever made. Doubtless other automata found their way to his workshop and aided him in his study of a profession which he still hoped to follow. During these discouraging times he was often assisted financially by one Monsieur G——, who either advanced money on his automata or bought them outright. In the same year, 1844, he retired to a suburb of Paris, and there, he asserts, he built his famous writing and drawing figure.

Poster for the Emile-Houdin benefit at St. James's Theatre in 1848. From the Harry Houdini Collection.

The next year, 1845, he was assisted by Count de L'Escalopier, a devotee of conjuring and automata, who advanced the money to fit up and furnish a small theatre in the Palais Royal. Robert-Houdin went about the work of decorating and furnishing this theatre with a view to securing the most dramatic and brilliant effects, surrounding his simple tricks with a setting that made them vastly different from the same offerings by his predecessors. He was what is called to-day an original producer of old ideas. On June 25th, 1845, he gave his first private performance before a few friends. On July 3d of the same year his theatre of magic was opened formally to the public. The programme of this performance is shown on page 37.

It will be noted that the famous writing and drawing figure was not then included in Robert-Houdin's répertoire, nor does it ever appear on any of his programmes. He exhibited it at the quinquennial exhibition in 1844, received a silver medal for it, and very soon sold it to the late P. T. Barnum, who exported it to America.

Poster used by Robert-Houdin when he played at Sadler's Wells, London, in 1853. He never refers to this engagement in his writings because he was not proud of having appeared in a second-class theatre, while his rival, Anderson, held the fashionable audiences at the St. James's, where Robert-Houdin had worn out his welcome. From the Harry Houdini Collection.

This question naturally arises: If Robert-Houdin built the original writing and drawing figure, why could he not make a duplicate and include it in his programme? Surely it was one of the most remarkable of the automata which he claims as the creations of his brain and hands.

In 1846 he claims to have invented second sight, and at the opening of the season in 1847 he presented as his own creation the suspension trick. During the interim he played an engagement in Brussels which was a financial failure.

In 1848 the Revolution closed the doors of Parisian theatres, Robert-Houdin's among the rest, and he returned to clockmaking and automata building, until he received from John Mitchell, who had met with great success in managing Ludwig Döbler and Phillippe, an offer to appear in London at the St. James's Theatre. This engagement was a brilliant success and for the first time in his career Robert-Houdin reaped big financial returns.

Later Robert-Houdin toured the English provinces under his own management and made return trips to London, but his tour under Mitchell was the most notable engagement of his career.

Robert-Houdin's grave, in the cemetery at Blois, France. From a photograph taken by the author, especially for this work, and now in the Harry Houdini Collection.

In 1850, while playing in Paris, he decided to retire, and to turn over his theatre and tricks to one Hamilton. A contemporary clipping, taken from an English newspaper of 1848, goes to prove that Hamilton was an Englishman who entered Robert-Houdin's employ. Hamilton signed a dual contract, agreeing to produce Robert-Houdin's tricks as his acknowledged successor and to marry Robert-Houdin's sister, thus keeping the tricks and the theatre in the family. During the next two years Robert-Houdin spent part of his time instructing his brother-in-law in all the mysteries of his art. In July, 1852, he played a few engagements in Germany, including Berlin and various bathing resorts, and then formally retired to his home at St. Gervais. Here he continued to work along mechanical and electrical lines, and in 1855 he again came into public notice, winning awards at the Exhibition for electrical power as applied to mechanical uses. In 1856, according to his autobiography, he was summoned from his retirement by the Government to make a trip to Algeria and there intimidate revolting Arabs by the exhibition of his sleight-of-hand tricks. These were greatly superior to the work of the Marabouts or Arabian magicians, whose influence was often held responsible for revolts. What Robert-Houdin received for performing this service is not set forth in any of his works. He spent the fall of 1856 in Algeria.

Bas-relief on Robert-Houdin tombstone. From a photograph taken by the author, especially for this work, and now in the Harry Houdini Collection.

From the date of his return to St. Gervais to the time of his death, June 13th, 1871, Robert-Houdin devoted his energies to improving his inventions and writing his books, though, as stated before, it was generally believed by contemporary magicians that in the latter task he entrusted most of the real work to a Parisian journalist whose name was never known.

He was survived by a wife, a son named Emile, and a step-daughter. Emile Houdin managed his father's theatre until his death in 1883, when the theatre was sold for 35,000 francs. The historic temple of magic still stands under the title of "Théâtre Robert-Houdin," under the management of M. Melies, a maker of motion picture films.

The last photograph taken of Robert-Houdin and used as the frontispiece for the original French edition of his "Memoirs," published in 1868.

During my investigations in Paris, I was shocked to find how little the memory of Robert-Houdin was revered and how little was known of France's greatest magician. In fact, I was more than once informed that Robert-Houdin was still alive and giving performances at the theatre which bears his name.

Contemporary magicians of Robert-Houdin and men of high repute in other walks of life seem to agree that Robert-Houdin was an entertainer of only average merit. Among the men who advanced this theory were the late Henry Evanion of whose deep interest in magic I wrote in the introduction, Sir William Clayton who was Robert-Houdin's personal friend in London, Ernest Basch who saw Robert-Houdin in Berlin, and T. Bolin of Moscow, Russia, who bought all his tricks in Paris and there saw Robert-Houdin and studied his work as a conjurer.

Robert-Houdin's contributions to literature, all of which are eulogistic of his own talents, are as follows:

"Confidence et Révélations," published in Paris in 1858 and translated into English by Lascelles Wraxall, with an introduction by R. Shelton Mackenzie.

"Les Tricheries des Grecs" (Card-Sharping Exposed), published in Paris in 1861.

"Secrets de la Prestidigitation" (Secrets of Magic), published in Paris in 1868.

"Le Prieuré" (The Priory, being an account of his electrically equipped house), published in Paris in 1867.

"Les Radiations Lumineuses," published in Blois in 1869.

"Exploration de la Rétinue," published in Blois, 1869.

"Magic et Physique Amusante" (œuvre posthume), published in Paris in 1877, six years after Robert-Houdin's death.

In his autobiography, Robert-Houdin makes specific claim to the honor of having invented the following tricks: The Orange Tree, Second Sight, Suspension, The Cabalistic Clock, The Inexhaustible Bottle, The Pastry Cook of the Palais Royal, The Vaulting Trapeze Automaton, and the Writing and Drawing Figure.

His fame, which has been sung by writers of magic without number since his death, rests principally on the invention of second sight, suspension, and the writing and drawing automaton. It is my intention to trace the true history of each of these tricks and of all others to which he laid claim as inventor, and show just how small a proportion of the credit was due to Robert-Houdin and how much he owed to magicians who preceded him and whose brain-work he claimed as his own.

CHAPTER II

THE ORANGE-TREE TRICK

ROBERT-HOUDIN, on page 179 of the American edition of his "Memoirs," thus describes the orange-tree trick, which he claims as his invention: "The next was a mysterious orange-tree, on which flowers and fruit burst into life at the request of the ladies. As the finale, a handkerchief I borrowed was conveyed into an orange purposely left on the tree. This opened and displayed the handkerchief, which two butterflies took by the corners and unfolded before the spectators."

On page 245 of the same volume he presents the programme given at the first public performance in the Théâtre Robert-Houdin, stating:

"The performance will be composed of entirely novel Experiments invented by M. Robert-Houdin. Among them being The Orange-Tree, etc."

Now to retrace our steps in the history of magic as set forth in handbills and advertisements of earlier and contemporaneous newspaper clippings describing their inventions.

Under the title of "The Apple-Tree" this mechanical trick appeared on a Fawkes programme dated 1730. This was 115 years before Robert-Houdin claimed it as his invention. In 1732, just before Pinchbeck's death, it appeared on a programme used by Christopher Pinchbeck, Sr., and the younger Fawkes. In 1784 it was included in the répertoire of the Italian conjurer, Pinetti, in the guise of "Le Bouquet-philosophique." In 1822 the same trick, but this time called "An Enchanted Garden," was featured by M. Cornillot, who appeared in England as the pupil and successor of Pinetti.

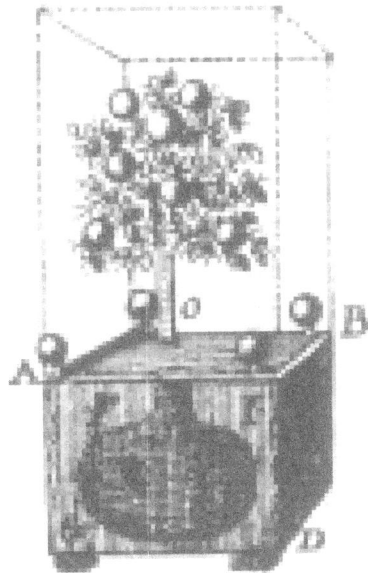

Diagram of the orange-tree trick, from Wiegleb's "The Natural Magic," published in 1794.

The trick was first explained in public print by Henri Decremps in 1784 when his famous exposé of Pinetti was published under the title of "La Magie Blanche Dévoilée," and in 1786-87 both Halle and Wiegleb exposed the trick completely in their respective works on magic.

That Robert-Houdin was an omnivorous reader is proven by his own writings. That he knew the history and tricks of Pinetti is proven by his own words, for in Chapter VI. of his "Memoirs" he devoted fourteen pages to Pinetti and the latter's relations with Torrini.

Now to prove that the tree tricks offered by Fawkes, Pinchbeck, Pinetti, Cornillot, and Robert-Houdin were practically one and the same, and to tell something of the history of the four magicians who featured the trick before Robert-Houdin had been heard of:

Christopher Pinchbeck, Sr. This is the oldest and rarest authentic mezzotint in the world pertaining to the history of magic. From the Harry Houdini Collection.

Unquestionably, the real inventor of the mysterious tree was Christopher Pinchbeck, who was England's leading mechanical genius at the close of the seventeenth century and the beginning of the eighteenth. He was a man of high repute, whose history is not that of the charlatan, compiled largely from tradition, but it can be corroborated by court records, biographical works, and encyclopædias, as well as by contemporaneous newspaper clippings.

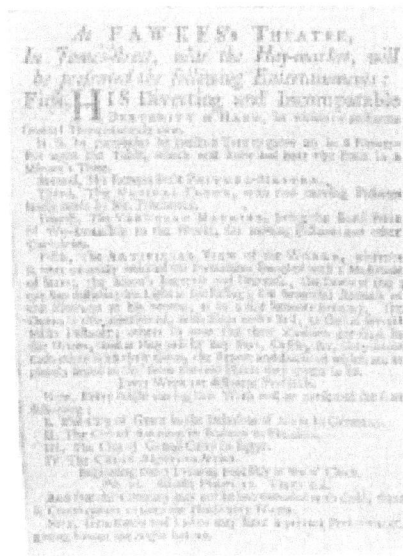

Advertisement from the London Daily Post during 1730, showing the orange tree as offered by the senior Fawkes, just previous to his death. From the Harry Houdini Collection.

According to Vol. XLV. of the "Dictionary of National Biography," edited by Sidney Lee and published in 1896 by Smith, Elder & Co., 15 Waterloo Place, London: "Christopher Pinchbeck was born about 1670, possibly in Clerkenwell, London. He was a clockmaker and inventor of the copper and zinc alloy called after his name. He invented and made the famous astronomico-musical clock. In Appleby's *Weekly Journal* of July 8th, 1721, it was announced that 'Christopher Pinchbeck, inventor and maker of the astronomico-musical clock, is removed, from St. George's Court (now Albion Place) to the sign of the "Astronomico-Musical Clock" in Fleet Street, near the Leg Tavern. He maketh and selleth watches of all sorts and clocks as well for the exact indication of the time only as astronomical, for showing the various motions and phenomena of planets and fixed stars.' Mention is also made of musical automata in imitation of singing birds and barrel organs for churches, as among Pinchbeck's manufactures.

"Pinchbeck was in the habit of exhibiting collections of his automata at fairs, sometimes in conjunction with a juggler named Fawkes, and he entitled his stall 'The Temple of the Muses,' 'Grand Theatre of the Muses,' or 'Multum in Parvo.' The *Daily Journal* of August 27th, 1729, announced that the Prince and Princess of Wales went to the Bartholomew Fair to see his exhibition, and there were brief advertisements in *The Daily Post* of June 12th, 1729, and the *Daily Journal* of August 22d and 23d, 1729. There is still a large broadside in the British Museum (1850 c. 10-17) headed 'Multum in Parvo,' relating to Pinchbeck's exhibition, with a blank left for place and date, evidently intended for use as a poster. He died November 18th, 1732; was buried November 21st, in St. Denison's Church, Fleet Street.

"In a copy of the *Gentlemen's Magazine*, printed 1732, page 1083, there is an engraved portrait by I. Faber, after a painting by Isaac Wood, a reproduction of which appears in 'Britten's

Clock and Watch Maker,' page 122. His will, dated November 10th, 1732, was proved in London on November 18th."

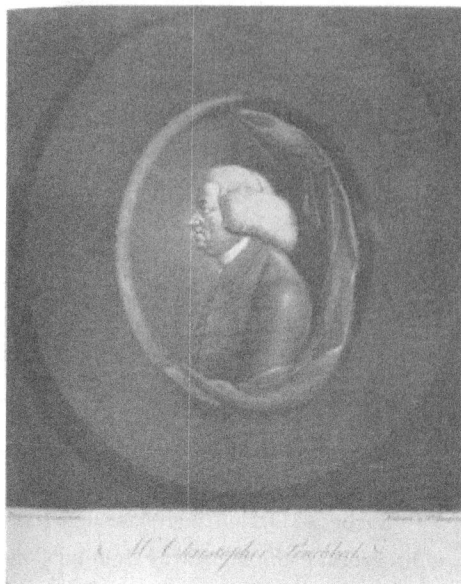

A very rare mezzotint of Christopher Pinchbeck, Jr., combining the work of Cunningham, the greatest designer, and William Humphrey, the greatest portrait etcher of his day. From the Harry Houdini Collection.

During one of his engagements at the Bartholomew Fair, Pinchbeck probably met Fawkes, the cleverest sleight-of-hand performer that magic has ever known, and the two joined forces. Pinchbeck made all the automata and apparatus thereafter used by Fawkes, and, in Fawkes, he had a master-producer of his tricks. Christopher Pinchbeck never appeared on the program used by Fawkes, save as the maker of the automata or apparatus, but directly after the death of the elder Fawkes, and a few months before his own, the elder Pinchbeck appeared with the son of his deceased partner, and was advertised as doing "the Dexterity of Hand" performance. This indicates that he was inducting young Fawkes into all the mysteries of the profession at which the two elder men, as friends and business partners, had done so well.

Christopher Pinchbeck was survived by two sons, Edward and Christopher, Jr. Edward, the elder, succeeded to his father's shop and regular business. He was born about 1703, and was well along in years when he entered into his patrimony, which he advertised in *The Daily Post* of November 27th, 1732, as follows: "The toys made of the late Mr. Pinchbeck's curious metal are now sold only by his son and sole executor, Mr. Edward Pinchbeck."

This announcement settles forever the oft-disputed question as to whether the alloy of copper and zinc which bears the name of Pinchbeck was invented by Christopher Pinchbeck, Sr., or by his son Christopher, Jr.

All newspaper and magazine descriptions of the automata invented by the elder Pinchbeck indicate that his hand was as cunning as his brain was inventive, for they showed the most delicate mechanism, and included entire landscapes with figures of rare grace in motion.

The best portrait of Isaac Fawkes in existence. The original, now in the Harry Houdini Collection, is supposed to have been engraved by Sutton Nichols. It is said that there is only one more of these engravings extant.

"Christopher, the second son of Christopher Pinchbeck the elder," continues the biographical sketch, "was born about 1710 and possessed great mechanical ingenuity. While the elder son, Edward, was made executor and continued his father's trade in a quiet, conservative fashion, the younger son struck out along new lines and became even more famous as an inventor than his brilliant father had been.

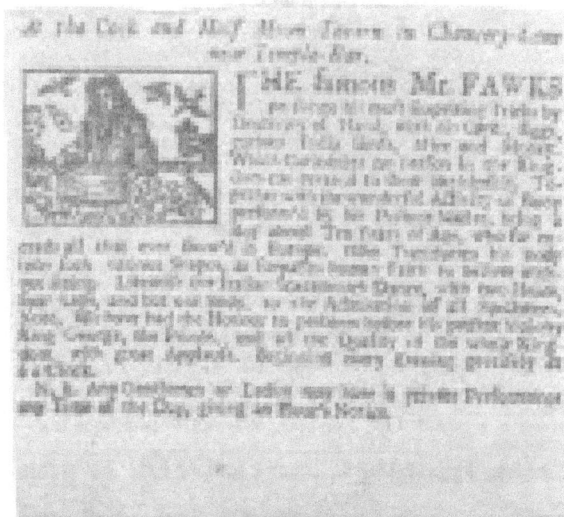

An early Fawkes advertisement, clipped from a London paper of 1725. From the Harry Houdini Collection.

"He was a member and at one time president of the Smeatonian Society, the precursor of the Institution of Civil Engineers. In 1762, he devised a self-acting pneumatic brake for preventing accidents to the men employed in working wheel-cranes. In *The Gentlemen's Magazine* for June, 1765, page 296, it is recorded that Messrs. Pinchbeck and Norton had made a complicated astronomical clock for the Queen's house, some of the calculations of the wheel having been made by James Ferguson, the astronomer. There is no proof that Pinchbeck and Norton were ever in partnership, and there are now two clocks answering to the description at Buckingham Palace, one by Pinchbeck, with four dials and of a very complicated construction, and another by Norton.

"Pinchbeck took out three patents: the first (No. 892), granted 1768, was for an improved candlestick with a spring socket for holding the candle firmly, and an arrangement whereby the candle always occupied an upright position, however the candlestick might be held. In 1768 (patent No. 899) he patented his nocturnal remembrancer, a series of tablets with notches, to serve as guides for writing in the dark. His snuffers (No. 1119) patented 1776, continued to be made in Birmingham until the last forty years or so, when snuffers began to go out of use. In 1774, he presented to the Society of Arts a model of a plough for mending roads. Pinchbeck's name first appears in the London directory in 1778, when it replaced that of Richard Pinchbeck, toyman, of whom nothing is recorded.

"Christopher Pinchbeck, Jr., was held in considerable esteem by George III., and he figures in Wilkes' London Museum (ii-33) in 1770 in the list of the party who called themselves the King's friends. He died March 17th, 1783, aged 73, and was buried in St. Martin's-in-the-Fields. His will, which was very curious, is printed in full in *The Horological Journal* of November, 1895. One of his daughters married William Hebb, who was described as 'son-in-law and successor of the late Mr. Pinchbeck at his shop in Cockspur Street' (imprinted on Pinchbeck's portrait), whose son Christopher Henry Hebb (1772-1861) practised as a surgeon in

Worcester. There is in existence a portrait of Christopher Pinchbeck the younger, by Cunningham, engraved by W. Humphrey."

The mezzotints of the Pinchbecks, father and son, herewith reproduced, are extremely rare, and when I unearthed them in Berlin I felt myself singularly favored in securing two such treasures of great value to the history of magic. S. Wohl, the antiquarian and dealer from whom they were purchased, acquired them during a tour of old book and print shops in England, and thought them portraits of one and the same person; but by studying the names of the artists and the engravers on the two pictures, it will be seen that they set forth the features of father and son, as indicated by the biographical notes quoted above.

Of the early history of Fawkes, whose brilliant stage performance lent to the Pinchbeck automata a new lustre, little is known. It is practically impossible to trace his family history. His Christian name was never used on his billing nor published in papers or magazines, and after repeated failures I was about to give up the task of discovering it, when in 1904, aided by R. Bennett, the clerk of St. Martin's-in-the-Fields Parish Church, Trafalgar Square, London, England, I came upon the record of his burial. This record, which I found after many days' search among musty, faded parchments, showed that his Christian name was Isaac, and that he died May 25th or 29th, 1731, and was buried in St. Martin's-in-the-Fields Parish Church.

The records further show that he was buried in the church vault, the coffin being carried by six men. Prayers were said in the church, candles were used, and the great bell was tolled. As the fees amounted to £6 12s., a goodly sum for those days, all signs indicate that the funeral was on a scale more costly and impressive than the ordinary.

Fawkes was worth at his death £10,000, which was considered an enormous sum in those days. Every penny of this he made performing at the fairs.

The earliest announcements of Fawkes' performance in my collection are dated 1702 and include advertisements headed "Fawkes and Powel," "Fawkes and Phillips," and "Fawkes and Pinchbeck." Powel was the famous puppet man, Phillips a famous posture master (known to-day as contortionist), and Pinchbeck was the greatest of mechanicians. Fawkes seems to have possessed a singular gift for picking out desirable partners.

From this mass of evidence, I am producing various clippings. By a peculiar coincidence one of these I believe offers the most authentic and earliest record of "two a night" performances in England.

In my collection are a number of other clippings from the press of the same year, in April and May, 1728, but none of them says "twice a night," therefore I judge that the custom of giving two performances in a night was tried previously to April, 1728, and then abandoned, or after the first of May.

In the London *Post* of February 7th, 1724, Fawkes announced an exhibition "in the Long Room over the piazza at the Opera House in the Haymarket." At this time he also advertised the fact that he was about to retire and was exposing all his tricks. The clipping of that date from my collection has the following foot-note: "Likewise he designs to follow this business no longer than this season; so he promises to learn any lady or gentleman his fancies in dexterity of hand for their own diversion."

When Fawkes was not in partnership with some puppet showman, he always advertised his own puppets as "A court of the richest and largest figures ever shown in England, being as big as men and women!" His admission charges varied, but 12 pence seemed his favorite figure. About six years before his death he had his own theatre in James Street, near the Haymarket, in which he exhibited for months at a time before and after fairs.

I reproduce a clipping from my collection showing Fawkes' last program. Here it will be seen that his first trick was causing a tree to grow up in a flower-pot on the table, and bear fruit in a minute's time. In *The Gentlemen's Magazine*, that oft-quoted and most reliable periodical, of February 15th, 1731, readers were informed that the Algerian Ambassadors witnessed Fawkes' performance.

At their request, he showed them "a prospect of Algiers, and raised up an apple-tree which bore ripe fruit in less than a minute's time, which several of the company tasted of."

Fawkes, too, had a son, and thus the partnership and the friendship which had existed between the elder Fawkes and the elder Pinchbeck were carried on by the second generation. All of the marvellous apparatus made by Pinchbeck the elder, for Fawkes, may have been bequeathed by the latter to his son, but, in 1732, Pinchbeck the elder and Fawkes the younger were in a booth together, and Pinchbeck was advertised as doing "the dexterity of hand" performances. After Christopher Pinchbeck, Sr., died, young Fawkes started out on his own account. In 1746, according to an advertisement in my collection, a Fawkes and a Pinchbeck were together again, so the son of Pinchbeck must have joined the younger Fawkes for exhibition purposes. The accompanying clippings from contemporary publications trace the history of young Fawkes, and prove that the tree which bore fruit in a minute's time was still on his programme.

Reproduction of page 1226 of Hone's "Every-Day Book" in the Harry Houdini Collection. This is a portrait of Fawkes, engraved on a fan by Setchels in 1721 or 1728. Fans like these were distributed at the Bartholomew Fair.

For many years it was supposed that only one portrait of Fawkes was in existence, but it now seems that three were made. I publish them all, something which no one has ever before been able to do. One was taken from a Setchels fan published about 1728, although some authorities say 1721. It appeared in Hone's "Every-Day Book," page 1226. Another, I believe, was engraved by Sutton Nicols, as Hone mentions it in his description of Fawkes. In the fan engraving, it will be noticed that there appears a man wearing a star on his left breast. It is said that this is Sir Robert Walpole, who was Prime Minister while Fawkes was at the height of his success, and who was one of the conjurer's great admirers. Hogarth also placed Fawkes in one of his engravings as the frontispiece of a most diverting brochure on "Taste," in which he belittles Burlington Gate. This makes the third portrait from my collection herewith reproduced.

According to an article contributed by Mons. E. Raynaly in the *Illusionniste* of June, 1903, the orange tree next appeared in the répertoire of a remarkable peasant conjurer, whose billing Mons. Raynaly found among "Affiches de Paris." This performer was billed as the Peasant of North Holland, and gave hourly performances at the yearly fairs at Saint-Germain.

It is more than possible that he purchased this trick from Fawkes or Pinchbeck, having seen it at the Bartholomew Fair in England.

He featured the orange tree as follows: "He has a Philosophical Flower Pot, in which he causes to grow on a table in the presence of the spectators trees which flower, and then the flowers fall, and fruit appears absolutely ripe and ready to be eaten."

His posters are dated 1746-47 and 1751.

The next programme on which the mysterious tree appears is a Pinetti handbill, dated in London, 1784, when the following announcement was made:

"Signore Pinetti will afterwards present the assembly with a Tree called Le Bouquet-philosophique composed of small branches of an orange-tree, the leaves appearing green and natural. He will put it under a bottle, and at some distance, by throwing some drops of water of his own composition, the leaves will begin to change and the bouquet will produce natural flowers and various fruits."

Masquerade and opera at Burlington Gate. Reproduction of Hogarth's engraving entitled "Taste," belittling the artistic taste of London. This caricature verifies the Fawkes advertisement, reproduced on page 64, for here the conjurer is pictured leaning from the window of the "long room" and calling attention to his performances. From the Harry Houdini Collection.

Pinetti is one of the most fascinating and picturesque figures in the history of magic. His full name was Joseph Pinetti de Willedal, and, like Pinchbeck and Fawkes, he was a man of parts and readily made friends with the nobility. In fact, there is some question as to whether he did not come of a noble family.

He was born in 1750 in Orbitelle, a fortified town once claimed by Tuscany. What can be gleaned regarding his early history goes to prove that his family connections were excellent and his education of the best. One of his portraits, reproduced herewith, shows a half-crown of laurel decorating the frame, and on one side of the bust is a globe, while in the rear of the picture is a stack of books. This would establish his claim that he was once a professor of physics and geography. In fact, the legend beneath the portrait, being translated from the French, runs:

"I. I. Pinetti Willedal de Merci, Professor and Demonstrator of Physics, Chevalier of the Order of St. Philipe, Geographical Engineer, Financial Counselor of H.R.H. Prince of Linbourg Holstein, Born in Orbitelle in 1750."

A wood-cut used by Pinetti during his engagement at Hamburg, Germany, in October, 1796. From the Harry Houdini Collection.

As it has so often happened in the history of savants and students, there ran in Pinetti's blood a love of the mysterious with that peculiar strain of charalatanism which went to make up the clever performer in old-time magic. Evidently, he resigned his duties as a professor for the more picturesque life of the travelling magician, and he is first heard from in this capacity in the French provinces in 1783. His fame quickly carried him to Paris, where in 1784 he appeared before the court of Louis XVI. His arrival was most opportune, for just then all Paris and, for that matter, all Europe had been aroused to a new interest in magic by the brilliant Cagliostro.

From Paris he went to London, playing at the Haymarket and creating a sensation equal to that which he made in France. Later he toured Germany, playing in Berlin and Hamburg. Next, he went back to his native land, Italy, but later returned to Germany for a second engagement. In 1789, he appeared in Russia and never left that country. There he married a Russian girl, daughter of a carriage manufacturer. They had two children. Pinetti would have left enormous wealth, but in his later years he became interested in ballooning, the sensation of the hour, and spent his entire fortune on balloon experiments. He died in Bartichoff, Volhinie, aged fifty years.

Henri Decremps, the French author who exposed and endeavored to ruin Pinetti, but succeeded only in immortalizing him.

Pinetti was a man of rare inventive genius and almost reconstructed the art of conjuring, so numerous were his inventions. For half a century after his death his successors drew upon Pinetti's inventions and répertoire for their programmes. Naturally such ability aroused bitter jealousies, especially as Pinetti made no attempt to conciliate his contemporaries, either magicians or writers on magic. He issued one book, whose title-page reads:

"Amusements Physiques et Differentes Expériences Divertissements, Composées et Executées, tant à Paris que dans les diverses Courts de l'Europe. Par M. Joseph Pinetti de Willedal, Romain, Chevalier de l'Ordre Mérite de Saint-Phillipe, Professeur de Mathématiques et de Physiques, Protégé par toute la Maison Royale de France, Pensionnaire de la Cour de Prusse, etc., 1785."

The work, however, was not a clear and lucid explanation of his methods and tricks. In fact some of his contemporaries claimed that he deliberately misrepresented his methods of performing tricks. Among these writers was Henri Decremps, a brilliant professor of mathematics and physics in Paris, who proceeded to expose all of Pinetti's tricks in the book referred to in the preceding chapter, "La Magie Blanche Dévoilée." This work was in five volumes and was so popular in its day that it was translated into nearly every modern language. The following explanation of the trick is taken from page 56 of the English translation, entitled "The Conjurer Unmasked":

"The branches of the tree may be made of tin or paper, so as to be hollow from one end to the other in order that the air which enters at the bottom may find its exit at the top of the branch. These branches are so adjusted that at intervals there appear twigs made from brass wire, but the whole so decorated with leaves made from parchment that the ensemble closely resembles nature.

"The end of each branch is dilated to contain small pieces of gummed silk or very fine gold-beater's skin, which are to catch the figures of the flowers and fruit when the latter expand by the air driven through the branches to which they were fastened by a silk thread.

"The tree or nosegay is then placed on a table, through which runs a glass tube to supply air from beneath the stage, where a confederate works this end of the trick, and causes the tree to 'grow' at the prearranged signal."

Later it was described as being accomplished entirely by springs, and real oranges were first stuck on the tree by means of pegs or pins, and the leaves were so secured around them that at first appearance they could not be seen. Then a piston was used to spread all the leaves, another that forced the blossom up through the hollow branches, etc.

Pinetti's personality was almost as extraordinary as his talents. A handsome man who knew how to carry himself, acquiring the graces and the dress of the nobility, he became rather haughty, if not arrogant, in his bearing. He so antagonized his contemporaries in the fields of magic and literature that he was advertised as much by his bitter enemies as by his loving friends. Many of his methods of attracting attention to himself were singularly like those employed by modern press agents of theatrical stars. He never trusted to his performances in theatres and drawing-rooms to advertise his abilities, but demonstrated his art wherever he appeared, from barber-shops to cafés.

Perhaps the best pen pictures of Pinetti and his methods are furnished by E. G. Robertson in his "Memoirs." Robertson was a contemporary of Pinetti, and, like him, a pioneer in ballooning. His "Memoirs," written in the French language, were published in 1831. The following extracts from this interesting book tell much of Pinetti's life in Russia and of his professional history as tradition and actual acquaintance had presented it to M. Robertson:

"Pinetti had travelled a great deal and for a long time had enjoyed a great European reputation. He had done everything to attain it. There was never a man that carried further the art of the 'charlatisme.' When he arrived in a town where he intended to give a show, he took good care to prepare his public by speeches, which would keep it in suspense. In St. Petersburg, great and incredible examples of mystification and of prestidigitation were told about him.

"One day he went to a barber-shop to get shaved, sat down in the chair, had the towel tied around his neck, and laid his head back ready for the lather. The barber left him in this position to get hot water, and when he returned, guided by force of habit, he applied the lather where the chin should be, but he found feet, arms, hands, and body in a coat, but no head! Such lamentations! No more head! What could it mean? He opened the door, and, frightened to death, ran away. Pinetti then went to the window and called the barber back. He had put his head in his coat in such a clever way, covering it with his handkerchief, that the surprise and the fright of the barber were quite natural. Of course, this barber did not fail to spread over the whole town that he had shaved a man who could take his head off and on to his wish.

Frontispiece of Pinetti's book, "Amusements Physiques," published in Paris, 1785, one of the first treasures of the Evanion Collection purchased by the author.

"Pinetti met in a summer-garden a young Russian who sold small cakes. He bought a few cakes, bit into them, and complained of finding a hard substance. The youth protested, but Pinetti opened the cake before him and found inside a gold piece. The magician pocketed the gold piece, bought another cake, then a third cake, and in each case found a new gold piece inside. He tried to buy the rest of the cakes. The passers-by had in the mean time come round the seller, and everybody wanted to buy as well. The market seemed to be all right, a ducat for a kopeck! Twelve francs for a cent! The young man refused to sell any more, hurried away, and when alone opened the cakes that were left. He found only the substances of which the cakes were made—nothing else. He had two left, so he hurried back to offer these to Pinetti. Pinetti bought them from him, opened them and showed in each one the gold piece, which the young man could not find in the two dozen cakes which he had spoilt. The poor boy bit his lips and looked at Pinetti with wondering, frightened eyes. This little adventure was advertised here, there, and everywhere, and was told in the clubs and in the society gatherings, and very soon the name of Pinetti gave the key to the enigma, and Pinetti was in demand by everybody.

"When Pinetti came on the stage, he had the knack of attracting members of the nobility around his table, by letting them learn some small secrets. This would render them confederates in working his tricks. He would appear in rich suits, embroidered in gold, which he changed three and four times in the evening. He would not hesitate to deck himself in a quantity of foreign decorations. In Berlin it was told how Pinetti would go through the streets, in a carriage drawn by four white horses. He was clad in fine embroidery and decorated with medals of all nations. Several times it happened that, as he passed by, the soldiers would call arms and salute, taking him for a prince. One day the King of Prussia rode out in his modest carriage drawn by two horses. Ahead of him drove the supposed prince. When the King witnessed the mistake made by his soldiers, he made inquiries as to the rank of this man to whom his men were paying such honor, then gave the Cavalier Pinetti twenty-four hours to get beyond Prussia's borders."

Whatever may be said of Pinetti's charlatanism, it must be admitted that he gave to the art of conjuring a great impetus which was felt for several generations. It is not remarkable, therefore, that when the French magician Cornillot appeared in London in 1822 he announced himself as the pupil and successor of Pinetti. This was when Robert-Houdin was seventeen years of age, twenty-three years before he made his professional début, and on Cornillot's programme we find another version of the now famous and almost familiar tree trick. As will be seen from the accompanying reproduction of a Cornillot handbill, the tree now appears as "An Enchanted Garden," and, if the wording of the bill is to be believed, Cornillot had improved the trick and was using more than one tree or plant.

Cornillot remained in England for some time and is classed among the conjurers of good repute. Another bill in my collection shows that he played at the Theatre of Variety, Catherine Street, Strand, in October, 1823. He was then assisted by several singers and dancers, including the famous Misses Hamilton and Howe, pupils of M. Corri. In his company was also an Anglo-Chinese juggler, who, in addition to feats of juggling, "swallows an egg, a sword, and a stone, a la Ramo Samee."

To sum up the evidence against Robert-Houdin in this particular trick: Four magicians of high repute gave public performances before Robert-Houdin knew and operated the orange-tree trick. Three eminent writers exposed it clearly and accurately. Robert-Houdin, as an indefatigable student of the history of magic, must have known of the trick and its *modus operandum*. He may have purchased it from Cornillot, or as a clever mechanician he had only to reproduce the trick invented by his predecessors, train his confederate in its operation—and—by his cleverly written autobiography—attempt to establish his claim to its invention.

CHAPTER III

THE WRITING AND DRAWING FIGURE

IN his "Memoirs" Robert-Houdin eulogizes the various automata which he claims to have invented. The picturesque fashion in which he describes the tremendous effort put forth ere success crowned his labors would render his arguments most convincing—if stern historical facts did not contradict his every statement.

One of the most extraordinary mechanical figures which he exploits as his invention was the writing and drawing figure, which he exhibited at the Quinquennial Exhibition in 1844, but never used in his public performances, though he asserts that he planned to exhibit it between performances at his own theatre. This automaton, he says, laid the foundation of his financial success and opened the way to realizing his dream of appearing as a magician.

Writing and drawing figure claimed by Robert-Houdin as his invention. From Manning's Robert-Houdin brochure.

On page 196 of his "Memoirs," American edition, he starts his romantic description of its conception and manufacture. According to this he had just planned what promised to be the most brilliant of his mechanical inventions when financial difficulties intervened. He was obliged to raise two thousand francs to meet a pressing debt. He applied to the ever-convenient Monsieur G——, who had bought automata from him before. He described the writing and drawing figure minutely to his patron, who immediately agreed to advance two thousand five hundred francs, and if the figure was completed in eighteen months, two thousand five hundred francs more were to be paid for it, making five thousand francs in all. If the figure was never completed, then Monsieur G—— was to reimburse himself for the amount advanced by selecting automatic toys from Robert-Houdin's regular stock.

After liquidating his debt, Robert-Houdin retired to Belleville, a suburb of Paris, where for eighteen months he worked upon the figure, seeing his family only twice a week, and living in the most frugal fashion.

He employed a wood-carver to make the head, but the result was so unsatisfactory that in the end he was obliged, not only to make all the complicated machinery which operated the figure, but to carve the head itself, which, he adds, in some miraculous fashion, resembled himself. This resemblance, however, cannot be traced in existing cuts of the figure.

The chapter devoted to this particular automaton is so diverting that I quote literally from its pages, thus giving my readers an opportunity to take the true measure of the writer and the literary style of his "Memoirs." Here is his description of his moment of triumph:

"I had only to press a spring in order to enjoy the long-waited-for result. My heart beat violently, and though I was alone I trembled at the mere thought of this imposing trial. I had just laid the first sheet of paper before my writer and asked him this question: 'Who is the author of your being?' I pressed the spring, and the clockwork started—began acting. I dared hardly breathe through fear of disturbing the operations. The automaton bowed to me, and I could not refrain from smiling on it as on my own son. But when I saw the eyes fix an attentive glance on the paper—when the arm, a few seconds before numb and lifeless, began to move and trace my signature in a firm hand—the tears started in my eyes and I fervently thanked Heaven for granting me success. And it was not alone the satisfaction I experienced as an inventor, but the certainty I had of being able to restore some degree of comfort to my family, that caused my deep feeling of gratitude.

"After making my Sosia repeat my signature a thousand times, I gave it this question: 'What o'clock is it?' The automaton, acting in obedience to the clock, wrote, 'It is two in the morning.' This was a timely warning. I profited by it and went straight to bed."

Specimens of penmanship executed by the Droz writing automaton in 1796 and 1906 respectively. From the brochure issued by the Society of History and Archæology, Canton of Neuchatel, Switzerland.

Robert-Houdin injects a little humor into this chapter, for he relates that as Molière and J. J. Rousseau consulted their servants, he decided to do likewise; so early the next morning he invited his portress and her husband, Auguste, a stone-mason, to be present at the first performance of the figure. The mason's wife chose the question, "What is the emblem of fidelity?" The automaton replied by drawing a pretty little greyhound, lying on a cushion. The stone-mason wished to see the works, saying: "I understand about that sort of thing, for I have always greased the vane on the church steeple, and have even taken it down twice."

When the work was completed, according to page 208 of the American edition of his "Memoirs," he returned to Paris, collected the remaining two thousand five hundred francs due him from Monsieur G——, to whom he delivered the figure, and two thousand francs more on an automatic nightingale made for a rich merchant of St. Petersburg. Incidentally he mentions that during his absence his business had prospered, but he fails to state who managed it for him, and here is where I believe credit should be given Opre, the Dutch inventor, who was unquestionably Robert-Houdin's assistant for years.

In 1844 he claims to have borrowed the writing and drawing figure from the obliging Monsieur G—— to exhibit it at the Quinquennial Exposition, where it attracted the attention of Louis Philippe and his court, thus insuring its exhibitor the silver medal.

At this point Robert-Houdin deliberately drops the writing and drawing figure, leaving his readers to believe that it was returned to its rightful owner, Monsieur G——, but, unfortunately for his claims, another historian steps in here to cast reflections on Monsieur G——'s ownership of the figure. This writer is the world's greatest showman, the late P. T. Barnum, who purchased the figure at this same exposition of 1844, paying for it a goodly sum, and this incident is one of the significant omissions of the Robert-Houdin "Memoirs." Either Robert-Houdin sold the figure to Mr. Barnum for Monsieur G——, or such a person as Monsieur G—— never existed, for in his own book Mr. Barnum writes:

"When I was abroad in 1844 I went to Paris expressly to attend the 'Quinquennial Exposition'—an exhibition then held every five years. I met and became well acquainted with a celebrated conjurer, as he called himself, Robert-Houdin, but who was not only a prestidigitateur and legerdemain performer, but a mechanic of absolute genius. I bought at the exposition the best automaton he exhibited and for which he obtained a gold medal. I paid a round price for this most ingenious little figure, which was an automaton writer and artist. It sat on a small table, pencil in hand; and, if asked, for instance, for an emblem of 'fidelity,' it would instantly draw the picture of a handsome dog; if love was wanted, a cupid was exquisitely pencilled. The automaton would also answer many questions in writing. I took this curiosity to London, where it was exhibited for some time at the Royal Adelaide Gallery, and then I sent it across the Atlantic to my American Museum, where it attracted great attention from the people and the press. During my visit, Houdin was giving evening legerdemain performances, and by his pressing invitation I frequently was present. He took great pains, too, to introduce me to other inventors and exhibitors of moving figures, which I liberally purchased, making them prominent features in the attractions of the American Museum."

The late P. T. Barnum, the world's greatest showman, who bought the writing and drawing figure from Robert-Houdin, and wrote at length of the French conjurer in his autobiography. Born July 5, 1810. Died April 7, 1891. From the Harry Houdini Collection.

The figure of Cupid as executed by the Droz drawing figure. From the brochure issued by the Society of History and Archæology, Canton of Neuchatel, Switzerland.

Barnum then continued to describe Robert-Houdin's greatness and his cleverness in the use of electricity. The showman was always a welcome guest at the magician's house, and he relates how, at luncheon time, Robert-Houdin would touch a knob and through the floor would rise a table, laden with inviting viands. These details in the Barnum book make it all the more inexplicable that Robert-Houdin should omit all mention of the great showman's name in his "Memoirs."

Hanger advertising the Professor Faber talking machine, exhibited by P. T. Barnum during 1873 in his museum department. This automaton was the first talking figure. From the Harry Houdini Collection.

Just at this time the amusement-seeking public seemed greatly interested in automata, so it was only natural that Barnum, great showman that he was, should scour Europe for mechanical figures. Soon after he purchased the writing and drawing figure claimed by Robert-Houdin, he brought to America a talking figure invented by Professor Faber of Vienna, to which he refers most entertainingly in his address to the public dated 1873:

"The Museum department contains 100,000 curiosities, including Professor Faber's wonderful talking machine, costing me $20,000 for its use for six months; also the National Portrait Gallery of one hundred life-size paintings, including all the Presidents of the United States, etc.; John Rogers' groups of historic statuary; almost an endless variety of curiosities, including numberless automaton musicians, mechanicians, and moving scenes, etc., etc., made in Paris and Geneva."

It can be imagined how wonderful this talking machine must have been when Barnum gave it special emphasis, selecting it from the hundreds of curios he had on exhibition. As this talking machine is probably forgotten, I will reproduce the bill used at the time of its appearance in London, England.

When Barnum was in London in 1844, with Gen. Tom Thumb, who was then performing at the Egyptian Hall, he first saw the automatic talking machine and engaged it to strengthen his show. Thirty years later Prof. Faber's nephew was the lecturer who explained to the American public the automaton's mechanism and also the performer who manipulated the machine.

Barnum always speaks of the talking automaton as being a life-size figure, but the pictures used for advertising purposes show that it was only a head.

The fate of both the talking automaton and the writing and drawing figure is shrouded in mystery. If they were in the Barnum Museum when the latter was swept by fire in 1865, they were destroyed. If they had been taken back to Europe, they may now be lying in some cellar or loft, moth-eaten and dust-covered, ignominious end for such ingenious brain-work and handicraft.

So much for the claims of Robert-Houdin. Now to disprove them.

The earliest record of a writing figure I have found is in the "Dictionary of Arts, Manufactures, and Mines," compiled by Andrew Ure, M.D., and published in New York in 1842 by Le Roy Sunderland, 126 Fulton Street. On page 83, under the heading of "Automaton," is this statement:

"Frederick Von Knauss completed a writing machine at Vienna in the year 1760. It is now in the model cabinet of the Polytechnic Institute, and consists of a globe two feet in diameter, containing the mechanism, upon which sits a figure seven inches high and writes, upon a sheet of paper fixed to a frame, whatever has been placed beforehand upon a regulating cylinder. At the end of each line it raises and moves its hand sideways, in order to begin a new line."

Portrait and autograph of Pierre Jacquet-Droz. Born 1721, died 1790. From the brochure issued by the Society of History and Archæology, Canton of Neuchâtel, Switzerland.

This does not answer the description of the figure which Robert-Houdin claims, but it is interesting as showing that mechanical genius ran along such lines almost a hundred years before Robert-Houdin claims to have invented the famous automaton.

The writing and drawing figure claimed by Robert-Houdin as his original invention can be traced back directly to the shop door of Switzerland's most noted inventor, Pierre Jacquet-

Droz, who with his son, Henri-Louis, laid the foundation of the famous Swiss watch-and music-box industry.

In the latter part of the eighteenth century, probably about 1770, the Jacquet-Drozes turned out a drawing figure which also inscribed a few set phrases or titles of the drawings. In mechanism, appearance, and results it tallies almost exactly with the automaton claimed by Robert-Houdin as originating in his brain. The Jacquet-Droz figure showed a child clad in quaint, flowing garments, seated at a desk. The Robert-Houdin figure was modernized, and showed a court youth in knee breeches and powdered peruque, seated at a desk. The Jacquet-Droz figure drew a dog, a cupid, and the heads of reigning monarchs. The Robert-Houdin figure, made seventy-five years later, by some inexplicable coincidence drew a dog as the symbol of fidelity, a cupid as the emblem of love, and the heads of reigning monarchs.

The history of the Jacquet-Drozes is written in the annals of Switzerland as well as the equally reputable annals of scientific inventions, and cannot be refuted.

Pierre Jacquet-Droz was born July 28th, 1721, in a small village, La-Chaux-de-Fonds, near Neuchâtel, Switzerland. According to some authorities, his father was a clock-maker, but the brochure issued by "Société d'Histoire et d'Archéologie" of the city of Neuchâtel, which has recently acquired many of the Jacquet-Droz automata, states that he was the son of a farmer and was sent to a theological seminary at Basle. Here the youth's natural talent for mechanics overbalanced his interest in "isms" and "ologies," and he spent every spare moment at work with his tools. On his return to his native town he turned his attention seriously to clock- and watch-making, constructing a marvellous clock with two peculiar hands which, in passing each other, touched the dial and rewound the clock.

Henri-Louis Jacquet-Droz, son of Pierre Jacquet-Droz, and the superior of his father as a mechanician. Born Oct. 13th, 1752, died November 15th, 1791. From the Jaquet-Droz brochure, issued by the Neuchâtel Society of History and Archæology.

At this time, his work attracted the attention of Lord Keith, Governor of Neuchâtel, then a province of Prussia, who induced the young inventor to visit the court of Ferdinand VI. of Spain, providing the necessary introductions. Pierre Jacquet-Droz remained for some time in

Madrid and made a clock of most complicated pattern. This was a perpetual calendar. For hands, he utilized artificial sunbeams, shooting out from the sun's face which formed the dial, to denote the hours, days, etc. With the money received from the Spanish monarch he returned to Switzerland to find that his son, Henri-Louis, had inherited his remarkable inventive gifts. He sent his boy to Nancy to study music, drawing, mechanics, and physics. During his son's absence in all probability he produced the first of the marvellous automata which made the Jacquet-Drozes famous the modern world over, namely, the writing figure.

With the return of Henri-Louis Jacquet-Droz from college commenced what may be termed the golden age of mechanics in Switzerland. Associated with father and son were the former's pupils or apprentices, Jean-Frédéric Leschot, Jean-David Maillardet, and Jean Pierre Droz, a blood relation who afterward became director of the mint at Paris and a mechanician of rare talent. Jean Pierre Droz is credited with having invented a machine for cutting, stamping, and embossing medals on the face and on the edges at one insertion.

Jean-Frédéric Leschot. Born 1747, died 1824. Portrait published by Société des Arts de Genève. Presented to the author by Mons. Blind (Magicus) of Geneva.

The output of this shop and its staff of gifted workers included the first Swiss music box, the singing birds which sprang from watches and jewel caskets, the drawing figure which was an improvement on the writing figure, the spinet player, and the grotto with its many automatic animals of diminutive size but exquisite workmanship. Years were spent in perfecting the various automata, and none of them have been equalled or even approached by later mechanicians and inventors.

Henri-Louis Jacquet-Droz was conceded to be the superior of his father, Pierre Jacquet-Droz. In a German encyclopædia which I found at the King's Library, Munich, it is stated that when Vaucanson, celebrated as the inventor of "The Flute Player," "The Mechanical Duck," "The Talking Machine," etc., saw the work of the younger Droz, he cried loudly, "Why, that boy commences where I left off!"

According to the brochure issued by the Society of History and Archæology, Canton of Neuchâtel, and an article contributed by Dr. Alfred Gradenwits to *The Scientific American* of June 22d, 1907, the writing and drawing figures are made and operated as follows:

The Jacquet-Droz writing automaton. From the brochure issued by the Society of History and Archæology, Canton of Neuchâtel, Switzerland.

"The writer represented a child of about four years of age, sitting at his little table, patiently waiting with the pen in his hand until the clockwork is started. He then sets to work and, after looking at the sheet of paper before him, lifts his hand and moves it toward the ink-stand, in which he dips the pen. The little fellow then throws off an excess of ink and slowly and calmly, like an industrious child, begins writing on the paper the prescribed sentence. His handwriting is careful, conscientiously distinguishing between hair strokes and ground strokes, always observing the proper intervals between letters and words and generally showing the sober and determined character of the handwriting usual at the time in the country of Neuchâtel. In order, for instance, to write a T, the writer begins tracing the letter at the top, and after slightly lifting his hand halfway, swiftly traces the transversal dash, and continues writing the original ground stroke.

"How complicated a mechanism is required for insuring these effects will be inferred from the illustration, in which the automaton is shown with its back opened. In the first place a vertical disk will be noticed having at its circumference as many notches as there are letters and signs. Behind this will be seen whole columns of cam-wheels, each of a special shape, placed one above another, and all together forming a sort of spinal column for the automaton.

"Whenever the little writer is to write a given letter, a pawl is introduced into the corresponding notch of the disk, thus lifting the wheel column and transmitting to the hand, by the aid of a complicated lever system and Cardan joints arranged in the elbow, the requisite movements for tracing the letter in question. The mechanism comprises five centres of motion connected together by chains.

"In the 'Draftsman,' the mechanism is likewise arranged in the body itself, as in the case of the 'Writer.' The broad chest thus entailed also required a large head, which accounts for the somewhat bulky appearance of the two automatons. With the paper in position and a pencil in hand, the 'Draftsman' at first traces a few dashes and then swiftly marks the shadows, and a dog appears on the paper. The little artist knowingly examines his work, and after blowing away the dust and putting in a few last touches, stops a moment and then quickly signs, 'Mon Toutou' (My pet dog). The motions of the automaton are quite natural, and the outlines of his drawings extremely sharp. The automaton when desired willingly draws certain crowned heads now belonging to history; for example, a portrait of Louis XV., of Louis XVI., and of Marie Antoinette."

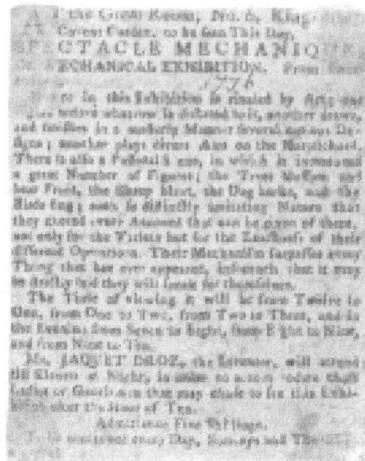

The automata made by the Jacquet-Drozes and their confrères were exhibited in all the large cities of Great Britain and Continental Europe. According to the programmes and newspaper notices in my collection, Henri-Louis Jacquet-Droz acted as their first exhibitor. As proof I am reproducing a Droz programme from the London *Post*, dated 1776.

In support of this advertisement, note what the same paper says in what is probably a criticism of current amusements:

Heads of King George and Queen Charlotte, executed in their presence by the Jacquet-Droz drawing figure in 1774. From the brochure issued by the Society of History and Archæology, Canton of Neuchâtel, Switzerland.

"This entertainment consists of three capital mechanical figures and a pastoral scene, with figures of an inferior size. The figure on the left-hand side, a beautiful boy as large as life, writes anything that is dictated to him, in a very fine hand. The second on the right hand, of the same size, draws various landscapes, etc., etc., which he finishes in a most accurate and masterly style. The third figure is a beautiful young lady who plays several elegant airs on the harpsichord, with all the bass accompaniments; her head gracefully moving to the tune, and her bosom discovering a delicate respiration. During her performance, the pastoral scene in the centre discovers a variety of mechanical figures admirably grouped, all of which seem endued, as it were, with animal life, to the admiration of the spectator. The last curiosity is a canary bird in a cage, which whistles two or three airs in the most natural manner imaginable. Upon the whole, the united collection strikes us as the most wonderful exertion of art which ever trod before so close on the heels of nature. The ingenious artist is a young man, a native of Switzerland."

The inventory of Jacquet-Droz, Jr., dated 1786, quotes the "Piano Player" as valued at 4,800 livres, the "Drawing Figure" at 7,200 livres, while the "Writer" had been ceded to him by his father for 4,800 livres, in consideration of certain improvements and modifications which Henri-Louis Jacquet-Droz made in the original invention. This shows that while the elder Droz did not die until 1790, his son controlled the automata previous to this date, for exhibition and other purposes.

During his later years Henri-Louis Jacquet-Droz was induced to take the automata to Spain. His tour was under the direction of an English manager, who, possibly for the purpose of securing greater advertisement, announced the figures as possessed of supernatural power. This brought them under the ban of the Inquisition, and Jacquet-Droz was thrown into prison. Eventually he managed to secure his freedom, and, breathing free air once more, like the proverbial Arab, he silently folded his tent and stole away, leaving the automata to their fate. Henri-Louis Jacquet-Droz died in Naples, Italy, in 1791, a year after his father's death.

A de Philipsthal programme of 1803 before the writing and drawing figure came under his control. From the Harry Houdini Collection.

Poster used, March 22nd, 1811, by de Philipsthal and Maillardet during their partnership, on which the writing and drawing figure is featured. From the Harry Houdini Collection.

The English manager, however, tarried in Spain. The figures were "tried" and as they proved motionless the case was dropped. The Englishman then claimed the automata as his property and sold them to a French nobleman. Their owner did not know how to operate them, so their great value was never realized by his family. After his death, during a voyage to America, they lay neglected in the castle of Mattignon, near Bayonne. After changing hands many times, about 1803 they passed into the hands of an inventor named Martin, and were controlled by his descendants for nearly a hundred years. One of his family, Henri Martin, of Dresden, Germany, exhibited them in many large cities, and advertised them for sale at 15,000 marks in the *Muenchener* Blaetter of May 13th, 1883. After Martin's death, his widow succeeded in disposing of them to Herr Marfels, of Berlin, who had them repaired with such good results that in the fall of 1906 he sold them for 75,000 francs, or about $15,000, to the Historical Society of Neuchâtel. In April, 1907, the writing figure, the drawing figure, and the spinet player were on exhibition in Le Locle, Chaux-de-Fonds, and Neuchâtel.

So far we have traced only the original writing and drawing figure. This has been done purely to show that even if Robert-Houdin had been capable of building such an automaton, he would not have been its real inventor, but would merely have copied the marvellous work of the Jacquet-Drozes. Now to trace the figure which in 1844 he claimed as his invention.

With the fame of the Neuchâtel shop spreading and the demand for Swiss watches increasing, Maillardet and Jean Pierre Droz, apprentices or perhaps partners of Pierre Jacquet-Droz and Henri-Louis Jacquet-Droz, removed to London and there set up a watch factory. About this time Maillardet invented a combination writing and drawing figure which was pronounced by experts of the day slightly inferior to the work of the two Jacquet-Drozes. However, it must have been worthy of exhibition, for it appeared at intervals for the next fifty years in the amusement world, particularly in London. At first Maillardet was not its exhibitor nor was his name ever mentioned on the programmes and newspaper notices, but later his name appeared as part owner and exhibitor. As the Swiss watches had created a veritable sensation and were snatched up as fast as produced, it is quite likely that he had no time to play the rôle of showman.

The figure first appeared in London in 1796, when the London *Telegraph* of January 2nd carried the advertisement reproduced on the next page.

Haddock had no particular standing in the world of magic, and it is more than likely that he rented the automata which he exhibited, or merely acted as showman for the real inventors.

In quite a few works on automata, notably Sir David Brewster's "Letters on Natural Magic," Collinson is quoted as having interviewed Maillardet as the inventor of the combination writing and drawing figure. *The Franklin Journal* of June, 1827, published in Philadelphia, Pa., credits this figure to Maillardet and gives the following description: "It was the figure of a boy kneeling on one knee, holding a pencil in his hand, with which he executed not only writing but drawings equal to those of the masters. When the figure began to work, an attendant dipped the pencil in ink, and fixed the paper, when, on touching a spring, the figure wrote a line, carefully dotting and stroking the letters."

The Robert-Houdin figure did not kneel, but this change could be made by a mechanician of ordinary ability.

The writing and drawing figure does not reappear on amusement programmes in my collection until 1812, when it was featured by De Philipsthal, the inventor of "Phantasmagoria."[The nature of the inventions grouped under this title can best be judged from the reproduction of a De Philipsthal programme, dated 1803-04, and reproduced in the course of this chapter. All evidence goes to prove, however, that De Philipsthal did not control the writing and drawing figure exclusively, but that it was the joint property of himself and his partner, Maillardet. One of their joint programmes is also reproduced. Wherever De Philipsthal appears as an independent entertainer, the writing and drawing figure is missing from his billing. Later the writing and drawing automaton came into the possession of a Mr. Louis, who, as it will be seen from the billing, acted as assistant engineer to De Philipsthal and Maillardet. Louis evidently controlled the wonderful little automaton in the years 1814-15.

The last De Philipsthal programme in my possession is dated Summer Theatre, Hull, September 15th, 16th, 17th, 18th and 19th, 1828, when he advertises only "rope dancers and mechanical peacock," and features "special uniting fire and water" and "firework experiments." He must have died between that date and April, 1829, for a programme dated at the latter time announces a benefit at the Théâtre Wakefield for the widow and children of De Philipsthal, "the late proprietor of the Royal Mechanical and Optical Museum." This benefit programme contains no allusion to the writing and drawing figure, which goes to prove that it had not been his property, or it would have been handed down to his estate.

In May, 1826, an automaton was exhibited at 161 Strand, a bill regarding which is reproduced. This mechanical figure, however, should not be confounded with the original and genuine writing and drawing figure. It seems to have lacked legitimacy and, from what I can learn from newspaper clippings, was worked like "Zoe," with a concealed confederate, or, like the famous "Psycho" featured by Maskelyne, it was worked by compressed air. This bill is interesting solely because I believe that this fake automaton exhibited at 161 Strand was the first figure of the sort foisted on the public after the Baron Von Kemplen chess-player, which is described in Halle's work on magic, published in 1784.

In 1901, while in Germany, I saw a number of these automaton artists, all frauds. The figure sat in a small chair before an easel, ready to draw portraits in short order. The figure was shown to the audience, then replaced on the chair, whereupon a man under the platform would thrust his arm through the figure and draw all that was required of the automaton. The fake was short-lived, even at the yearly fairs, and now has sunk too low for them.

During this interim, that is between 1821 and 1833, the famous little figure seems to have been in the possession of one Schmidt, who, according to the programmes in my collection, exhibited it regularly.

In 1833 Schmidt is programmed in London, playing at the Surrey Theatre, when the writing and drawing figure is one of twenty-four automatic devices. A program, which, judging from its printing, is of a still later date, announces Mr. Schmidt and the famous figure at New Gothic Hall, 7 Haymarket, for a short period previous to the removal of the exhibit to St. Petersburg. The dates of other programmes in my collection can be judged only from the style of printing which changed at different periods of the art's development. Some of these indicate that the writing and drawing figure was on exhibition during the early 40's in London at Paul's Head Assembly Rooms, Argyle Rooms, Regent Street, etc.

It is more than likely, according to Robert-Houdin's own admission regarding his study of automata and his opportunities to repair those left at his shop, that at some time the writing and drawing figure was brought to Paris to be exhibited, needed repairing, and thus reached his shop. Whether it was bought by Monsieur G——, whose interest in automata is featured in Robert-Houdin's "Memoirs," and brought to Robert-Houdin to repair, or whether Robert-Houdin bought it for a song, and repaired it to sell to advantage to his wealthy patron, cannot be stated, but I am morally certain that Robert-Houdin never constructed, in eighteen months, a complicated mechanism on which the Jacquet-Drozes spent six years of their inventive genius and efforts. Modern mechanicians agree that such a performance would have been a physical impossibility, even had Robert-Houdin been the expert mechanician he pictured himself.

To sum up the evidence: The writing and drawing figure as turned out by the Jacquet-Drozes was known all over Europe. It is not possible that a man so well read and posted in magic and automata as Robert-Houdin did not know of its existence and mechanism. And if Robert-Houdin had invented the same mechanism it is hardly possible that his design would have run in precisely the same channel as that of Jacquet-Droz and Maillardet, in having the figure draw the dog, the cupid, and the heads of monarchs.

In those days, humble mechanicians, however well they were known in their own trade, were not exploited by the public press. Nor did they employ clever journalists to write memoirs lauding their achievements. And so it happened that for years the names of Jacquet-Droz and Maillardet were unsung; their brainwork and handicraft were claimed by Robert-Houdin, who had mastered the art of self-exploitation. To-day, after a century and a half of neglect, the laurel wreath has been lifted from the brow of Robert-Houdin, where it never should have been placed, and has been laid on the graves of the real inventors of the writing and drawing figure, Pierre Jacquet-Droz and Henri-Louis Jacquet-Droz and Jean-David Maillardet.

CHAPTER IV

THE PASTRY COOK OF THE PALAIS ROYAL

CONCERNING this trick, which Robert-Houdin claims as his invention, he writes on page 79 of his "Memoirs," American edition: "The first was a small pastry cook, issuing from his shop door at the word of command, and bringing, according to the spectator's request, patties and refreshments of every description. At the side of the shop, assistant pastry cooks might be seen rolling paste and putting it in the oven."

By means of handbills, programmes, and newspaper notices of magical and mechanical performances, this trick in various guises can be traced back as far as 1796. Nine reputable magicians offered it as part of their repertoire, and at times two men presented it simultaneously, showing that more than one such automaton existed. The dates of the most notable programmes or handbills selected from my collection are as follows:

1, Haddock, 1797. 2, Garnerin, 1815. 3, Gyngell, 1816 and 1823. 4, Bologna, 1820. 5, Henry, 1822. 6, Schmidt, 1827. 7, Rovere, 1828. 8, Charles, 1829. 9, Phillippe, 1841.

In 1827 Schmidt and Gyngell joined forces, yet both before and after this date each performer had the wonderful little piece of mechanism on his programme. In 1841, four years before Robert-Houdin appeared as a public performer, Phillippe created a sensation in Paris, presenting among other automata "Le Confiseur Galant." In 1845, when Robert-Houdin included "The Pastry Cook of the Palais Royal" in his initial programme at his own theatre in Paris, Phillippe was presenting precisely the same trick at the St. James Theatre, London.

Of this goodly company, however, Rovere and Phillippe deserve more than passing notice, as both were the contemporaries of Robert-Houdin, and Rovere was his personal friend. Both also appear in Robert-Houdin's "Memoirs."

The trick appears first, not as a confectioner's shop with small figures at work, but as a fruitery, then again as a Dutch Coffee-House and a Russian Inn, from which ten sorts of liquor are served. Finally, in 1823, it is featured under the name that later made it famous, the Confectioner's Shop.

Haddock, the Englishman who had the writing and drawing figure in his possession for some time, featured the fruitery on his programmes dated 1796. One of his advertisements from the London *Telegraph* is reproduced on page 106, in connection with the history of the writing and drawing figure, but for convenience I am quoting here Haddock's own description of the fruitery trick, which was even more complicated than the famous Pastry Cook of the Palais Royal:

A Bologna poster of 1820 which features an automatic distiller who draws eight different liquors from one cask. From the Harry Houdini Collection.

"A model of the neat rural mansion, and contains the following figures: First, the porter, which stands at the gate, and on being addressed, rings the bell, when the door opens, the fruiteress comes out, and any lady or gentleman may call for whatever fruit they please, and the figure will return and bring the kind required, which may be repeated and the fruit varied as often as the company orders: it will likewise receive flowers, or any small article, carry them in, and produce them again as called for. As the fruits are brought out, they will be given in charge of a watch-dog, which sits in front of the house, and on any person taking or touching them will begin to bark, and continue to do so until they are returned. The next figure belonging to this piece is the little chimney-sweeper, which will be seen coming from behind the house, will enter the door, appear at the top of the chimney, and give the usual cry of 'Sweep' several times, descend the chimney, and come out with his bag full of soot."

In 1820, Haddock's programme, including the fruitery, appears with only a few minor changes as the répertoire of Bologna, a very clever conjurer who afterward became the assistant of Anderson, the Wizard of the North, and who made most of the latter's apparatus. On the Bologna programme, for a performance to be given at the Great Assembly Room, Three Tuns Tavern, the shop trick is described thus: "A curious Mechanical Fruiterer and Confectioner's Shop, kept by Kitty Comfit, who will produce at Command such Variety of Fruit and Sweetmeats as may be asked for."

The marvellous little shop does not appear again on programmes of magic until 1815, when Garnerin features it as "The Dutch Coffee-House." On the programme used by Garnerin in that year for a benefit which he gave for the General Hospital at Birmingham, England, it is featured as No. 10: "A Dutch Coffee-House, a very surprising mechanical piece, in which there is the figure of a Girl, six inches high, which presents, at the Command of the Spectators, ten different sorts of Liquors."

This programme is of such historical value that I reproduce it in full. It will show that this particular mechanical trick is by no means the most important feature of Garnerin's répertoire. In fact, his fame is based on his ballooning, and he is said to have been the inventor of the parachute. The ascension of the nocturnal balloon, also scheduled on this programme, is an imitation of the one which Garnerin arranged in honor of Bonaparte's coronation in 1805. On that occasion, the balloon started at Paris and descended in Rome, a distance of five hundred miles which was covered in twenty-two hours.

Garnerin was a contemporary of both Pinetti and Robertson and was with them in Russia when Pinetti dissipated his fortune in balloon experiments. In their correspondence, both Pinetti and Robertson spoke slightingly of Garnerin, but the Frenchman's programmes all indicate that he was not only a successful aëronaut, but a magician who could present a diverting entertainment.

A Gyngell poster of 1816, featuring the Russian Inn, with service of various kinds of liquor. From the Harry Houdini Collection.

In 1816 the elder Gyngell featured the trick on his programmes as "The Russian Inn," and in 1823 he changed it to "The Confectioner's Shop." These programmes are reproduced as the most convincing evidence against the claims of Robert-Houdin.

The Gyngell family is one of the most interesting in the history of magic. The Christian name of the founder of the family I have never been able to ascertain, though programmes give the initial as G. He was celebrated as a Bartholomew Fair conjurer. His career started about 1788, and his contemporaries were Lane, Boaz, Ball, Jonas, Breslaw, and Flocton. At one time

Gyngell and Flocton worked together, and Thomas Frost in his book, "The Lives of Conjurers," claims that at Flocton's death Gyngell received a portion of the former's wealth.

The original Gyngell, a portrait reproduced from the book on magic written by this famous Bartholomew Fair conjurer. From the Harry Houdini Collection.

Associated with him in his performances were his brother, two sons, and a daughter. The latter was not only a clever rope-dancer but a musician of more than ordinary ability and she often constituted the entire "orchestra."

On Gyngell's programme offered in 1827 he proves himself a great showman, for he features Herr Schmidt's "Mechanical Automatons, Phantasmagoria, a laughing sketch entitled Wholesale Blunders, his son on the flying wire, during which he would throw a somersault through a balloon of real fire, a broadsword dance by Miss Louise and Master Gyngell, and Miss Louise's performance on the tight rope, clowned by Master Lionel."

On a programme used in Hull, October 29th, 1827, a lottery was featured as follows: "On which occasion the first hundred persons paying for the gallery will be entitled by ticket to a chance of a Fat Goose, and the same number in the pit to have the same chance for a fat turkey. To be drawn for on the stage, in the same manner as the State Lottery."

According to Thomas Frost, Gyngell died in 1833 and was buried in the Parish Church, Camberwell. His children, however, continued the work so excellently planned by their father.

The programmes herewith reproduced I purchased from Henry Evanion, who secured them directly from the last of the Gyngell family, as the accompanying letter, now a part of my collection, will show:

DOVER, February 10th, 1867.

MR. EVANION:

DEAR SIR—Yours of the 5th inst. I received just as I was leaving Folkestown, and it was forwarded from Guilford.

I am sorry I have not one of my old bills with me, neither do I think any of my family could find one at home. I may have some among my old conjuring things, and when I return to Guilford I will look them over and send you what I can find. I was sorry I was not at home when you were in Guilford, for I feel much pleasure in meeting a responsible professional. I am not certain when I shall return, but most likely not for six weeks. I will keep your address; so should you change your residence, write to me about that time.

I was looking over some old papers some time last summer, and found a bill of my father's, nearly 60 years ago, when his great trick was cutting off the cock's head and restoring it to life again. And a great wonder it was considered and brought crowded rooms.

I was Master Gyngell, the wonderful performer on the slack wire; and now in my 71st year I am lecturer, pyrotechnist, and high-rope walker, for I did that last summer. My life has been a simple one of ups and downs.

I am, dear sir, yours truly,

J. D. G. GYNGELL.

The signature of this letter, "J. D. G. Gyngell," clears up considerable uncertainty regarding the names of the two Gyngell sons. At times the clever young tight-rope performer has been spoken of as Joseph, and at others as Gellini. It is quite probable that the two names were really part of one, and the full baptismal name was "Joseph D. Gellini." It was as Gellini Gyngell that he met Henry Evanion at Deal, February 20th, 1862, when the latter was performing as a magician at the Deal and Walmer Institute, while Gellini Gyngell gave an exhibition of fireworks and a magic-lantern display on the South Esplanade. A fine notice of both performances was published in the Deal *Telegram* of February 23d, when the hope was expressed that Gyngell's collection, taken among those who enjoyed his outdoor performance, repaid him for his admirable entertainment. Gyngell was landlord of the Bowling Green Tavern at this time, and travelled as an entertainer only at intervals.

The next appearance of the trick is in a book published by M. Henry, a ventriloquist, who played London and the provinces from 1820 to 1828. During an engagement at the Adelphia Theatre, London, which according to the programme was about 1822, Henry published a book entitled "Conversazione; or, Mirth and Marvels," in which he interspersed witty conversation with descriptions of his various tricks. On page 11 he thus describes the automaton under consideration:

"Illusion Third. A curious mechanical trick; an inn, from which issues the hostess for orders, upon receiving which, she returns into the inn and brings out the various liquors as called for by the audience, and at last waiting for the money, which, having received, goes in and shuts the door. Mr. Henry says he has produced the inn in preference to palaces, though more stupendous and magnificent, thinking, as a certain author wrote, the heartiest welcome is to be found at the inn."

In the same year Henry issued a challenge open to the whole world, defying any performer to equal his manipulation of the cup and ball trick. He also employed as an adjunct of his conjuring performances Signor de Fedori of Rome, an armless wonder, who used his feet to play the drum, violin, and triangle.

A contemporary of Henry was Charles, the great ventriloquist, who varied his performance as did all ventriloquists of his day, by presenting "Philosophical and Mechanical Experiments" to make up a two-hour-and-a-half performance. Charles made several tours of the English provinces, and played in London at intervals. On a London programme which is undated, but which announces M. Charles as playing at Mr. Wigley's Large Room, Spring Gardens, the second automaton on his list is described as "The Russian Inn, out of which comes a little Woman and brings the Liquor demanded for." Two of his programmes dated Theatre Royal, Hull, April, 1829, now in my collection, carry a pathetic foot-note written in the handwriting of the collector through whom they came into my possession: "The audiences on both the evenings were extremely small, and the money was refunded."

By referring to the chapter on the writing and drawing figure, Chapter III, Page 113, a Schmidt programme of 1827 will be found, in which he features "The Enchanted Dutch Coffee-

House, an elegant little building. On the traveller ringing the bell, the door opens, the hostess attends and provides him with any liquor he may call for."

Schmidt seems to have confined his exhibitions to London and the provinces and was often connected with other magicians, including Gyngell and Buck. The latter was an English conjurer, best known as the man who was horribly injured when presenting "The Gun Delusion." This consisted of having a marked bullet shot at the performer, who caught it between his teeth on a plate, or on the point of a needle or knife. Some miscreant loaded the gun with metal after Buck had it prepared for the trick, and the unfortunate performer's right cheek was literally shot away.

In 1828 Jules de Rovere, a French conjurer, whose fame rests principally on the fact that he coined the new title "prestidigitator," appeared at the Haymarket Theatre, London, and also toured the English provinces. A clipping from the Oxford *Herald* of that year includes this description of his automaton: "One of the clowns vanishes from the box, and instantly at the top of the hall a little lady, in a little hotel brilliantly illuminated, gives out wines and liquors to them who ask for them, without any apparent communication with the artiste, and yet the lady is only six inches high."

In the late 30's Rovere made his headquarters in Paris, and there he and Robert-Houdin met. The latter refers to this meeting on page 153 of his "Memoirs," when writing of the misfortunes which had overtaken Father Roujol, whose shop had once been headquarters for conjurers: "Still I had the luck to form here the acquaintance of Jules de Rovere, the first to employ a title now generally given to fashionable conjurers."

And after Rovere, Phillippe, who is by far the most important presenter of the Pastry Cook of the Palais Royal, as bearing upon Robert-Houdin's claims.

For Phillippe's early history we must depend largely upon Robert-Houdin's "Memoirs." According to these, Phillippe started life as a confectioner or maker of sweets, and his real name was Phillippe Talon. According to an article published in *L'Illusionniste* in January, 1902, he was born in Alias, near Nîmes, December 25th, 1802, and died in Bokhara, Turkey, June 27th, 1878.

Reproduction of pastel portrait of Phillippe. Only known likeness of the conjurer in existence. Made for him by a Vienna artist. Original now in the Harry Houdini Collection.

Like many a genius and successful man, his early history was written in a minor key. According to Robert-Houdin his sweets did not catch the Parisian fancy, and he went to London, where at that time French bonbons were in high favor. But for some reason he failed in London, and went on to Aberdeen, Scotland, where he was very soon reduced to sore straits. In his hour of extremity his cleverness saved the day. In Aberdeen at the same time was a company of actors almost as unfortunate as himself. They were presenting a pantomime which the public refused to patronize. The young confectioner approached the manager of the pantomime and suggested that they join forces. In addition to the regular admission to the pantomime each patron was to pay sixpence and receive in return a paper of mixed sugar plums and a lottery ticket by which he might gain the first prize of the value of five pounds. In addition, Talon promised not only to provide the sweets free of cost to the management, but to present a new and startling feature at the close of the performance.

The novel announcement crowded the house, the pantomime and the bonbons alike found favor, but the significant feature of the performance was young Talon's appearance in the finale in the rôle of "Punch," for which he was admirably made up. He executed an eccentric dance, at the finish of which he pretended to fall and injure himself. In a faint voice he demanded pills to relieve his pain, and a fellow-actor brought on pills of such enormous size that the audience stopped sympathizing with the actor and began to laugh. But the pills all disappeared down the dancer's throat, for Talon was not only an able confectioner and an agile dancer, but a sleight-of-hand performer. From that hour he exchanged the spoon of the confectioner for the wand of the magician. The fortunes of both the pantomime and Phillippe, as he now called himself, improved. Quite probably he remained with the pantomime company until the close of the season and then struck out as an independent performer.

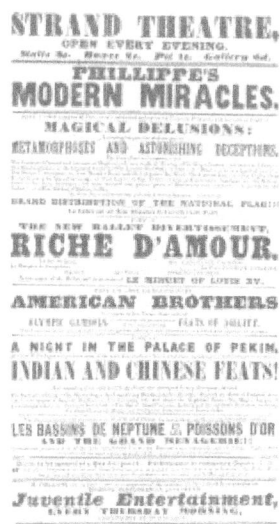

Poster used by Phillippe during his engagement at the Strand Theatre, London, 1845-46. From the Harry Houdini Collection.

Another story which is gleaned from a biography of John Henry Anderson, the Wizard of the North, tells how Phillippe started his career as a pastry cook in the household of one Lord Panmure, and I quote this literally from the Anderson book, because I believe it to be truthful, as material gathered from Anderson literature has proved to be:

"It was at this time that he came in contact with a person who afterward, under the designation of M. Phillippe, became celebrated in France as a magician. Phillipee (for so was he named in Scotland) was originally a cook in the services of the late Lord Panmure. Leaving that employment, he settled down and remained for a number of years in Aberdeen. He heard of the fame of the youthful magician, was induced to visit his 'temple,' and was struck with his performances; and having made the acquaintance of Mr. Anderson, he solicited from him and obtained an insight into his profession, and fac-similes of his then humble apparatus. Phillippe improved to such a degree upon the knowledge he thus acquired that, leaving England for France, he earned the reputation of being one of the most accomplished magicians ever seen in the country."

The date of his initial performance is not known, but he must have remained in Scotland, perfecting his act, for the earliest Phillippe programme in my collection is dated February 3d, 1837, when he opened at Waterloo Rooms, Edinburgh, and announced:

"The high character which Mons. Phillippe has obtained from the Aberdeen, Glasgow, Greenock and Paisley Press, being the only four towns in Britain where he has made his appearance, is a sufficient guarantee to procure him a visit from the inhabitants of this enlightened Metropolis, where talent had always been supported when actually deserved."

Phillippe and his Scotch assistant, Domingo. The latter became famous as a magician under the name of Macallister, introducing in America Phillippe's gift show. From a lithograph in the Harry Houdini Collection.

Evidently, however, Phillippe made rapid progress, for a programme dated Saturday, April 21st, 1838, shows that his last daytime or matinée performance in Waterloo Rooms was given under the patronage of such members of the nobility as the Right Honorable Lady Gifford, the Right Honorable Lady H. Stuart Forbes, etc. In an Edinburgh programme, dated probably 1837, he is shown as performing his tricks, clad in peculiar evening clothes, knickerbockers and waistcoat matching, with a mere suggestion of the swallow-tail coat. In his 1838 bill he is shown clad in the flowing robes of the old-time magician, and he advertises the Chinese tricks, notably the gold-fish trick, which demanded voluminous draperies.

According to Robert-Houdin, Phillippe built a small wooden theatre in Glasgow. Humble as this building was, however, it brought a significant factor into Phillippe's life. This was a young bricklayer named Andrew Macallister who had a natural genius for tricks and models, and who became Phillippe's apprentice, later appearing as Domingo, his assistant on the stage, wearing black make-up.

In either Edinburgh or Dublin Phillippe met the Chinese juggler or conjurer who taught him the gold-fish trick and the secret of the Chinese rings.

Armed with these two striking tricks, Phillippe determined to satisfy his yearning to return to his native land, and in 1841 he appeared at the Salle Montesquieu, Paris. Later, the Bonne-Nouvelle, a temple of magic, was opened for Phillippe in Paris, and there he enjoyed the brilliant run to which Robert-Houdin refers in his "Memoirs."

Phillippe was an indefatigable worker and traveller, and one brilliant engagement followed another. During the 40's he appeared, according to my collection of programmes, all over Continental Europe, and in most of his programmes this paragraph is featured:

"PART III.

"An unexpected present at once gratuitous and laughable, composed of twelve prizes, nine lucky and three unfortunate, in which the general public will participate."

He also continued to distribute bonbons from an inexhaustible source, probably a cornucopia, calling this trick "a new system of making sweetmeats, or Le Confiseur Moderne."

During his first engagement in Vienna he had painted for advertising purposes a pastel portrait, showing him clad in his magician's robes at the finale of the gold-fish trick. From this picture his later cuts were made. By some mistake he left the original pastel in Vienna, where I bought it at a special sale for my collection. It remains an exquisite piece of color work, even at this day. So far it is the only real likeness of Phillippe I have been able to unearth.

In 1845-46 he was at the height of his popularity in London, where he had a tremendous run. In June, 1845, we find him playing at the St. James Theatre, under Mitchell's direction, and on September 29th, under his own management, he moves to the Strand, where he is still found in January of 1846. During all this time he featured The Pastry Cook of the Palais Royal under the title of "Le Confiseur Galant."

1. Cuisine de Parafaragamus; 2. Le Chapelier de 1943; 3. Le Paon magique; 4. La Bouteille enchantée; 5. La Chaîne hydonstaine; 6. La Tête infernale; 7. Le Chapeau merveilleux; 8. L'Arlequin savant; 9. Le Confiseur galant et le Liquoriste impromptu; 10. Le Bassin de Neptune ou les poissons d'or et la ménagerie prodigieuse; 11. Éclairage de tout le

As proofs that Phillippe used the pastry-cook trick both before and during Robert-Houdin's career as a magician, I offer several programmes containing accurate descriptions of the automaton, and also a page illustration from a current publication dated Paris, 1843, which shows the confectioner or pastry-cook standing in the doorway of his house, while the key explaining the various tricks reads: "No. 9. Le Confiseur galant et le Liquoriste impromptu."

Robert-Houdin devotes nearly an entire chapter to the history of Phillippe and a description of his tricks and automata, yet curiously forgets to mention the pastry cook, which he later claims as his own invention.

Ernest Basch, formerly of Basch Brothers, conjurers, and the richest manufacturer of illusions in the world, claims that the original trick is now in his possession. Herr Basch is located in Hanover, Germany, where he builds large illusions only. The wonderful mechanical house passed to Basch by a bequest on the death of Baron von Sandhovel, a wealthy resident of Amsterdam, Holland. Von Sandhovel had bought the trick from the heirs of Robert-Houdin on the death of the latter, because he believed it to be the brain and handwork of Opre, a Dutch mechanician of great talent. Ernest Basch shares this belief, and with other well-read conjurers thinks that Opre was Robert-Houdin's assistant and built most of his automata, including The Pastry Cook of the Palais Royal, The Windmill or Dutch Inn, Auriel and Debureau, The French Gymnasts, The Harlequin, and The Chausseur.

Opre was a man of ability, but lacked presence and personality properly to present his inventions. So far I have found his name in three places only: On the frontispiece of a Dutch book on magic, published in Amsterdam; in Ernest Basch's correspondence about conjurers; and on page 77 of Robert-Houdin's "Memoirs," when he speaks of Opre as the maker of the Harlequin figure which Torrini asked Robert-Houdin to repair during their travels.

With such convincing proof, some of which was contemporary, that other men had exhibited The Pastry Cook of the Palais Royal in its identical or slightly different guise, it was daring indeed of Robert-Houdin to claim it as his own invention.

David Leendert Bamberg, of the second generation of the Bamberg family. Born 1786; died 1869. The above daguerrotype was presented to the author by Herr Ernest Basch, and is the only one in existence.

The most direct information regarding Opre comes through that eminent family of conjurers known as the Bambergs of Holland. At this writing, "Papa" (David) Bamberg, of the fourth generation, is prominent on the Dutch stage, and his son Tobias David, known as Okito, of the fifth generation, is a cosmopolitan magician, presenting a Chinese act.

According to the family history, traceable by means of handbills, programmes, and personal correspondence, the original Bamberg (Eliazar) had a vaulting figure in his collection of automata in 1790, fifty years before Robert-Houdin became a professional entertainer. This figure was made by Opre, to whom all conjurers of that time looked for automata and apparatus. David Leendert Bamberg, of the second generation, who also had the vaulting figure, was the intimate friend and confidant of Opre and was authority for the statement that Opre's son sold in Paris the various automata made by his father, which later Robert-Houdin claimed as his own invention. It may be noted that Robert-Houdin never invented a single automaton after he went on the stage in 1845, and as Opre died in 1846, the coincidence is nothing if not significant.

CHAPTER V

The Obedient Cards.

To trace here the history of three very common tricks claimed by Robert-Houdin as his own inventions would be sheer waste of time, if the exposure did not prove beyond doubt that in announcing the various tricks of his répertoire as the output of his own brain he was not only flagrant and unscrupulous, but he did not even give his readers credit for enough intelligence to recognize tricks performed repeatedly by his predecessors whom they had seen. Not satisfied with purloining tricks so important that one or two would have been sufficient to establish the reputation of any conjurer or inventor, he must needs lay claim to having invented tricks long the property of mountebanks as well as reputable magicians.

The tricks referred to are the obedient card, the cabalistic clock, and the automaton known as Diavolo Antonio or Le Voltigeur au Trapèze.

Card trick as featured by Anderson in 1836-37. From a poster in the Harry Houdini Collection.

The obedient-card trick, mentioned on page 245 of the American edition of his "Memoirs," as "a novel experiment invented by M. Robert-Houdin," can be found on the programme of every magician who ever laid claim to dexterity of hand. Whether they accomplished the effect by clock-work or with a black silk thread or a human hair, the result was one and the same. It has also been worked by using a fine thread with a piece of wax at the end. The wax is fastened to the card, and the thread draws it up. The simplest method of all is to place the thread over and under the cards, weaving it in and out as it were, and then, by pulling the thread, to bring the different cards selected into view.

So common was the trick that its description was written in every work on magic published from 1784 to the date of Robert-Houdin's first appearance, and in at least one volume printed as early as 1635. The majority of French encyclopædias described the trick and exposed it according to one method or another, and Robert-Houdin admits having been a great reader of encyclopædias.

The trick first appears in print in various editions of "Hocus Pocus," twenty in all, starting with 1635. The majority contain feats with cards, showing how to bring them up or out of a pack with a black thread, a hair spring, or an elastic.

In 1772 the rising-card trick was shown in Guyot's "Physical and Mathematical Recreations," also in the Dutch or Holland translations of the same work. In 1791 it was minutely explained by Hofrath von Eckartshausen, who wrote five different books on the subject of magic. The fourth, being devoted principally to the art of the conjurer, was entitled "Die Gauckeltasche, oder vollständiger Unterricht in Taschenspieler u. s. w.," which translated means "The Conjurer's Pocket or Thorough Instructions in the Art of Conjuring." The title was due to the fact that in olden days, conjurers worked with the aid of a large outside pocket. The five books, published under the general title of "Aufschlüsse zur Magie," bear date of Munich, Germany.

On page 138 of the third edition of Gale's "Cabinet of Knowledge," published in London in 1800, will be found a description of the rising-card trick as done with pin and thread, and the same book shows how it is accomplished with wax and a hair. This book seems to have been compiled from Philip Breslaw's work on magic, "The Last Legacy," published in 1782. Benton, who published the English edition of Decremps' famous work on magic, exposing Pinetti's répertoire, also described the trick. "Natural Magic," by Astley, the circus man, and Hooper's "Recreations," in four volumes, published in 1784, expose the same trick.

the Art of (OR) Slaght of Hand

Reproduction of frontispiece in Breslaw's book on magic, "The Last Legacy," published in 1782. Original in the Harry Houdini Collection.

As to magicians who performed the trick, their names are legion, and only a few of the most prominent conjurers will be mentioned in this connection.

J. H. Anderson's birth place as drawn by him from memory. The following is written under the sketch in his own handwriting: "A rough sketch of the farm house called 'Red Stanes,' on the estate of Craigmyle, Parish of Kincardine O'Neil, Aberdeenshire. The house was built by my grandfather, John Robertson, in the year 1796, and in it I was born on the 15th day of July, 1814. John Henry Anderson." Photographed from the original now in the possession of Mrs. Leona A. Anderson, by the author.

The man who obtained the best effects with this trick was John Henry Anderson, who startled the world of magic and amusements by his audacity, in 1836, nine years before Robert-Houdin trod the stage as a professional entertainer.

Anderson was born in Kincardine, Scotland, in 1814, and started his professional career as an actor. He must have been a very poor one, too, for he states that he was once complimented by a manager for having brought bad acting to the height of perfection.

John Henry Anderson, wife and son, from a rare photograph taken in 1847 or 1848. Said to be an especially good likeness of Mrs. Anderson and the only one extant. Photograph loaned by Mrs. Leona A. Anderson, daughter-in-law of the "Wizard of the North."

Cover design of Anderson's book, exposing the Davenport Brothers; now a very rare book. From the Harry Houdini Collection.

Anderson was first known as the Caledonian magician, then assumed the title of the Wizard of the North, which he said was bestowed on him by Sir Walter Scott. Thomas Frost belittles this statement, on the grounds that Scott was stricken with paralysis in 1830. However, Anderson became famous in 1829, so he should be given the benefit of the doubt. He was the greatest advertiser that the world of magic has ever known, and he left nothing undone that might boom attendance at his performances. He started newspapers, gave masked balls, and donated thousands of dollars to charities. He was known in every city of the world, and, when so inclined, built his own theatres. He sold books on magic during his own performances, and would sell any trick he presented for a nominal sum. His most unique advertising dodge was to offer $500 in gold as prizes for the best conundrums written by spectators during his performances. To make this scheme more effective, he carried with him his own printing-press and set it up back of the scenes. While the performance was under way, the conundrums handed in by the spectators were printed, and, after the performance, any one might buy a sheet of the questions and puns at the door. As everyone naturally wanted to see his conundrum in print, Anderson sold millions of these bits of paper. In 1852, while playing at Metropolitan Hall, New York City, he advertised his conundrum contest and sold his book of tricks, etc., and such notables as Jenny Lind and General Kossuth entered conundrums.

He was among the first performers to expose the Davenport Brothers, whose spiritualistic tricks and rope-tying had astonished America. Directly on witnessing a performance and solving their methods, Anderson hurried back to England and exposed the tricks.

To sum up his history, he stands unique in the annals of magic as a doer of daring things. He rushed into print on the slightest pretext, was a hard fighter with his rivals and aired his quarrels in the press, and he was a game loser when trouble came his way. Not a brilliant actor or performer, he yet had the gift of securing excellent effects in his *mise en scène*. He made and lost several fortunes, generally recouping as quickly as he lost. He was burned out several times, the most notable fire being that of Covent Garden, London, in 1856. He was liked in spite of his eccentricities, but when he died, February 3d, 1874, his fortune was small.

Anderson billing of 1838, featuring obedient cards as "Napoleon's Trick." From the Harry Houdini Collection.

Anderson had numerous imitators, including M. Jacobs, "Barney" Eagle, and E. W. Young, all of whom used the rising-or obedient-card trick. They copied not only his tricks, but the very names he had used and the style of his billing. All three of these men were professional magicians before Robert-Houdin appeared, and Anderson was his very active contemporary.

A Jacobs bill is here reproduced, showing the card trick featured among other attractions. The lithograph of Jacobs used in this connection is an actual likeness and I believe it to be as rare as it is timely.

Lithograph used by E. W. Young, who copied all of John Henry Anderson's billing and featured the obedient-card trick. This setting shows how cumbersome was the apparatus employed by magicians before Wiljalba Frikell proved that he could score with apparently no apparatus. Original in the Harry Houdini Collection.

Frontispiece from Eagle's book, in which he exposes Anderson's gun delusion. Said by Henry Evanion, who knew Eagle, to be a fine likeness. From the Harry Houdini Collection.

Young's name has been handed down in history because he made money on Anderson's reputation, by the boldest of imitations, assuming the title of Wizard of the North with his own name in small type. One of his bills is also reproduced.

Barnedo or "Barney" Eagle is the man of the trio of the imitators who deserves more than passing notice. He became Anderson's bitterest enemy, and their rivalry made money for the printers.

Eagle could neither read nor write, but having a quick brain he hired a clever writer to indite his speeches and duplicated Anderson's show so closely that Anderson's pride was hurt. He therefore decided to expose Eagle, and thousands of bills, constituting a virulent attack upon his imitator, were distributed. One of these is reproduced. It is so rare that I doubt whether another is in existence.

An Anderson poster, exposing "Barney" Eagle's tricks. Only bill of this sort in existence. From the Harry Houdini Collection.

"BARNEY" ALIAS THE IMPOSTOR WIZARD

Window poster issued by Anderson to belittle his imitator "Barney" Eagle and show how the latter secured royal patronage. From the Harry Houdini Collection.

As Eagle had advertised that he was patronized by royalty, Anderson had another bill printed, showing Eagle playing before the King at the Ascot race-track, and an assistant passing the hat in mountebank fashion. In revenge, Eagle had a book published, in which he exposed Anderson's best drawing trick, The Gun Delusion, in which the magician allowed any one from the audience to shoot a gun at him using marked bullets. These bullets were caught in his mouth or on the point of a knife. This trick became as common as the obedient-card trick.

In the face of such overwhelming evidence, Robert-Houdin's claim to having invented the obedient-card trick is nothing short of farcical.

A "Barney" Eagle poster on which the obedient-card trick is featured as "The Walking Cards." From the Harry Houdini Collection.

The Cabalistic or Obedient Clock

There might be said to exist a very reasonable doubt as to the exact date at which Robert-Houdin produced the cabalistic clock which he included among his other doubtful claims to inventions.

On page 250 of the American edition of his "Memoirs" he has the Cabalistic Clock on his opening programme for July 3d, 1845, but in the appendix of the French edition he states that the clock first made its appearance at the opening of the season of 1847. In nearly all his statements he is equally inaccurate.

The mysterious clock might be termed the obedient clock, for the trick consists in causing the hand or hands to obey the will of the conjurer or the wishes of the audience.

The hands will point to a figure, move with rapidity, or as slowly as possible, or in time to music. In fact the performer has full control of the hands—he can make them do his every bidding.

The mysterious clock is a trick as old as the obedient-card trick, if not older. It was explained according to various methods in books before Robert-Houdin's appearance on the stage. In fact, the majority of old-time conjuring books explain mysterious clocks carefully.

Before electricity was introduced, magnets were employed, but the earliest method was to make use of thread wound about the spindle of the clock hand, and that method is still the very best used to-day, owing to its simplicity. The clock, on being presented to the audience, may be hung or placed in the position best suited to the particular method by which it is being "worked."

It shows a transparent clock face, such as you see in any jewelry shop. Some magicians utilize only one hand, which permits the easy use of electricity or magnet, while others employ two and even three hands. When more than one hand is used the hours and minutes are indicated simultaneously and, if cards are pasted on the clock face, the largest hand is used to find the chosen cards.

The clock may be placed on a pedestal, in an upright position, or hung in midair on two ribbons or strings. It can be hung on a stand made expressly for the purpose, on the style of a music stand, or it can be swung in a frame. In fact, as stated before, it is usually placed so as to facilitate the method of working.

M. Jacobs, magician, ventriloquist, and bold imitator of John Henry Anderson. From a rare lithograph now in the Harry Houdini Collection.

When the cabalistic clock is taken off the hook or the stand on which it is placed, and handed to one of the spectators to hold, the latter places the hand on the pin in the centre of the glass face, and revolves it. The arrow or hand is worked by a counterweight, controlled by the performer, who has it fixed before he hands it to the innocent spectator. The clock can be purchased from any reliable dealer of conjuring apparatus, in almost any part of the world.

For a clock worked by counterweight the hand of thin brass is prepared in the centre, where there is a weight of peculiar shape which has at the thin or tapering end a small pin. This pin is fixed permanently to the weight and can be revolved about the small plate on which it is riveted. Through this plate there is a hole, exactly in the centre. This hand has all this covered with a brass cap, and, to make the arrow point to any given number, you simply move the weight with your thumb. The pin clicks and allows you to feel it as it moves from one hole to another. With very little practice you can move this weight, while in the act of handing it to some one to place it on the centre of the clock face; and when spun, the weight, of its own accord, will land on the bottom, causing the hand to point where it is forced by the law of gravity. The plate on which the weight is fastened is grooved or milled, so that it answers to the slightest movement of your thumb.

When the clock is on the stage and the hand moves simply by the command of the performer or audience, it is manipulated by an assistant behind the scenes, either by the aid of electricity or by an endless thread which is wrapped about the spindle and runs through the two ribbons or strings that hold the clock in midair. Some conjurers work the clock so arranged as to make a combination trick; first by having it worked by the concealed confederate; then, taking the clock off the stand and bringing it down in the midst of the audience. But for this trick you can use only one hand.

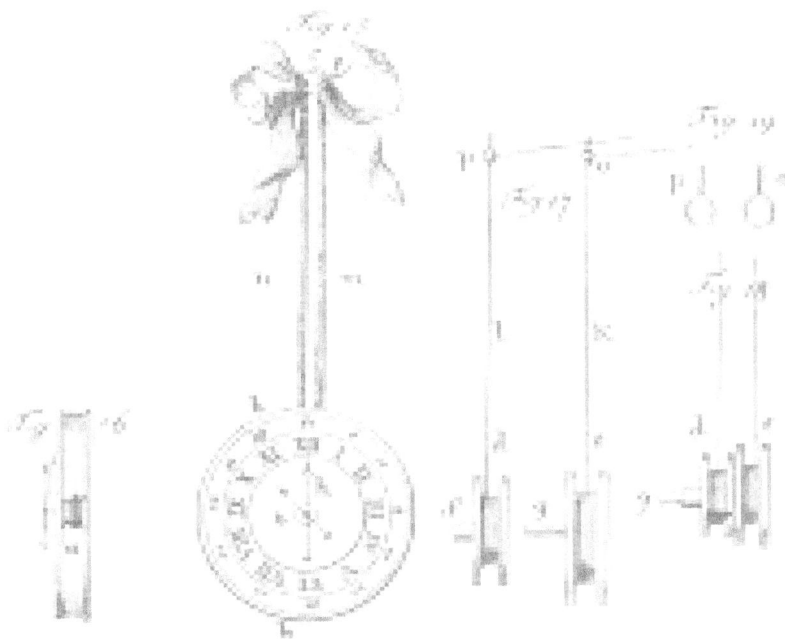

The above diagram exposes the magic clock trick, as offered in the time of Hofrath von Eckartshausen, a German writer on magic in the eighteenth and the nineteenth centuries. Fig. 15 shows the clock in position for the trick, hung against the rear wall or "drop." Gaily-colored ribbons hide thin leather tubes through which run two sets of stout silk thread or catgut, connecting with the hour and minute hands. The thread then passes through the two iron rings, p and o in Figures 17 and 19, which are screwed to the ceiling; thence to the hidden confederate, who manipulates the clock hands as the hour and minute are announced by magician or spectator. Fig. 16 shows the two faces of the clock, with the fine connecting rod around which the string is wound to manipulate the hands. This mechanism is hidden by a flat brass band which encircles the edges of the two transparent faces. From Eckartshausen's "The Conjurer's Pocket," edition of 1791.

Years ago, when I introduced this trick in my performance, I called a young man on my stage and asked him to place the hand on the spindle. It would then revolve and stop at any number named. But first I made him inform the audience the number he had chosen, which gave me time to fix the weight with my thumb. I then gave him the hand, but he was a skilled mechanic, and possibly knew the trick. Instead of holding the clock by the ring at the top, which was there for that purpose, he grasped the dial at the bottom, causing the number 6 instead of 12 to be on top. When the hand started to turn, of course it would have stopped at the wrong number. I managed to escape humiliation by pretending I was afraid he would break the clock by letting it fall, so took it away from him, holding it myself.

Reproduction of rare engraving of Johann Nep. Hofzinser, who invented the clock worked by a counter-weight, and who was one of the world's greatest card tricksters. Original in the Harry Houdini Collection.

The mechanic walked off the stage winking at me in the most roguish manner.

Robert-Houdin worked The Mystic Bell trick in connection with The Clock. This was manipulated in the same way. The bell was worked with thread, pulling a small pin, which in turn caused the handle to fall against the glass bell. Naturally, having electricity at his command at that time, he made use of that force whenever it suited his fancy.

I am positive that Robert-Houdin presented the electrical clock, because T. Bolin, of Moscow, visited Paris and bought the trick from Voisin, the French manufacturer of conjuring apparatus. The trick which Robert-Houdin presented, according to his claims, was with the clock hanging in midair to prove that it was not electrically connected, but the truth of the matter is that the strings which held the clock suspended in midair concealed the wires through which his electrical current ran.

In my library of old conjuring books the thread method is ably described by Hofrath von Eckartshausen, mentioned earlier in this chapter. In fact in the pictorial appendix of this work he gives this trick prominence by minutely illustrating the same. He makes use of two hands, and to make the trick infallible he explains that the best way would be to use two glass disks, have them held together by a brass rim, and your threads will work with absolute certainty. The spectators imagine that they are seeing only one glass clock.

Johann Conrad Gutle, the well-known delver after secrets of natural magic, also explains several cabalistic clock tricks in his book published in 1802.

Reproduction of a triple colored lithograph. This section features Breslaw in stage costume. Original in the Harry Houdini Collection.

I am reproducing herewith a number of programmes describing the effect of the trick and proving that it was no novelty when Robert-Houdin "invented" it. In fact the trick was so common that only the supreme egotism of the man can explain his having introduced it into the pages of his book as an original trick. The mysterious clock worked by the counterweight, which has been described, is credited as having been the invention of Johann Nep. Hofzinser.

Katterfelto, the bombastic conjurer, who is famous for having sold sulphur matches in 1784, before the Lucifer match is supposed to have been discovered. Reproduced from a rare copy of "The European Magazine," dated June, 1783, now in the Harry Houdini Collection.

In an advertisement, published in the *London Post* of May 23d, 1778, included in my collection, this announcement, among others of much interest, will be found:

"PART II.—Breslaw will exhibit many of his newly invented deceptions with a grand apparatus and experiments and particularly the Magic Clock, Sympathetic Bell, and Pyramidical Glasses in a manner entirely new."

In 1781, while showing at Greenwood's Rooms, Haymarket, London, Breslaw heavily advertised, "Particularly an experiment on a newly invented mechanical clock will be displayed, under the direction of Sieur Castinia, just arrived from Naples, the like never attempted before in this metropolis."

There is every reason to believe that Katterfelto, the greatest of bombastic conjurers, used the electrical clock in his performances, as he made a feature of the various late discoveries, and in his programme of 1782 he advertises "feats and experiments in Magnetical, Electrical, Optical, Chymical, Philosophical, Mathematical, etc., etc." Among implements and instruments or articles mentioned I found Watches, Caskets, Dice, Cards, Mechanical Clocks, Pyramidical Glasses, etc., etc.

Gyngell, Sr., the celebrated Bartholomew Fair conjurer, whose career started about 1788, had on his early programmes, "A Pedestal Clock, so singularly constructed that it is obedient to the word of command." On the same programme (Catherine Street Theatre, London, February 15th, 1816) I find "The Russian Inn," "The Confectioner's Shop," and "The Automaton Rope Vaulter." This programme is reproduced in full in Chapter IV.

Without devoting further space to Robert-Houdin's absurd claim to having invented this clock, we will proceed to discuss his claims to the automaton rope walker, which he called a trapeze performer.

The Trapeze Automaton

Though "Diavolo Antonio" or "Le Voltigeur Trapeze" was not a simple trick, but a cleverly constructed automaton, worked by a concealed confederate, it was a common feature on programmes long before Robert-Houdin claimed it as his invention. Yet with the daring of one who believes that all proof has been destroyed, he announces on page 312 of the American edition of his "Memoirs" that he invented "The Trapeze Performer" for his season of 1848. In the illustrated appendix of his French edition he states that the figure made its first appearance at his Paris theatre, October 1st, 1849. He thus describes the automaton:

"The figure is the size of an infant, and I carry the little artist on my arm in a box. I put him on the trapeze and ask him questions, which he answers by moving his head. Then he bows gracefully to the audience, turning first this way, then that; suspends himself by his hands and draws himself up in time to the music. He also goes through the motions of a strong man, hangs by his head, hands, and feet, and with his legs making the motions of aërial telegraphy."

Reproduction of an illustration in "Aufschlüsse zur Magie," by Hofrath von Eckartshausen, showing the automatic rope vaulter as exhibited in 1784 by Pinetti. Original in the Harry Houdini Collection.

Decremps in his exposé, "The Conjurer Unmasked," published in 1784, thus describes the automaton and its work: "Our attention was next called to observe an automaton figure, that vaulted upon a rope, performing all the postures and evolutions of the most expert tumblers, keeping exact time to music. By seeing Mr. Van Estin wind up the figures, and being shown the wheels and levers contained in the body of the automaton, caused us to believe it moved by its own springs, when Mr. Van Estin thus explained the deception: 'To make a figure of this kind depends a great deal on the proportion and the materials with which it is composed: The legs and thighs are formed out of heavy wood, such as ash or oak; the body of birch or willow, and made hollow, and the head, for lightness, of papier-maché. The figure is joined by its hands to a bar of iron, that passes through a partition, and is turned by a confederate; the arms are inflexible at the elbows, but move freely at the shoulders by means of a bolt that goes through the body; and the thighs and legs move in the same manner at the hips and knees, and are stayed by pieces of leather to prevent them from bending in the wrong way. The bar is covered with hollow twisted tubes, and ornamented with artificial flowers, so as no part of it can be seen to turn; the confederate by giving the handle a quarter of a turn to the left, the automaton, whose arms are parallel to the horizon, lift themselves by little and little, till they become vertical and parallel to the rest of the body; if in following the same direction, the other part of the body moves forward; and by watching the motions through a hole, he seizes the instant that a leg passes before the bar, to leave the automaton astride; afterward he balances it by jerks, and causes it to take a turn around, keeping time with the music as if it was sensible of harmony.

"N.B.—Three circumstances concur here to favor the illusion: First, by the assistance of a wire, the confederate can separate the bar from the automaton, which, falling to the ground, persuades one it loses itself by real machinery. Secondly, in winding up the levers shown in the body, confirms the spectators in the idea that there is no need of a confederate. Thirdly, the tubes that are twisted around the bar, except where the automaton is joined to it, seem to be the rope itself, and being without motion, as is seen by the garlands which surround them, it cannot be suspected that the bar turns in the inside, from whence it is concluded that the figure moves by its own machinery."

According to one of de Philipsthal's advertisements, page 103, the trapeze automaton which he featured was six feet in height. But Pinetti programmes show that he had a smaller figure known as the rope vaulter. This is probably the trick exposed in Decremps' book.

On page 108 will be found a Louis programme of 1815, on which a figure is thus featured:

"TWO ELEGANT AUTOMATA

As large as nature, the one representing a beautiful POLONNESE, the other a little boy.

Nothing can surpass the admirable construction of these Pieces. The large figure seems almost endowed with human Faculties, exhibiting the usual feats of a Rope-Dancer, in the fullest imitation of life. The small Figure is invested with equally astonishing powers of action. To such ladies as are spectators it must be a very pleasing circumstance that these exertions do not excite those disagreeable sensations which arise from the sight of Figures fraught with life, performing feats attended with so much danger."

By referring to page 113 the reader will find a Schmidt programme, dated 1827, on which the figure is featured as follows:

"THE ROPE DANCER,

Whose surprising performances surpass, in agility, attitudes, and evolutions, every Professor of the art, keeping correct time to the music of the machinery."

A Gyngell programme, dated 1823, which is reproduced in the chapter devoted to "The Pastry Cook of the Palais Royal," page 125, reads as follows: "Two automatons, one of which will execute wonderful feats on the tight rope, and the other dance a characteristic hornpipe."

As Gyngell figured in the amusement world from 1788 to 1844, the little figure must have been tolerably well known to the magic-loving public of England by the time Robert-Houdin appeared in London in 1848.

A magician named York, who appeared in London in 1844, the year before Robert-Houdin made his professional début, featured under date of January 29th "two automatons, one of which will execute wonderful feats on the Tight Rope, and the other dance a characteristic Hornpipe."

Bologna announced for his performance at the Sans Pareil Theatre, Strand, London, under date of March 18th, 1812, "The Two Automaton Rope Dancers from St. Petersburg, whose Feats of Agility were never equalled, and cannot be surpassed, will perform together in a style of Excellence hitherto unknown in this country."

De Philipsthal also featured a pair of automatic tight-rope performers from 1804 until his death; and in the early 30's the figures were exhibited by his widow. By referring to Chapter III. a De-Philipsthal programme of 1806 is reproduced as evidence.

From 1825 to 1855 J. F. Thiodon played London and the provinces, advertising on his programmes:

"FOURTH PIECE.—The Wonderful and Unrivalled Automaton on the Flying Rope. The only one of this construction in the Kingdom; and forms a more extraordinary Novelty from the circumstances of its not being fastened on the Rope by the Hands, like others hitherto exhibited. The Rope will be in continual Motion, and the Figure will sit perfectly easy and in a graceful attitude while on the Swing, and perform the most surprising Evolutions, scarcely to be distinguished from a Living Performer, as it moves with the utmost Correctness, without any apparent Machinery."

From this overwhelming evidence, it can be argued beyond doubt that if Robert-Houdin even constructed the automaton he merely copied figures presented by both his predecessors and his contemporaries, and he was fully aware of the existence of several such automata when he advertised his as an original invention. They were made by many mechanicians.

In the illustrated appendix of the French edition of his "Memoirs" he goes further; he deliberately misrepresents the mechanism of the figure and insinuates that the automaton is a self-working one. This is not true, as it was worked by a concealed confederate, as described above by Decremps.

Robert-Houdin even used the garlands of flowers to hide the moving bars as Pinetti and others of his predecessors had done. The truth was not in him.

CHAPTER VI

THE INEXHAUSTIBLE BOTTLE

WHILE Robert-Houdin claims to have invented "The Inexhaustible Bottle" for a special programme designed to create a sensation at the opening of his season of 1848, in the illustrated appendix of the original French edition of his "Memoirs" he states that it had its premier presentation December 1st, 1847. These discrepancies occur with such frequency that it is difficult to refute his claims in chronological order. Perhaps he adopted this method intentionally, to confuse future historians of magic, particularly concerning his own achievements.

In order to emphasize the brilliancy of this trick, Robert-Houdin turned boastful in describing it. On page 348 of the American edition of his "Memoirs," he states that the trick had created such a sensation and was so much exploited in the London newspapers that the fame of his inexhaustible bottle spread to the provinces, and on his appearance in Manchester with the bottle in his hand the workmen who made up the audience nearly mobbed him. In fact, the description of this scene is the most dramatic pen-picture in his "Memoirs."

The truth, sad to state, is that the bottle trick did not create the sensation he claims for it in London, nor did the press eulogize it. It was classed with other ordinary tricks, and twenty London papers bear mute testimony to this fact. In a complete collection of press clippings regarding his first London appearance, only four of the London papers mention the trick. *The Times*, the great conservative English paper, in reviewing Robert-Houdin's performance in its issue of May 3d, 1847, ignored the trick entirely. The four London papers which made mention of the bottle trick, and then only in a passing comment, were *The Chronicle*, *The Globe*, *The Lady's Newspaper*, and *The Court Journal*. Any one acquainted with the two last-named periodicals will know that they rarely reach the hands of the humble artisans in Manchester. *Punch*, London's great comic paper, gave the trick some space, however.

The trick of pouring several sorts of liquors from the same bottle has been presented in various forms and under different names. To prove the futility of Robert-Houdin's claims I will explain the mystery of this trick, which is of an interesting nature.

To all intents and purposes the bottle used looks like glass; but it is invariably made of tin, heavily japanned. Ranged around the central space, which is free from deception, are five compartments, each tapering to a narrow-mouthed tube which terminates about an inch or an inch and a half from within the neck of the bottle. A small pinhole is drilled through the outer surface of the bottle into each compartment, the holes being so placed that when the bottle is grasped with the hand in the ordinary way, the performer covers all but one of the pinholes with his fingers and thumb. The centre section is left empty, but the other compartments are filled with a funnel which has a tapering nozzle made specially for this purpose.

The trick is generally started by proving to the audience that the bottle is empty. It is then filled with water, which is immediately poured out again, all this time the five pinholes

197

being covered tightly with the hand or fingers which are holding the bottle. When a liquor is called for, the performer raises the finger over the air-hole above that particular liquor, and the liquor will flow out. When a large number of liquors may be called for, the performer has one compartment filled with a perfectly colorless liquor, which he pours into glasses previously flavored with strong essences. Certain gins and cordials can be simulated in this fashion.

Various improvements have been made in this bottle trick. For instance, after the bottle has yielded its various sorts of liquors, it is broken, and from the bottle the performer produces some borrowed article which has been "vanished" in a previous trick and then apparently forgotten. This may have been a ring, glove, or handkerchief, which will be discovered tied around the neck of a small guinea-pig or dove taken from the broken bottle.

This is accomplished by having the bottle especially constructed. Its compartments end a few inches above the bottom of the bottle and the portion below having a wavy or cracked appearance, is made to slip on and off. The conjurer goes through the motions of actually breaking the bottle by tapping it near the bottom with a small hammer or wand, and the appearance of the guinea-pig or lost article causes surprise, so that the pretended breaking of the bottle passes unnoticed.

Again, this bottle can be genuine, with no loose bottom at all, and a small article can be inserted, but this makes a great deal of trouble, and the effect is not greatly increased. In doing the trick thus, I was always compelled to have an optician cut the bottom from the bottle, and then at times even he would break it.

To explain further how the article is "loaded" into the bottle, the performer borrows several articles, for example a ring and two watches. He will place the ring and watches into a funnel at the end of a large horse-pistol, and shoot them at the target. The two watches appear on the target or in a frame or any place that he may choose. In obtaining the articles, he may have wrapped them up in a handkerchief which he has hidden in the front of his vest. Alexander Herrmann was exceptionally clever in making this exchange, his iron nerve and perpetual smile being great aids in the trick.

The performer now places the duplicate handkerchief on the table in full view of the audience, and walks to another table for a gun. While reaching for this gun, he places the original articles which he borrowed behind his table on a servante, so that his hidden assistant may reach for them, place the two watches on the "turn-about target," tie the ring on the neck of the guinea-pig, shove him into the bottle, and insert the false bottom. The trick is then ready in its entirety.

The magician calls for something to use as a target, and the assistant responds with the revolving target or frame. When the conjurer shoots, the two watches appear on the target or in the frame. This part of the trick is accomplished by having the centre of the target revolve, or, if the frame is used, by having a black velvet curtain pulled up by rapid springs or strong rubbers.

While all this is going on, some one has brought on the stage the loaded bottle, and as no attention is called to this, by the time the watches have been restored to the owners the conjurer introduces the bottle trick, pours out the various liquors, and eventually breaks the bottle and reproduces the borrowed article tied about the neck of the guinea-pig or dove.

Many names have been given to this trick. The old-time magicians who remained for months in one theatre had to change their programmes frequently, so for one night they would present the bottle without breaking it, and on the next they would break the bottle, so as to vary the trick.

This bottle trick originated in "The Inexhaustible Barrel." The first trace that I can find of this wonderful barrel is in "Hocus Pocus, Jr., The Anatomie of Legerdemain," written by Henry Dean in 1635 (Second Edition). On page 21 is described a barrel with a single spout, from which can be drawn three different kinds of liquors. This was worked precisely on the same principle as was the inexhaustible bottle trick centuries later, by shutting up the air-holes of compartments from which liquors were not flowing.

Its first public appearance, according to the data in my collection, clipped from London papers of 1707 and 1712, was when the "famous water-works of the late ingenious Mr. Henry Winstanly" were exhibited by his servants for the benefit of his widow; and the exhibition included a view of "the Barrel that plays so many Liquors and is broke in pieces before the Spectators."

In 1780 Dr. Desaguliers presented in London a performance entitled "A Course of Experimental Philosophy wherein the Principles of Mechanics, Hydrostatics, Pneumatics, and Optics are proved and demonstrated by more than 300 Experiments."

In the course of these lectures he produced a sort of barrel, worked by holding the fingers over the air-holes. He also exposed the real source of strength of the notorious strong man of his day, John Carl von Eckeberg, who allowed horses to pull against him, permitted heavy stones to be broken on his bare chest, and who broke heavy ropes simply by stretching or straightening his knees. These lectures and exposés made Dr. Desaguliers so famous that he has been given considerable space in Sir David Brewster's "Letters on Natural Magic," published in London in 1851, in which book the various deceptions used by strong men are fully described. In fact the book is one that should be in every conjurer's library.

The old Dutch books explain the barrel trick, and in 1803 Charles Hutton, professor of Woolwich Royal Academy, translated four books from Ozanam and Montucla, exposing quite a number of old conjuring tricks. The barrel trick will be found on page 94 of Volume II.

The first use of "The Inexhaustible Bottle" by modern conjurers I found in an announcement of Herr Schmidt, a German performer, who for a time controlled the original writing and drawing figure, as will be found by reference to Chapter III., which is devoted to the history of that automaton. The programme published in that chapter is dated 1827, and does not include the famous bottle, because it was no longer a novelty in Herr Schmidt's répertoire; but the advertisement reproduced herewith, dated 1821, schedules the bottle trick thus: "The Bottle of Sobriety and Inebriety, proving the inutility of a set of decanters, when various liquors can be produced by one." Thus Schmidt antedated Houdin's offering of the trick by more than a quarter of a century.

Next the bottle turned up in 1835 in London, where it was presented by a German who styled himself "Falck of Koenigsberg, Pupil of the celebrated Chevalier Pinnetty," and who introduced the programme with which Döbler made such a sensation in 1842.

Mr. Falck opened at the Queen's Bazaar, Oxford Street, London, November 8th, 1835. Before opening, however, he gave a private performance for the press, and received quite a number of notices. A half-column clipping in my collection, dated November 4th, 1835, which I think is cut from *The Chronicle* or *The Globe*, mentions the trick among other effects like "Flora's Gift," "The Card in the Pocket," etc., and adds that the "exchange of wine was so that if once in Mr. Falck's company, we should not wish to exchange it, for he poured three sorts of wine, Port, Sherry, and Champagne, out of one bottle. Then he put them together, and from such a mixture produced sherry in one glass, and port in another."

From this notice it will be seen that Falck had "The Inexhaustible Bottle," and had some method of returning all the liquors not drunk back into the bottle and then pouring out two different kinds of liquor.

Perhaps he resorted to chemicals, but one thing is evident—the bottle was used for six different kinds of liquors at one and the same time.

Phillippe from 1836 to 1838 featured "An Infernal Bottle" trick, also "The Inexhaustible Bottle" trick. The trick also was seen on programmes used by John Henry Anderson, the Wizard of the North, in the same years. According to these programmes Phillippe and Anderson showed the bottle empty, filled it with water, and then served five different liquors.

On April 30th, 1838, Anderson thus announced the trick on a programme used at Victoria Rooms, Hull:

"Handkerchiefs will be borrowed from three gentlemen; the magician will load his mystic gun, in which he will place the handkerchiefs; he will fire a bottle containing wine, the bottle will be broken and the handkerchiefs will appear."

Programmes in my collection show that Anderson presented the trick, serving various sorts of liquors, when he played London in 1840, but little attention was drawn to the wonderful bottle. In 1842 Ludwig Döbler, Germany's best-beloved magician, came to London and featured what he termed "The Travelling Bottle."

"THE GREAT WIZARD OF THE NORTH."

Reproduction of a political cartoon in Punch, published during Anderson's London engagement, April, 1843, proving that the "Inexhaustible Bottle Trick" was used by Anderson before Robert-Houdin was a professional entertainer. From the Harry Houdini Collection.

Ludwig Döbler in his prime, taken about 1839. The original of this rare picture was discovered by the author in a small print shop in Moscow, Russia. It is now a part of his Collection.

Ludwig Leopold Döbler was born in Vienna in 1801. He was the best-beloved magician who ever trod the stage. He started life as an engraver of metals, but his fancy turned to necromancy. He gave his best performances in his native city. In 1841 he was touring Holland, and in a letter now in my possession, which he wrote to a director and editor in Vienna under date of March 15th, 1842, he informs his friend that he has sent all his baggage to London from Amsterdam, and is on a visit to Paris. He regrets that he has not all of his apparatus with him, but has given several performances, and mentions the fact that "to-morrow I am engaged to give a performance in the private parlor of Rothschild and then by the Count Montaliset, minister of the King's mansions." He also informs his friend that he expects to visit Paris the next season and build his own theatre. He states a fact most interesting to all magicians, namely, that he has rented the St. James Theatre in London for two thousand francs ($400) a night, or more than $2,400 rent for one week. Döbler drew such big audiences and made so much money that he refused to give private performances, only breaking this rule when presenting his show before H. M. Queen Victoria and the Prince Consort.

He played the provinces, then went over to Dublin, where, although unable to speak English, he was a veritable sensation. In 1844 Döbler played a return date at the St. James Theatre, London, and this time he had Anderson as a rival at the Théâtre Royal Adelphia.

Döbler amassed a fortune very rapidly; in fact he retired in 1847, and never again appeared on the stage. He always explained his early retirement by saying: "The public loves me, and I want it to always love me. I may return and be a failure, so it is best to know just when to stop." He died in a little village near Tunitz, on April 17th, 1864, when one of God's noblemen was laid to rest.

"The Travelling Bottle" alluded to by Döbler in his programmes was nothing more or less than "The Inexhaustible Bottle." The following excerpt from the London *Chronicle* during Döbler's engagement at the St. James Theatre, April, 1842, is illuminating:

Döbler's farewell programme in verse, used when he played his last engagement in the Josephstadter Theatre, Vienna. Original given by Döbler personally to Henry Evanion; now in the Harry Houdini Collection.

Ludwig Döbler in his prime, offering his most popular trick, "The Creation of Flowers." From a rare lithograph in the Harry Houdini Collection.

"DÖBLER—ST. JAMES THEATRE.—Among the illusions that more particularly struck our fancy was one entitled 'The Travelling Bottle,' where Herr Döbler, filling a common bottle with water, transformed this water into a collection of wines of all countries, amicably assembled together in one receptacle, and he fills out first a glass of sherry, then one of port, then one of champagne, and so on."

The critic then describes how the bottle was broken, and the borrowed handkerchief was found inside the bottle.

Probably because of the prominence which Herr Döbler gave to this trick it attracted more attention when Anderson presented it during his London run of 1843. He announced it as "Water vs. Wine, or Changing Water into Different Liquids—Sherry, Port, Champagne, Gin, Milk, Rum, and Water."

The London *Sun* of April 18th, 1843, says:

"Mr. Anderson, besides the feats by which his reputation was established in his former exhibitions in the metropolis, performed with perfect ease and success some of greater difficulty than those by which Herr Döbler astonished the world, such as serving several kinds of wines from the same bottle."

The Morning Advertiser (London) of the same date said:

"With the utmost ease he produced from an empty bottle wine, water, port, sherry, and champagne, and immediately afterward, under a blaze of wax and gas, he broke the same bottle and produced from it half a dozen cambric handkerchiefs, which had previously been deposited under lock and key at a considerable distance."

Macallister, the Scotch brick-mason, who became the pupil and assistant of Phillippe, as described in the chapter on "The Pastry Cook of the Palais Royal," also claimed the bottle trick as his invention. I have been unable to obtain any of the early programmes used by Macallister, but I am reproducing the one he utilized during his engagement at the Bowery Theatre, New York City, in 1852. This was not his first appearance in New York, however. In December, 1848, and January, 1849, he played at the same theatre, and announced that he had just concluded a successful engagement at the Grand Theatre Tacon, Havana, Cuba.

Although Macallister claims to have invented "The Inexhaustible Bottle" trick, it is more likely that, having been connected so long with Phillippe, he knew the secret several years before Robert-Houdin appeared in public. But as Macallister also claimed to have invented the peacock and the harlequin automata, both of which are recognized as the inventions of his predecessors, his claim cannot be given serious consideration.

He advertised to produce twenty-two kinds of liquors from one bottle, and therefore he must have utilized the essence glasses in connection with the bottle.

What must have been Robert-Houdin's feeling when, on arriving in London in 1848, he found another magician, Compars Herrmann, heavily advertised at the Théâtre Royal, and already offering each and every trick included by the Frenchman in his répertoire. Even the much-vaunted bottle was in Herrmann's list of tricks. No one seems able to tell where Compars Herrmann obtained the tricks he used, but he must be given credit for never advertising them as his own inventions. His record in this respect was clean throughout his life as a mysterious entertainer.

The programme presented by Herrmann at the Théâtre Royal during Robert-Houdin's opening week at the St. James Theatre is herewith reproduced. Herrmann remained some time in London, playing at the Adelphia, then at the Royal Princess, and finally at the Surrey Theatre. A bill used by Herrmann at the Princess is reproduced on page 232. It evidently proved satisfactory to the public and he used it without change for many years. Probably the most notable warfare waged over the honor of having invented this trick arose between Robert-Houdin and Henri Robin, who were contemporaries.

Henri Robin, generally conceded to have been the most polished conjurer in the history of magic. From the Harry Houdini Collection.

Robin, whose right name was Dunkell, was of Holland birth and died in Paris in 1874. He was at his prime about 1839-40, when he toured the Continent. He was popular in London, Paris, and both the English and French provinces. A polished man, famous for the elegance of his speech and manners, he conducted his performance and all his business in a quiet, conservative fashion. In both Paris and London, he had playhouses named temporarily in his honor, Salle de Robin, and at one time in London he also appeared at the Egyptian Hall. He published his own magazine, *L'Almanach d'Cagliostro*, an illustrated periodical which was quite pretentious.

Robin presented all the tricks and automata that Robert-Houdin claimed as his original inventions, and in the famous controversy, Robert-Houdin came out second best. Robin proved that he had used the bottle trick before Robert-Houdin did, by showing back numbers of his magazine, whose illustrations pictured Robin performing the trick at his theatre in Milan, Italy, July 6th, 1844, or three years before Robert-Houdin presented it in Paris.

Robin, however, never wrote an autobiography nor any exhaustive work dealing with the history of magic, while Robert-Houdin did. The latter set forth his claims over other magicians so skilfully that for more than half a century the intelligent and thoughtful reading public has been deceived and has accepted his statements as authoritative. According to an article published in *L'Illusionniste*, scientists to this day, in explaining the law of physics as operated by the use of air-holes in the inexhaustible bottle, refer to it as the "Robert-Houdin bottle," when in reality the honor of its invention belongs to some obscure mechanic or magician whose name must remain forever unsung by writers on magic.

CHAPTER VII SECOND SIGHT

EVIDENTLY second sight was the foundation-stone of Robert-Houdin's success. Reading between the lines of his autobiography, one finds that this was the trick which carried him into the salons of fashion and royalty. Before he introduced second sight into his répertoire, his tricks were so commonplace that they did not arouse the interest of the court circle, whose approval furnished the seal of success.

This trick of second sight he claims body and soul, as the favorite child of his brain. He even goes as far as to relate a story to prove that the trick came to him in the form of an inspiration. I quote directly from the American edition of his "Memoirs," page 255:

"My two children were playing one day in the drawing-room at a game they had invented for their own amusement; the younger had bandaged his elder brother's eyes and made him guess the objects that he touched, and when the latter happened to guess right they changed places. This simple game suggested to me the most complicated idea that ever crossed my mind. Pursued by the notion, I ran and shut myself in my workshop, and was fortunately in that happy state when the mind follows easily the combinations traced by fancy. I rested my head in my hands, and in my excitement laid down the first principles of second sight."

Robert-Houdin and his son Emile, presenting second sight. Here the bell is used as it was by Henri Robin. From an illustration in the original French edition of the Robert-Houdin "Memoirs."

Then, picking up the long idle quill of Baron Munchausen, he proceeds to explain the methods by which he perfected the trick and trained his son. To the layman these methods read most entertainingly. To the experienced conjurer or his humblest assistant they appeal as absurd and impossible, a sheer waste of time, of which a man who reproduced the tricks of his predecessors as rapidly as Robert-Houdin did, would not be guilty.

Robert and Haidee Heller from photographs taken at the time that they were presenting second sight according to the Robert-Houdin method by an electric code. From the Harry Houdini Collection.

He claims to have trained the eye and memory of his son, by leading the latter past shop windows, and after allowing him one glance, demanding the names of articles seen at this single glance. When the boy could mention forty things after passing the window, his education was pronounced good. Robert-Houdin also tells in his "Memoirs" of spending hours with his son in poring over an enormous collection of coins, medals, etc., which severe lesson helped them both in future performances. To the conjurer, this tale is farcical. Not only was there no need of forcing the boy to become a coin expert, but the task was one which could not be accomplished in the brief time which Robert-Houdin allowed himself for perfecting the trick.

The only knowledge required about coins is to recognize a coin when you see it. Some one may hand a coin of peculiar stamp, and the operator must signal to his medium the metal and all he knows about it. Of course, if both know the various coins, then they can understand each other with less signaling than if the coins were unfamiliar to either.

Inaudi, the French calculator, can look at a blackboard filled with numbers for a few seconds, then turn his back upon them and add the entire amount that he has just seen and memorized. But let the reader understand that Inaudi is peculiarly gifted by nature, while second sight is a trick in which the person on the stage known as the medium is assisted by words, signs, prearranged movements, or articles or figures in rotation, which to the layman have the appearance of being unprepared. At a familiar cue, however, the operator touches articles that have been memorized, a ring, a watch, a scarf-pin, a lady's fan, an opera glass, all in rotation. At a snap of the fingers the medium will know that the articles are to be named in consecutive order, and only after the snap of the fingers or another cue agreed upon.

Robert-Houdin presented the trick for the first time at his own theatre, February 12th, 1846. Unquestionably at this time he employed the speaking code, wherein the answer is contained in the question asked of the medium by the performer. As he describes scene after scene in which he and his son participated, it is almost possible for a conjurer or any one interested in magic to follow his code. Apparently, the amusement-loving public became familiar with his speaking code, for three years later, according to the illustrated appendix of the French edition of his "Memoirs," he adopted a code of signals, which he states was especially arranged to confuse those whom he terms his "fearless discoverers."

A mysterious bell was used in this connection, but he admits that it mattered not whether the bell struck or was silent, his son could name the object under consideration or answer the question. While Robert-Houdin asserts that he did not employ electricity for working his silent code, investigations make it almost certain that this was the method used. It is known throughout the world of conjuring that in 1850-51 Robert Heller (William Henry Palmer) reproduced Robert-Houdin's entire répertoire of tricks, with the exception of the suspension, and all worked precisely by Robert-Houdin's methods. In the second-sight trick, which he first presented with a young man as the medium, then later with Miss Haidee Heller, the medium was seated on a sofa fully equipped with wires and electric batteries. Heller's second sight was worked with both the speaking and silent codes. His confederate was concealed behind the scenes watching Heller through a peep-hole, or possibly he used another, seated in the audience, and had the wires strung under his chair, arranging the signal button so that it could be easily reached on the arm or front part of the seat. The receiving instrument was attached to the sofa on which the medium was seated. The latter would be silently informed as to what was being shown and would answer all questions. As proof that these statements are not mere hearsay, the Heller sofa can now be seen in the possession of Mr. Francis J. Martinka, of New York; and Dr. W. Golden Mortimer, who once presented "Mortimer's Mysteries," a show on the style of Heller's performance, furnishes the information that when Heller died in Philadelphia, November 28th, 1878, he engaged the dead magician's chief assistant, an expert electrician named E. J. Dale, who had acted as secret confederate, assisting the medium.

Poster used by Robert Heller during his Boston engagement in 1853. From the Harry Houdini Collection.

After travelling with Mortimer some time, Dale eventually returned to England, and retired from the profession. He opened a large shop in London under the firm name of H. & E. J. Dale, Manufacturing Electricians, 4 Little Britain, E. C., in October, 1882.

It was the easiest thing imaginable for Robert-Houdin to have his theatre arranged with secret confederates and wires back of the scenes, where a man with powerful opera-glasses could stand. The place being small, he could look all over the room and see the minutest article.

When not making use of the talking code, the simplest method employed by second-sight artists is to have a confederate in the audience, with either an electrical push button or a pneumatic bulb, who gives the medium the signal. This is received by a miniature piston, which requires only a small hole in the stage, while the medium has a matching hole in the sole of his shoe. This allows the piston to touch the sole of the foot whenever the confederate presses the bulb or pushes the button.

The author at the long-neglected grave of Robert Heller, in Mt. Moriah Cemetery, Philadelphia, U. S. A. From a photograph in the Harry Houdini Collection.

From this array of facts, it will be seen that second sight is and always has been a matter of well-drilled phrases or signals, prearranged rotation of articles, well-built apparatus or well-trained confederates, but never a feat of actual thought-transferrence.

Some of Robert-Houdin's ardent supporters insist that in claiming the invention or discovery of second sight, the French conjurer was merely an unconscious plagiarist, having stumbled upon, quite by accident, a trick which he did not know that others had offered before him.

Such a statement is illogical and absurd. Books of magic to which Robert-Houdin had access and which he admits having read describe the trick in a more or less crude form. Pinetti, whose tricks were fully described to Robert-Houdin by his old friend Torrini, used the second-sight mystification with excellent effect. Robert-Houdin could not have been ignorant of its existence as a trick. In making the claim to its discovery in his "Memoirs" he simply trusted to the ignorance of the reading public in the history of magic.

According to programmes and newspaper clippings in my collection, Philip Breslaw was the first conjurer to feature second sight in his performance. Breslaw was a clever German who so established himself in the hearts of amusement-loving Englishmen that he remained in England for forty years, dying in Liverpool in 1803. In 1781, while playing at Greenwood's Rooms, Haymarket, London, he announced as Part One of his entertainment:

"Mr. Breslaw will exhibit his new magical deceptions, Letters, Medals, Dice, Pocket pieces, Rings, etc., etc., and particularly communicate the thoughts of any person to another without the assistance of speech or writing."

Pinetti comes next as an eminent presenter of second sight. Between these two well-known conjurers there may have been various unimportant, unchronicled performers who made use of Breslaw's trick, but they have no place in the history of magic.

The trick appeared on a Pinetti programme at the Royal Haymarket, London, England, December 1st, 1784, almost sixty-two years before Robert-Houdin presented it as his original invention.

Clipping from the London Post, December 1st, 1784, in which Pinetti featured second sight. From the Harry Houdini Collection.

The London *Morning Post and Daily Advertiser* of December 1st, 1784, contains the above advertisement, reproduced from my collection.

The talking code employed by Pinetti was not original with him, as it dates back to the automaton worked by a concealed confederate who controlled the piston for the mechanical figure or pulled the strings to manipulate the dancing coins or moving head. It was novel only in its application to the supposed thought-transferrence by a human being instead of an automaton.

This code is described by various reliable authors. On page 388, Volume III. of Hooper's "Recreations," edition 1782, it is stated that the confederate worked the apparatus from another room. "By certain words, previously agreed on, make it known to the confederate," is the advice given to would-be conjurers.

Beckman in his "History of Inventions" relates that he knew an exhibitor of a "talking figure" whose concealed confederate was cued to answer certain questions, the answers being given in the manner of putting the question, also by different signs. These instructions will be found on page 311 of Volume II., edition of 1817.

Reproduction of front and back of original handbill distributed on London streets in 1831, to advertise Master M'Kean. From the Harry Houdini Collection.

Decremps undertook to expose Pinetti's method of working the second-sight trick in his famous book, but in this attempt, he scored one of the few failures which marked the bitter fight he waged against Pinetti. In his book "La Magie Blanche Dévoilée" (White Magic Exposed), first edition, 1784, he offers on page 40 "Les Cartes dévinées, les yeux bandés" (The Divination of Cards with the Eyes Blindfolded). In this feat Decremps explains that Pinetti would allow cards to be drawn, then a lady (Signora Pinetti) would appear on the stage, would be blindfolded, and would name all the cards that were drawn. Decremps explains the prearranged pack of cards for this trick, also outlining the manner of giving the medium the cue for certain phrases. For instance, while explaining to the audience that he will not speak at all, in the very sentences addressed to the spectators he informs the medium which cards have been selected.

Pinetti's code must have been clever, as Decremps was unable to explain the entire second-sight act. He has omitted the principal part of the mystification, that is, naming the articles held up for the performer to see.

That the card trick was only one test of his second-sight performance, and that Pinetti's medium did not retire after naming the cards, are facts shown by the following clipping from one of his announcements:

"Signora Pinetti will have the special honor and satisfaction of exhibiting various experiments of new discovery, no less curious than seemingly incredible, particularly that of her being seated in one of the front boxes with an handkerchief over her eyes, and guess at everything imagined and proposed to her by any person in the company."

Third on the list of second-sight performers, according to the data in my collection, was Louis Gordon M'Kean, who created a sensation at the Egyptian Hall Bazaar, Piccadilly, London, in 1831, or fifteen years before Robert-Houdin, according to his claims, "discovered" second sight. Young M'Kean was featured as possessing double, not second, sight, and one of his bills is reproduced on page 212.

Another programme in my collection, dated the Théâtre Scarboro, Friday evening, August 4th, 1837, announces "For a limited engagement of three nights the Three Talented Highlanders and most extraordinary Second-Sighted Young Highlanders."

Decoration on the broadside used to advertise a young Dutchwoman who created a sensation in the early part of the eighteenth century. From the Harry Houdini Collection.

These lads, I believe, were three brothers, one the original M'Kean, or the latter working in conjunction with two other boys trained to the tricks in order to secure more impressive results. The trio appeared eight years before Robert-Houdin became a professional entertainer.

Holland also contributed a successful performer of second-sight tricks, the medium in this case being a Dutchwoman who created a profound sensation while touring Germany in the early part of the eighteenth century. The billing used at the yearly fairs is an enormous poster which would be unintelligible if reduced to a size suitable for reproduction.

It is now a part of my collection and reads as follows:

Reproduction of original billing matter used by the mysterious lady who offered second sight in the United States in 1841-42-43. From the Harry Houdini Collection.

Reproduction of the cut used on the mysterious lady's handbills, distributed in America in 1841. From the Harry Houdini Collection.

"The Holland Maid, Twenty Years of Age, from Amsterdam, whose powers, both in her residence there and in all other places to which she has gone, have excited great astonishment and much applause, and she will also in this place endeavor to obtain the same tribute of public applause. She will after the exhibition place herself before the eyes of all the spectators on the outside and gravely stand thereon and at all times give an answer of assurance to any one present to whom her judgment in all questions gives the most accurate response. She contrives also by her acuteness to discover and reply to the least thought, not until then explored. She guesses the age of everyone, whether they be married or not; how many children they have, of what sex, and whether they be living or dead at the present time, etc. She does the like for any one having a chance in the lottery, as to what is its number, and what will be its share of gains. She also guesses at every one of the most different sorts of coin, and even at the year with which they were stamped. She guesses at every number which any one shall secretly set down, even though it amounted to upward a million. She moreover tells exactly whether any one be in the Army, under how many Monarchs he has served, in how many battles he has been engaged, and whether he has ever been wounded and how many wounds he has received. By throwing the Dice, she will every time exactly tell the very number of spots which may have been determined on."

This wordy announcement is signed by W. Sahm, of Holland.

In my collection, there is also an interesting handbill advertising the tour of "The Mysterious Lady" who offered second-sight tricks in the eastern part of the United States in 1842-43. Her name was never stated on the programmes, but the latter, together with a clipping dated Boston, February 20th, 1843, will suffice to prove my claim that she was offering second-sight before Robert-Houdin did, and therefore could not be copying his trick. She also appeared in England fully a year before Robert-Houdin "discovered" second sight.

Henri Robin and his wife featured second sight in Italy just when Robert-Houdin first offered it in Paris. It is barely possible that they antedated Robert-Houdin in the production of this trick, for I have in my collection a brochure entitled "Album des Soirées de M. et Mme. Robin," which contains an engraving of the couple offering second-sight, a short poem in honor of Mme. Robin's remarkable gifts as a second-sight artist, and a poem generally eulogistic of M. Robin's talents dated distinctly February 7th, 1846. Robert-Houdin presented second-sight for the first time, according to his own "Memoirs," on February 12th, 1846.

Second sight as offered by M. and Mme. Robin, in which Robin employed the bell and the goblet. From the latter she sipped liquor, claiming it tasted like the wine secretly named by a spectator. Robin's stage was equipped with electrical appliances. From the Harry Houdini Collection.

To prove the utter folly of Robert-Houdin's claims to having trained his son's eye and memory by patient effort so as to have a mutual transferrence of thought, I will next show that animals had been trained for years to do tricks by secret signals before the alleged "discovery" of second sight.

Two rare old bills in my collection advertise the marvellous "mind-reading" performances of a goose and a blindfolded dog respectively. The first, dated 1789, announces that a Mr. Beckett, a trunk-maker of No. 31 Haymarket, is exhibiting "a Learned Goose, just lately arrived from abroad.

"It performs the following tricks: performing upon cards, money, and watches, telling the time of the month, year, and date, also the value of any piece either English or foreign, distinguishing all sorts of colors and (most prodigiously and certainly unbelieving to those who know the intellects of a goose) she tells the number of ladies and gentlemen in the company or any person's thoughts; any lady or gentleman drawing a card out of the pack, though ever so secret, the Goose, blindfolded at the same time, will find out the card they drew. Admittance two shillings each person."

The second bill features Don Carlo, the Double-Sighted dog, which gave an exhibition of his mysterious skill at the Pavillion by special command, before King William and the royal family on December 17th, 1831. This dog was blindfolded and could present almost in duplicate the second-sight tests offered by the Highland lad who five days later gave a similar exhibition before the royal family at the same place.

Rare poster announcing the performance of the learned goose, one of the first of the second-sight animal artists. Traced from the original poster in the British Museum by the author.

This proof regarding the use of animals as "mediums" is offered not to belittle the human mediums, but to prove that from start to finish, from the day that Breslaw offered the trick to the present moment, when a number of skilful so-called mind-readers still mystify the public, some sort of speaking or signal code has been used. Robert-Houdin used both the speaking and the signal code, but so did Breslaw, and all evidence points to the fact that Robert-Houdin merely improved upon the trick employed by Breslaw, Pinetti, and others among his predecessors in magic, by utilizing the newly found assistant to the magician, electricity. In his tiny theatre it would have been entirely feasible to have had electric wires run from all points of the auditorium to the stage, thus doing away with both the speaking and ordinary signal codes, even the pneumatic tube. For this improvement, and this alone, should Robert-Houdin be given credit. Nearly all magicians improve or redress tricks or apparatus handed down to them by their predecessors, but Robert-Houdin was not willing to admit that he owed anything to his predecessors.

CHAPTER VIII

THE SUSPENSION TRICK

IN chapters XVI. and XVII. of the American edition of his "Memoirs," Robert-Houdin states that he closed his theatre during the months of July, August, and September, 1847, and devoted his time to producing new tricks for the coming season. He chronicles as the result of these labors the following additions to his répertoire: "The Crystal Box," "The Fantastic Portfolio," "The Trapeze Tumbler," "The Garde Française," "The Origin of Flowers," "The Crystal Balls," "The Inexhaustible Bottle," "The Ethereal Suspension," etc.

Had these inventions really been original with the man who claimed them as the result of his own brain-work and handicraft, three years would not have sufficed to bring them to the perfection in which they were presented at that time. It is not always the actual work that makes a trick a success, nor the material from which it is constructed, but it takes time to plan a new trick; and then after you have worked out the idea, it takes more time to make it practical. The same piece of apparatus may have to be made dozens of times, in as many shapes, before it is presentable. Therefore, when Robert-Houdin claims to have invented and built with his own hands the tricks mentioned in the list given above, it is time to prove the improbability and falsity of his statements.

Inventions are a matter of evolution, but as the tricks which Robert-Houdin presented in his new répertoire were not new, he was able to offer them as the result of three months' work. To the expert mechanician or builder of conjuring apparatus his claim is farcical. The majority of the tricks mentioned require skilled hands and infinite patience, if they work in a way that will completely deceive the public. Particularly is this true of the first suspension apparatus such as Robert-Houdin must have used. This included a steel corset or frame for the subject, and both the corset and the supporting rods had to be strong, invisible to the audience, and still be perfect in mechanism.

Robert-Houdin, with characteristic ambiguity, does not refer to a complicated mechanism, but lays stress on his ability to keep his tricks up-to-date and in line with popular movements of the hour. In writing of the suspension trick, he gives the impression that but for the sensation created by the use of ether as an anæsthetic he would never have thought out the new trick. His own words as presented on page 312 of the American edition of his "Memoirs" are reproduced in this connection:

"It will be remembered that in 1847 the insensibility produced by inhaling ether began to be applied to surgical operations; all the world talked about the marvellous effect of this anæsthetic and its extraordinary results. In the eyes of the people it seemed much akin to magic. Seeing that the surgeons had invaded my domain, I asked myself if this did not allow me to make reprisals. I did so by inventing my ethereal suspension, which I believe was far more surprising than any result obtained by my surgical brethren. This trick was much applauded, and I am bound to say that my arrangements were excellently made. This was the first time that I tried to direct the surprise of my spectators by gradually heightening it up to the next moment, when, so to speak, it exploded."

While Robert-Houdin, in his "Memoirs," claims to have invented the trick for the season of 1847-48, in the illustrated appendix of the French edition he states that the first production of the trick, with improvements, was in October, 1849. The improvement consisted of working the trick with a stool upon a platform, when, previous to this date, he had used only the ordinary platform and rod.

During the course of researches covering many years, during which I visited national libraries in various countries, the first trace of the suspension trick was discovered in the writings of Ian Batuta, who flourished about the thirteenth century. He mentions two conjurers who performed before the court of the Mogul in Delhi. One of the men assumed the form of a cube and rose into the air, where he remained suspended. The other man then took off his shoe, struck it against a rock, and it also rose and hung in midair, close to the suspended conjurer or human cube. On being touched on the neck, the cube descended to the ground, and the conjurer resumed his natural form.

The historical verity of this tale cannot be determined, and it may be classed with the familiar story which crops up periodically, describing the ball of cord thrown into the air for a youth to climb into the clouds. Once out of sight, the youth is said to draw the cord up after him; then presently a leg falls from the unseen heights, then another, followed by an arm, a rib or two, and so on until the entire body is scattered upon the ground, the head coming last with the neck standing upward. At the command of the magician, the body seems to crawl together, so runs the tale, and eventually the youth stands up to be examined by the astonished populace.

Reproduction of an engraving in an old German Encyclopædia in the Harry Houdini Collection, which credits to the Chinese the trick of climbing into the air and having the body fall down piecemeal and being set together again.

These stories belong in the very first of the travellers' tales. In 1356 Sir John Mandeville, called by some authorities "the Father of English Prose," after travelling thirty-four years, published a book detailing some of his marvellous "witnessings." Though many of his stories are absolutely impossible, yet so popular did his works become that, barring the Scriptures, more copies and manuscripts of the books containing his various "Magician Stories" have been handed down to posterity and exist to-day than any works of his contemporaries. Still, Mandeville did not mention this suspension trick, which is sometimes attributed to the Chinese and sometimes to the Hindoos.

In Cologne, Germany, I purchased an encyclopædia, published in 1684, from which I reproduce a double-page engraving, which shows the Chinese magicians doing the tricks previously accredited, in the stories of travellers, to Hindoo conjurers.

In "Lives of the Conjurers," Thomas Frost describes the suspension trick as offered about 1828 or 1829 at Madras by an old Brahmin with no better apparatus than a piece of plank with four legs. This he had formed into a stool, and upon it, in a little brass socket, he placed a hollow bamboo stick in a perpendicular position. Projecting from the stick was a kind of crutch, covered with a piece of common hide. These properties he carried with him in a bag, which was shown to all those who desired to witness his exhibition. The servants of the household then held a blanket before him, and, when it was withdrawn, he was discovered poised in midair about four feet from the ground, in a sitting posture, with the outer edge of one hand merely touching the crutch, while the fingers deliberately counted beads, and the other hand and arm were held in an upright position. The blanket was again held up before him, and the spectators caught a gurgling sound, like that occasioned by wind escaping from a bladder or tube. When the screen or blanket was again withdrawn, the conjurer was standing on the ground.

The Brahmin suspension as shown in an illustration found in Robin's l'Almanach de Cagliostro.

The mystery was supposed to have been solved when Sheshal, commonly known as "the Brahmin of the Air," exhibited the trick in 1832 in Madras. It was observed that his stool was ornamented with two inlaid stars, and it was suggested that one of these might conceal a socket for a steel rod, passing through the bamboo, and that another rod, screwed to the perpendicular one and concealed by the piece of hide, might be connected with a mechanism of the same metal, passing up the sleeve and down the back, and forming a circular seat. This conjecture probably was not far from the truth, for while Frost is by no means the greatest of authorities on magic and magicians, in this particular instance I believe that his explanation of the trick is correct.

The next authentic early information I have gathered regarding suspension concerns that wonderful performer who called himself Ching Lau Lauro. Presumably he was a Chinaman, and from the programmes in my collection he evidently appeared first in England, in 1828, when he was engaged to perform between scenes of various plays, including "Tom and Jerry," at the Coburg. I reproduce on page 231 one of Ching Lau Lauro's programmes.

About 1833, or possibly a year earlier, he cut out some of his singing, and introduced the suspension with which he closed his performance. At this time, he gave the entire programme. According to his programmes, in some places he excluded the public from the gallery, so I judge that his suspension was accomplished by the use of the iron rod from the back, which would have been in plain sight from the gallery. The stage would not permit the suspension to be worked out of range of the gallery gods.

A Compars Herrmann programme of 1848 in which suspension is featured. From the Harry Houdini Collection.

When Robert-Houdin went to London in 1848 he found in the field of magic a clever rival, Compars Herrmann; a few months later came John Henry Anderson, the Wizard of the North. Both of these men presented the suspension trick in precisely the same manner claimed by Robert-Houdin as his original invention of 1847. Neither Anderson nor Herrmann claimed the honor of having invented the trick, and it is more than likely that the mechanician who made their apparatus for the suspension trick made the one used by Robert-Houdin also. Herrmann, like Robert-Houdin, called the trick ethereal suspension. Anderson gave it the title of "Chloriforeene Suspension," as the reproduction of an Anderson lithograph on page 234 will prove.

During precisely the same period of time a brilliantly successful German conjurer, Alexander, was presenting the same trick in America, where he remained as a professional entertainer for ten years. In my collection, together with corroborative handbills and programmes, there will be found this statement from Alexander:

"The suspension was at first produced by me in 1845 or 1846, after reading in an Oriental annual, edited by several officers of the Indian Army, the trick of a fakir who made a companion sit in the air by using a bamboo stick. My trick had no success, because the sitting was too near the ground. I then made him stand in the air, and the effect was marvellous."

My meeting with Alexander, of which this correspondence was the result, marked an era in my search for material for this volume. Having read in a small book on magic, dated 1896, that a man named Heimburger, who had travelled in America as "Alexander the Conjurer," was living in his native town of Münster, in Westphalia, I determined to secure an interview with him if possible.

"Suspension Chloriforeene," as presented by Anderson and his son, from a lithograph used by him on his return from the Continent, December, 1848. From the Harry Houdini Collection.

On March 17th, 1903, while playing in Cologne, I boarded an express train and arrived in Münster bright and early. From the city directory, I learned that one Heimburger resided in Krumpentippen, 16. Hailing a passing droschke I was soon carried to my destination, where a bright-faced German girl opened the door and ushered me, without formality, into the presence of the man to whom I desired to pay my respects.

An old man, bent with years, snow-white of beard and gray of head, came forward slowly to greet me. Finding that he was quite deaf, I raised my voice and fairly trumpeted my mission, adding that I felt especially honored to stand in the presence of the only magician who, up to that date, had ever appeared at the White House, Washington, by request of the President of the United States, my native land. Alexander had been asked to entertain President Polk and his guests on several occasions, and the fact that I knew this seemed to please the old conjurer and pave the way to a pleasant and profitable interview.

In a few moments we were sitting side by side, and he was adding to my store of information by relating the most fascinating experiences, stories of fellow-magicians long since dead, and tales which he could corroborate by his own collection of bills, programmes, etc., his diary, and his personal correspondence. He had known Robert-Houdin, Frikell, Bosco, Count Pererilli, John Henry Anderson, Blitz, the original Bamberg of Amsterdam, Compars Herrmann, and many lesser lights among the old-time magicians. Robert-Houdin had told him personally that being pressed for time he had entrusted the writing of his "Memoirs" to a Parisian journalist.

Mrs. Leona A. Anderson, daughter-in-law of John Henry Anderson, as she appeared with him in the suspension trick about 1868. From the Harry Houdini Collection.

As he warmed up to these reminiscences, he held me spellbound. Had he risen from the grave to tell of his contemporaries, he could not have riveted my attention more securely.

Here was a man of eighty-four, whose memory quickened at the coming of one interested in his beloved art, whose eye brightened with each fresh detail of a long and successful professional life, and who, in fifty years of retirement, had not only written a book, but had kept in touch with the world of magic, giving me information which the most exhaustive encyclopædia could not yield, answering questions on topics never yet discussed in dusty parchments and fading scripts. It was like having the history of magic unrolled before my eager eyes, in a living, palpitating, human scroll.

It had been my intention to remain but a few hours in Münster, but the old master held me as if hypnotized and the hours fairly drifted past. Letter after letter, clipping after clipping, token after token, he spread before my fascinated eyes; and I allowed him to speak without question or interruption of any sort. Early in our interview he had remarked that he was beginning to feel old and that only the impetus of my presence was responsible for his unusual strength of speech. For over seventy years he had been collecting books on conjuring and kindred topics, which he was able to read in English, French, Spanish, and German.

The dinner hour found us still engrossed in conversation, and Frau Heimburger extended a most hospitable and cordial invitation for me to join the family circle. But my hunger was purely mental, and the true savor of the meal was the reminiscent chat of Herr Heimburger, who, from his post at the head of his household, looked as hale and hearty as if he had found the Elixir of Life which so many of his charlatan predecessors claimed to have "discovered."

Alexander Heimburger, a veteran conjurer who presented the suspension trick in 1845-46 during his American tour.
From a photograph in the Harry Houdini Collection.

In 1904, I paid the old master a second visit. To his professions of pleasure at meeting me once more, he added the gift of several rare programmes now in my collection, and when our hands met in a farewell clasp he told me that he had set all things in order and was ready for the coming of the Grim Reaper. Soon after that visit, however, I received a card with the following melancholy message:

My Dear Friend—Have not been very well of late, and have been expecting my last days. All preparations have been made and Death the Visitor arrived, but instead of calling for me, he has taken away my beloved wife. I am not capable of writing more. God be with you. From your old friend,

Alexander Heimburger.

Alexander Heimburger or, as he was billed, Alexander the Conjurer, was born December 4th, 1818. From 1844 to 1854 he toured North and South America, returning to his native country with the intention of there following his calling as a professional entertainer. But his fame had preceded him, and, as his fortune was large, his souvenirs and tales of travel many and interesting, he was taken up by the world of fashion and lionized. This practically closed his career as a conjurer, for in those days magicians occupied no such reputable position in the professional world as they do to-day, and to have returned to his stage work would have closed the doors of aristocracy to him. He married one of Münster's prettiest girls, who bore him six children, two sons and four daughters. So he passed the remainder of his days, living modestly but comfortably on the money he had amassed in America, entertained by a large circle of appreciative friends, and well content to live thus, far from the madding crowd in which the professional entertainer must move.

While the recollections of his public career and his meetings with other magicians, as well as notable men in other walks of life, were fresh, he wrote his book, "Der Moderne Zauberer" (The Modern Magician), which he claims, with much justice, is rated as one of the gems of German literature, as well as the best book ever written by a conjurer. It is built from extracts from his diary and is on the style of Sig. Blitz's book, but is far more diversified and interesting.

Alexander Heimburger, known in conjuring as Alexander the Conjurer, from a quaint illustration in "The North American," published in Mexico.

His scrap-book also told a most romantic tale of vicissitudes. A half-page article in the New York *Tribune*, dated October, 1845, showed Alexander arrayed in a Chinese costume, and producing huge bowls of water, flowers, and various sorts of heavy articles. This proves conclusively that Ching Ling Foo was not the first conjurer to offer this Chinese trick in America, as it is generally supposed. Alexander added that all the old-timers would change their programmes by introducing the Chinese tricks, and, to verify his statement, readers need only to see the following files in Astor Library, New York City: New York *Herald*, New York *Tribune*, and New York *Evening Gazette* of November 6th, 1845.

Herr Alexander had arrived in New York almost penniless, after a disastrous tour of other American cities. He tried to hire Niblo's Garden, but was informed that the auditorium was never opened in winter. Through the intercession of Mrs. Niblo, however, he finally secured it at a rental of twenty dollars per night. He opened to a small house and for three nights did not even pay expenses, but the fourth night witnessed a change in his fortunes and for three months he played literally to standing room. Then because he had no new tricks to offer, and his pride forbade his presenting his old répertoire until receipts grew lighter, he closed his New York season.

While playing in Saratoga, Alexander was approached by the late P. T. Barnum, who was accompanied by Gen. Tom Thumb. Alexander declined Mr. Barnum's offer because he thought to join the Barnum staff of entertainers would injure his professional rating. Barnum's admission fee was 25 cents, while Alexander charged 50 cents and $1.

About this time, the fame of Alexander attracted the attention of no less a personage than S. F. B. Morse, of telegraphic fame; and Alexander had on his programme one trick which mystified Morse, who honestly believed that the conjurer had discovered some new law of nature that might be of service to scientists.

Alexander called this trick "The Spirit Bell," and, worked by one method or another, it has been used by many magicians. Some employ a thread and hook, causing the clapper to strike by pulling the thread which runs through an innocent-looking ribbon on which the bell hangs. Others use an electric magnet. Herr Alexander placed his bell on top of a fancy case which he could set anywhere, and the bell would ring at command. The secret was a small bird, trained to jump from one rung of a tiny ladder to another, at word of command or the waving of a stick or wand which the bird could see from its point of imprisonment. Every time that it jumped from one rung to another, it would pull down a step which was so arranged that by the smallest overweight it would release a catch, which in turn would throw the hammer against the glass. When the bird stepped off, the hammer would again come back to its original position and be ready for the second blow. This bird he bought from a street fortune-teller, who had trained it to go up different steps of a ladder and select envelopes containing variously printed fortunes.

Alexander enjoyed personal acquaintance with President Polk, Henry Clay, Daniel Webster, Calhoun, and their fellow-statesmen in the United States. Through his friendship with

President Polk he carried to the West Indies and Brazil letters so influential that the aristocracy in these countries opened its doors to him. He was welcomed at the palace of Dom Pedro, and has in his possession letters from both the King and his consort, dated 1850.

So much for the history of a man who was brave enough to admit that he developed the suspension trick from principles laid down by humble Indian fakirs.

The crudest method used for accomplishing the suspension trick consisted of a steel corset, an iron rod painted to resemble wood, and a platform. The steel rod was fitted into a special place in the corset, also in the platform. This method was improved, first to make it a self-raising suspension, then eventually with a steel rod from the back of the stage, eliminating the use of both rods under the arms.

Spectators and reviewers commented on the rigid, almost painful, carriage of Robert-Houdin's son during the performance, which they laid to the effect of ether. Unquestionably Robert-Houdin used this crude corset-and-rod method of working the trick.

The fumes of ether which reached the audience, he admits, were caused by pouring a little ether over hot irons in the wings.

But whatever the method employed by Robert-Houdin to secure the effects of "suspension éthéréenne," he was merely introducing a century-old trick, which other contemporary magicians were also exhibiting. The name of the real maker of the apparatus may never be known, but some clever mechanician supplied Robert-Houdin, Compars Herrmann, and John Henry Anderson with precisely the same method of working the trick, at precisely the same time. Robert-Houdin alone was audacious enough to claim the invention as his own.

CHAPTER IX

THE DISAPPEARING HANDKERCHIEF

SUPREME egotism and utter disregard for the truth may be traced in all of Robert-Houdin's writings, but they reached a veritable climax when he indited chapter XVI. of his "Memoirs." During the course of this chapter he described the so-called invention and first production of the disappearing-handkerchief trick.

According to the American edition of his "Memoirs," page 303, he received a command to appear before Louis Philippe and his family at St. Cloud in November, 1846. During the six days intervening between the official invitation and his appearance before the royal family, he arranged a trick from which, he states, he had every reason to expect excellent results. On page 305 he goes even further in his claims and announces:

"All my tricks were favorably received, and the one I had invented for the occasion gained me unbounded applause."

He then gives the following description of the trick and its performance:

"I borrowed from my noble spectators several handkerchiefs, which I made into a parcel, and laid on the table. Then, at my request, different persons wrote on the cards the names of places whither they desired their handkerchiefs to be invisibly transported.

"When this had been done, I begged the King to take three of the cards at hazard, and choose from them the place he might consider most suitable.

"'Let us see,' Louis Philippe said, 'what this one says: "I desire the handkerchiefs to be found beneath one of the candelabra on the mantelpiece." That is too easy for a sorcerer; so we will pass to the next card: "The handkerchiefs are to be transported to the dome of the Invalides." That would suit me, but it is much too far, not for the handkerchiefs, but for us. Ah, ah!' the King added, looking at the last card, 'I am afraid, M. Robert-Houdin, I am about to embarrass you. Do you know what this card proposes?'

"'Will your Majesty deign to inform me?'

"'It is desired that you should send the handkerchiefs into the chest of the last orange-tree on the right of the avenue.'

"'Only that, Sire? Deign to order, and I shall obey.'

"'Very good, then; I should like to see such a magic act: I, therefore, choose the orange-tree chest.'

"The King gave some orders in a low voice, and I directly saw several persons run to the orange-tree, in order to watch it and prevent any fraud.

"I was delighted at this precaution, which must add to the effect of my experiment, for the trick was already arranged, and the precaution hence too late.

"I had now to send the handkerchiefs on their travels, so I placed them beneath a bell of opaque glass, and, taking my wand, I ordered my invisible travellers to proceed to the spot the King had chosen.

"I raised the bell; the little parcel was no longer there, and a white turtle-dove had taken its place.

"The King then walked quickly to the door, whence he looked in the direction of the orange-tree, to assure himself that the guards were at their post; when this was done, he began to smile and shrug his shoulders.

"'Ah! M. Robert-Houdin,' he said, somewhat ironically, 'I much fear for the virtue of your magic staff.' Then he added, as he returned to the end of the room, where several servants were standing, 'Tell William to open immediately the last chest at the end of the avenue, and bring me carefully what he finds there—if he does find anything.'

"William soon proceeded to the orange-tree, and, though much astonished at the orders given him, he began to carry them out.

"He carefully removed one of the sides of the chest, thrust his hand in, and almost touched the roots of the tree before he found anything. All at once he uttered a cry of surprise as he drew out a small iron coffer eaten by the rust.

"This curious find, after having been cleaned from the mould, was brought in and placed on a small ottoman by the King's side.

"'Well, M. Robert-Houdin,' Louis Philippe said to me, with a movement of impatient curiosity, 'here is a box; am I to conclude it contains the handkerchiefs?'

"'Yes, Sire,' I replied with assurance, 'and they have been there, too, for a long period.'

"'How can that be? The handkerchiefs were lent you scarce a quarter of an hour ago.'

"'I cannot deny it, Sire; but what would my magic powers avail me if I could not perform incomprehensible tricks? Your Majesty will doubtless be still more surprised when I prove to your satisfaction that this coffer as well as its contents was deposited in the chest of the orange-tree sixty years ago.'

"'I should like to believe your statement,' the King replied with a smile; 'but that is impossible, and I must, therefore, ask for proofs of your assertion.'

"'If your Majesty will be kind enough to open this casket they will be supplied.'

"'Certainly; but I shall require a key for that.'

"'It only depends on yourself, Sire, to have one. Deign to remove it from the neck of this turtle dove, which has just brought it to you.'

"Louis Philippe unfastened a ribbon that held a small rusty key with which he hastened to unlock the coffer. The first thing that caught the King's eye was a parchment, on which he read the following statements:

"'This day, the sixth of June, 1786, this iron box, containing six handkerchiefs, was placed among the roots of an orange tree by me, Balsamo, Count of Cagliostro, to serve in performing an act of magic which will be executed on the same day sixty years hence before Louis Philippe of Orléans and his family.'

"'There is, decidedly, witchcraft about this,' the King said, more and more amazed. 'Nothing is wanting, for the seal and signature of the celebrated sorcerer are placed at the foot of this statement, which, Heaven pardon me, smells strongly of sulphur.'

"At this jest the audience began to laugh.

"'But,' the King added, taking out of the box a carefully sealed packet, 'can the handkerchiefs, by possibility, be in this?'

"'Indeed, Sire, they are; but, before opening the parcel, I would request your Majesty to notice that it, also, bears the impression of Cagliostro's seal.'

"This seal, once rendered so famous by being placed on the celebrated alchemist's bottles of elixir and liquid gold, I had obtained from Torrini, who had been an old friend of Cagliostro's.

"'It is certainly the same,' my royal spectator answered, after comparing the two seals. Still, in his impatience to learn the contents of the parcel, the King quickly tore open the envelope, and soon displayed before the astonished spectators the six handkerchiefs, which, a few moments before, were still on my table."

While the use of the Cagliostro seal really formed no part of the trick, its possession by Robert-Houdin goes to show how indefatigably he collected conjuring curios and how quick he was to utilize any part of his collection, and score thereby a brilliant showing.

Cagliostro seals were by no means rare. This prince of charlatans had seals, like adventures, in great variety; and in this connection, it is not out of place to tell something of Cagliostro and thus explain why the parchment bearing his seal created such a sensation at St. Cloud.

Cagliostro has no match in the annals of magic. Not a conjurer in the sense of being a public entertainer, he yet mystified and bewitched his thousands. Something of a physician, more of an alchemist, and altogether a charlatan, he left behind him a trail of brilliant chicanery, daring adventure, and ignominious failure and undoing unequalled in the history of Europe.

Reproduction of a rare portrait of Seraphinia Feliciani, Comtesse de Cagliostro, wrongfully called Lorenzo in the Encyclopædia Britannica. From the Harry Houdini Collection.

Cagliostro was born Joseph Balsamo, in Palermo, Italy, June 8th, 1743. His parents were in humble circumstances and he started his career as a novice in the Convent of Benfratelli, from which he was expelled for incorrigibility. Then he plunged into a life of dissipation and cleverly planned, ofttimes brilliantly executed crimes. He fled Palermo after forging theatre tickets and a will, and duping a goldsmith out of sixty pieces of gold. At Messina he fell in with an alchemist named Althotas, a man of some learning who spoke a variety of languages. These two adventurers travelled in Egypt, and when Althotas died Cagliostro went to Naples and Rome, where he married a beautiful girdle-maker named Seraphinia Feliciani. This woman shared both his triumphs and his disgrace. In 1776 they arrived in London, where he announced himself as the Count di Cagliostro. The title was assumed, the name was borrowed from his mother's side of the house. Here for the first time, Cagliostro announced himself also a worker of miracles or wonders.

He exhibited two mysterious substances, "Materia Prima," with which he transmuted all baser metals into gold, and "Egyptian Wine," with which he claimed to prolong life. His wife, who was just past twenty, he declared was more than sixty, her youthful appearance being due to the use of his elixir. He founded a spurious Egyptian rite in connection with the Masonic order which has been recognized as a blot upon Masonic history, and he claimed thousands of Masonic dupes. All over the Continent he and his beautiful wife travelled, now healing the poor for nothing, now duping the rich, but always living in a most picturesque, voluptuous fashion. He dipped into spiritualism and mesmerism, but wherever he went his converts followed after.

In 1789, while in Rome, he was seized by that invincible power, the Holy Inquisition, and was condemned to death. Later Pope Pius VI. changed the sentence to life imprisonment. Confinement made him more daring than ever. He asked for a confessor, and when a Capuchin monk was permitted to enter his cell in this capacity Cagliostro endeavored to choke him and escape in his robes. The monk fought for his life so effectually that it was he, and not Cagliostro, who escaped. Cagliostro was literally buried alive in a subterranean dungeon, as punishment for his final offence, and his wife immured herself in a Roman convent, where she died in 1794.

Testot programme, featuring "Cabalistic Art" in 1826. From the Harry Houdini Collection.

In Paris, perhaps, Cagliostro enjoyed his greatest triumphs of charlatanism, and it is not remarkable that the appearance of his seal in the midst of Robert-Houdin's trick should seem almost uncanny to the royal family.

But to return to the disappearing-handkerchief trick. Robert-Houdin did not invent this trick. It was presented by a number of conjurers before Robert-Houdin was known in the world of magic. Robert-Houdin simply employed the trick familiar to both his predecessors and contemporaries and redressed it to tickle the fancy of his royal patron.

In England, this trick was known among old conjurers as "The Ne Plus Ultra of the Cabalistic Art." In 1826 one M. Félix Testot, who claimed to be a compatriot of Robert-Houdin, presented the trick in the British provinces, and one of his bills I am reproducing because it shows that the trick he offered the provincial Britons and the trick which Robert-Houdin offered the royal family at St. Cloud were identical. It also proves that London had seen the trick; and what London had seen, Paris, including Robert-Houdin, had heard of.

A programme used by "The Celebrated Mr. Marriot, Professor of Recreative Philosophy," in 1831, contains word for word the announcement of the trick used on Testot's bill, which goes to show that a popular test was to have articles passed from the Adelphia Theatre to the gun which was being watched by a sentinel.

February 22d, 1833, found a Mr. Jefferini at the Royal Clarence Theatre, Liverpool Street, King's Cross, Liverpool. He agreed to make "an article fly at the rate of five hundred miles an hour, from King's Cross to the Centre of Greece."

The original Buck featured on his programme a similar trick which he called "The Loaf Trick." On a bill dated October 26th, 1840, it is announced as follows: "Watch in a loaf. The magician will command any gentleman's watch to disappear. It will be found in a loaf at any baker's shop in Town." The senior Ingleby changed the trick somewhat, sending out to any market for a shoulder of mutton, which, on being cut, would yield up a card previously drawn by some spectator. He thus describes his trick in his book "Whole Art of Legerdemain," published in London in 1815:

"TRICK FOUR.

"To cut out of a Shoulder of Mutton a Card which one of the Company had previously drawn out of the Pack.

Only known portrait of the clever English conjurer, Buck. From an engraving in the Harry Houdini Collection.

"Having desired a person to draw a Card out of several which you hold to him, and to remember it, which he promises to do, you tell him it shall be in a shoulder of mutton which you will send for.

"Accordingly, you desire a servant to go to the butcher's and bring one. When brought, it is examined, and then ordered to be put down to roast. After performing some tricks, you recollect the shoulder of mutton, which is immediately brought half-roasted, and after cutting it for some time you at length find the card, and produce it.

"Explanation:

"Having forced a card on one of the company, your confederate has an opportunity, when the mutton is sent to be roasted, of conveying a thin duplicate of that card folded into a narrow compass into the fleshy part near the shank, which can be easily done by means of a sharp penknife.

"This trick, though remarkably simple, has created universal astonishment at the Minor Theatre, where it was frequently exhibited by Mr. Ingleby."

The method of performing the trick was so familiar to conjurers of Robert-Houdin's time and earlier that Henry Evans Evanion was able to describe it to me from actual witnessings. Acting on his explanation, on my return to America I offered the trick, without any great amount of preparation and without a hitch, at a matinée entertainment given by a secret organization. I will describe precisely how this was done, and allow my readers to judge of the similarity of the trick offered years ago by humble travelling magicians whose names have been written most faintly in the annals of conjuring, and the much-vaunted trick "invented" by Robert-Houdin for the entertainment of his sovereign.

The hall in which the matinée was given was located in Harlem, Borough of Manhattan, New York City, and I had decided that the handkerchiefs which were to make the flying journey should be "desired" by some one present to appear under the top step of the winding staircase in the Statue of Liberty, which is located in New York Harbor. This meant a half-hour ride from the hall to the boat in a Subway train; then a run across New York Harbor to the Statue. These boats left the dock on the hour and the half-hour, so I timed my performance to fill just half an hour, starting with some sleight-of-hand, the egg-bag trick, and swallowing a package of needles and bringing them up threaded, which latter trick was introduced into magical performances in Europe by K. K. Kraus in 1816.

Reproduction of a rare Buck handbill, dated 1844. From the Harry Houdini Collection.

Just before 3:30 o'clock I borrowed three handkerchiefs and tied them together for easier handling. I had three handkerchiefs, similarly tied together, under my vest, and just at 3:30, I switched the two sets of handkerchiefs, so that the handkerchiefs furnished by the spectators were under my vest and the bogus handkerchiefs in my hand. First I dropped the bogus handkerchiefs on the table-trap, picking up the opaque glass cover with which they were to be hidden, and, by a carefully rehearsed bit of carelessness, dropped and broke it. Then, leaving the bogus handkerchiefs on the table trap, I stepped toward the wings, apparently to secure another glass bell or cover. To all intents and purposes, I did not pass from the view of the audience, for fully half of my body was on the stage, but as my assistant handed me a new glass cover, he deftly extracted the real handkerchiefs from under my vest. Then, while I returned to the stage with my patter and description of the flight the handkerchiefs were about to make, my assistant, with the handkerchiefs in his pocket, walked unnoticed from the door, and, once out of sight, ran madly to the Subway station. There he boarded an express and reached the boat landing just in time to catch the 4 o'clock boat. At the Statue, my brother and a tinsmith were waiting for him. The handkerchiefs were placed in the tin box, securely soldered, and then this box was placed inside a second iron box, which was locked. The "plant" was then taken upstairs and hidden under the top step.

In the mean time, with my thoughts following my assistant every step of his trip, I was playing out my end of the game. The audience was supplied with blank cards on which they might write the name of the place where the handkerchiefs should reappear. This, of course, took some time, and when the cards, each folded to hide the writing thereon, were collected in a hat, I shook them up thoroughly, and then turned them out upon a plate, deftly adding, on the top, three cards which I had concealed in my hand. This was sleight-of-hand purely, and I next picked out those three prepared cards on each of which was written "Can you send the handkerchiefs under the top step of the Statue of Liberty?" Explaining that I had in my hand three cards chosen at haphazard, I wished the final choice to be made by a disinterested party. A baby was finally chosen to select the card. Naturally, I refused even to take the slip of paper from the baby's hand, and one of the lodge members read the question.

Murmurs of surprise and incredulity echoed from all over the hall. The test was too difficult! I then announced that if the audience would select its own committee, making sure to pick out men who could not be bribed, I would accompany them, and we would surely return with the handkerchiefs, sealed in double boxes, as found under the famous stairway. As an elaborate course luncheon was to be served, the committee had time to act, and away we went, leaving the lodge to its feast. So much time had been lost in selecting the committee that we reached the wharf just in time to catch the 5 o'clock boat. On landing I received a prearranged signal from my assistants that all was well, and as I watched my committee dash up the stairs I knew that their quest would be rewarded.

When the committee and the writer returned to the lodge-room, a mechanic was required to pry open the box. There lay the identical handkerchiefs furnished by my spectators, who could hardly believe their eyes.

On other occasions, I have asked my audience to select a spokesman, who in a loud voice would announce the point at which the handkerchiefs would be found, and then my man, waiting just outside the door, would mount his bicycle and pedal like mad for the hiding-place, naturally outstripping any committee appointed. But the first method, that of selecting the place beforehand and having all arrangements made, even to the three prepared cards, is safest and is probably the one used by Robert-Houdin to deceive the French monarch. I doubt if he even had three different cards prepared, as he claims. I believe he exaggerated his feat, for that would have been taking long chances.

For this trick, I claim not an iota of originality. I simply fitted it to the time, the place, and the audience, and that I believe is all Robert-Houdin did when he "invented" the disappearing handkerchief trick for the amusement of his sovereign.

CHAPTER X

ROBERT-HOUDIN'S IGNORANCE OF MAGIC AS BETRAYED BY HIS OWN PEN

STATEMENTS in Robert-Houdin's various works on the conjurer's art corroborate my claim that he was not a master-magician, but a clever purloiner and adapter of the tricks invented and used by his predecessors and contemporaries. Whenever, in these books, he attempts to explain or expose a trick which was not part of his répertoire, he betrays an ignorance which would be impossible in a conjurer versed in the finer and more subtle branches of his art. Neither do these explanations show that he was clever enough as a mechanic to have invented the apparatus which he claimed as his handiwork. He states that practice and still more practice are essential, yet no intelligent performer, amateur or professional, can study my collection of Robert-Houdin programmes, handbills, and press notices without realizing that his répertoire contained little or no trace of what should be the foundation of successful conjuring, sleight-of-hand. Changing his fingers over the various air-holes of the inexhaustible bottle was as near as he ever came to sleight-of-hand, even when he was in the height of his success.

According to the press notices he had a pleasing stage presence, and also dressed and set forth his tricks richly, but it must be borne in mind that then, as often to-day, the man sent by an editor to criticise a conjurer's performance knew little or nothing about the art and could not institute comparisons between different magicians. To-day Robert-Houdin would shine as an exhibitor of illusions or mechanical toys. A pistol shot, a puff of smoke—and his confederate or assistant has done the real work behind the scenes.

His lack of finesse as a sleight-of-hand performer is nowhere more clearly shown than in his own writings. On page 37 of his French exposé of the secrets of magic, entitled "Comment on Devient Sorcier" (page 51 of the English translation by Professor Hoffmann, "The Secrets of Conjuring and Magic"), he thus naïvely describes his masterpiece of coin-palming:

"I myself practised palming long and perseveringly, and acquired thereat a very considerable degree of skill. I used to be able to palm two five-franc pieces at once, the hand, nevertheless, remaining as freely open as though it held nothing whatever."

An amateur of his own day would have blushed to admit that he could palm but two coins. Men like T. Nelson Downs, "The Koin King," think nothing of palming twenty five-franc or silver dollars, or forty half-dollars, and even this record has been broken.

Even two writers who contributed to the translation and editing of his works, R. Shelton Mackenzie and Professor Hoffmann (Angelo J. Lewis), and who have drawn rich royalties for the same, apologize for his flagrant mis-statements, which, they realize, any man or woman with but a slight knowledge of conjuring must recognize.

His first contribution to the history of magic was his "Memoirs"; and while he does not feature exposures of tricks in this work, he offers, in passing, explanations of tricks and automata presented by other magicians. For the most part these explanations are obviously incorrect, and so prove that he was ignorant of certain fundamental principles of the art in which he claimed to have shone.

In the introduction of the American edition, published in 1850, Mr. Mackenzie, the editor, thus apologizes for one of Robert-Houdin's most flagrant mistakes in tracing the history of magic:

"One error which M. Houdin makes must not be passed over. His account of M. de Kempelen's celebrated automaton chess-player (afterward Maëlzel's) is entirely wrong. This remarkable piece of mechanism was constructed in 1769, and not in 1796; it was the Empress Maria-Theresa of Austria who played with it, and not Catherine II. of Russia; it was in 1783 that it first visited Paris, where it played at the Café de la Regence; it was not taken to London until 1784, and again in 1819; it was brought to America in 1825, by M. Maëlzel, and visited our principal cities, its chief resting-place being Philadelphia; M. Maëlzel's death was in 1838, on the voyage from Cuba to the United States, and not, as M. Houdin says, on his return to France; and the automaton, so far from being taken back to France, was sold by auction here, finally purchased by the late Dr. J. K. Mitchell, of Philadelphia, reconstructed by him, and finally deposited in the Chinese Museum (formerly Peale's), where it was consumed in the great fire which destroyed the National Theatre (now the site of the Continental Hotel, corner of Ninth and Chestnut Streets), and, extending to the Chinese Museum, burnt it down on July 5th, 1854. An interesting account of the Automaton Chess-Player, written by Prof. George Allen, of this city, will be found in 'The Book of the First American Chess Congress,' recently published in New York."

Signor Blitz, in his book "Fifty Years in the Magic Circle," corroborates the Mackenzie correction, by telling how he saw Maëlzel in Havana, Cuba, where the famous German met his professional Waterloo, first in small audiences, then in the death of his faithful confederate, Schlomberg. Finally, broken in health and spirit, Maëlzel sailed from Havana for Philadelphia, but death overtook him at sea. His body was consigned to the ocean's depths, and his few effects were sold to liquidate the cost of passage and other debts.

That Robert-Houdin should make an error concerning a world-famous automaton the history of which could be traced through contemporary periodicals and libraries, is almost inconceivable and proves the carelessness with which he gathered and presented facts.

His inability to grasp the principles on which other performers built their tricks is shown most clearly when he attempts to describe and explain the performances of the Arabian mountebanks whom he saw during his stay in Algiers. These tricks have been handed down from one generation to another, and now that Arabian conjurers and acrobats are imported for hippodrome and vaudeville performances in all civilized countries, the tricks described by Robert-Houdin are familiar to the general public. They are also copied by performers of other nationalities, and can be seen in circus side-shows and at fairs, as well as in the better grade of houses. Having worked on the same bill with genuine Arabian performers, I know just how the tricks are accomplished.

Robert-Houdin undertakes to explain these tricks in chapter XXII. of the American edition of his "Memoirs." So long as he quotes reliable authorities like the *Journal des Sciences,* the explanations are correct. Directly he attempts an independent exposure, he strikes far from the correct explanation.

On page 424 he states:

"In the following experiment, two Arabs held a sabre, one by the hilt, the other by the point; a third then came forward, and after raising his clothes so as to leave the abdomen quite bare, laid himself flat on the edge of the blade, while a fourth mounted on his back, and seemed to press the whole weight of his body on him.

"This trick may be easily explained.

"Nothing proves to the audience that the sabre is really sharpened, or that the edge is more cutting than the back, although the Arab who holds it by the point is careful to wrap it up in a handkerchief—in this, imitating the jugglers who pretend they have cut their fingers with one of the daggers they use in their tricks.

"Besides, in performing this trick, the invulnerable turned his back on the audience. He knew the advantage to be derived from this circumstance; hence, at the moment when about to lay himself on the sabre, he very adroitly pulled back over his stomach that portion of his clothing he had raised. Lastly, when the fourth actor mounted on his back, he rested his hands on the shoulders of the Arabs who held the sabre. The latter apparently maintained his balance, but, in reality, they supported the whole weight of his body. Hence, the only requirement for this trick is to have the stomach more or less pressed in, and I will explain presently that this can be effected without any danger or injury."

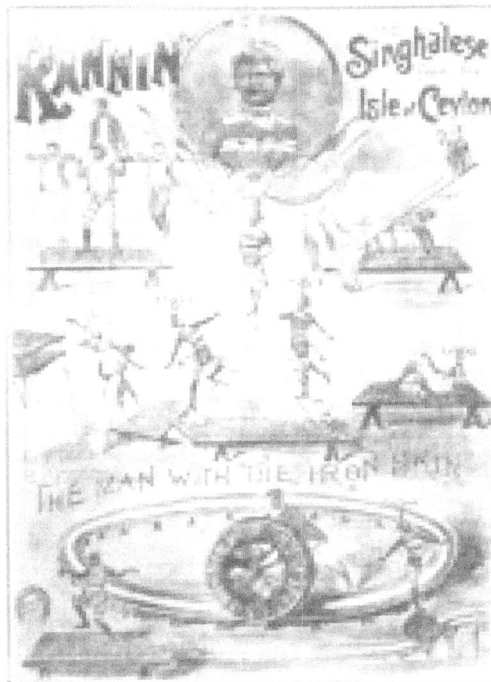

In this explanation, Robert-Houdin is entirely wrong. The real secret of lying on top of a sharp-edged razor, sword, or sabre rests on the fact that the performer does actually lie upon it in a perfectly motionless position. Were he to move but the width of a hair, backward or forward or sidewise, the weapon would slice his body, resulting in instant death or horrible mutilation. I have watched cheap performers of this class of work, in dime museums or fairs, walk up a ladder of sharp swords which I had previously held in my hand. They would place the foot down with infinite precision and then press it into place. This position will not result in cutting, but let the performer slip or slide and the flesh would be cut instantly. I have also seen an acrobat, working in a circus, select two razors in first-class condition, place them on a socket with the edges of the razors uppermost, and with his bare hands he would do what is known as a hand-stand on the keen edges of the blades. This trick of absolute balance is acquired by persistent practice from youth up.

Again Robert-Houdin errs wofully in comparing the sabre-swallower to the swallower of broken bottle-heels and stones. Sabre-swallowing is one trick, swallowing pebbles and broken glass belongs in quite a different class. And when I say this I do not mean powdered glass, but pieces of glass first broken, then chewed, and finally swallowed.

On page 426 Robert-Houdin puts the two tricks in the same class, as follows:

"When the trick of swallowing bottle-heels and pebbles was to be done, the Aïssaoua really put them in his mouth, but I believe, I may say certainly, that he removed them at the moment when he placed his head in the folds of the Mokadem's burnous. However, had he swallowed them, there would have been nothing wonderful about this, when we compare it with what was done some thirty years back in France by a mountebank called 'the Sabre-Swallower.'

"This man, who performed in the streets, threw back his head so as to form a straight line with his throat, and really thrust down his gullet a sabre, of which only the hilt remained outside his mouth.

"He also swallowed an egg without cracking it, or even nails and pebbles, which he caused to resound, by striking his stomach with his fist.

"These tricks were the result of a peculiar formation in the mountebank's throat, but, if he had lived among the Aïssaoua, he would have assuredly been the leading man of the company."

The sabre-swallower never releases his hold on the weapon. The pebble and bottle-heel swallower does—but brings them up again, by a system of retching which results from long practice. The Japanese have an egg-swallowing trick in which they swallow either small-sized ivory balls or eggs, and reproduce them by a retching so unnoticeable that they could easily show the mouth empty.

This trick dates back to the offerings of that celebrated water-spouter, Blaise Manfrede, or de Manfre, who travelled all over Europe. This man could swallow huge quantities of water and then eject it in streams or in small quantities or fill all sorts of glasses. In fact this one trick made him famous. *The European Magazine*, London, March, 1765, pages 194-5, gives a most diverting description of his trick, taken from an old letter, and here quoted:

"I have seen, at the September fair in Francfort, a man who professed drinking fifty quarts of water in a day, and indeed proved that he was capable of executing what he pretended to. I saw him perform frequently, and remember it as well as if it was but yesterday. He said he was an Italian; he was short and squat, his chest, face, forehead, eyes, and mouth very large. He pretended to be fifty years old, though he did not seem forty.

Blasius de Manfre or Blaise Manfrede, from a rare old woodcut in the Harry Houdini Collection.

"He was called the famous Blaise Manfrede, a native of Malta. At Francfort he frequently performed three times a day: for, besides his performances twice a day on the public stage (which nobody approached without paying), he attended private houses when called upon by great people.

"He called for a large bucket of fair warm water, and twenty little glass bottles, flat like cupping glasses, so that they could stand topside turvy. Some of these he filled with water, plunging them into the bucket with a good deal of ceremony, and usually swallowed two or three to wash his mouth and gargle his throat. He threw up the water again immediately, to shew the spectators that he had no drugs between his teeth, whence he could be suspected to derive any advantage.

"After this plausible prelude, he made an Italian harangue, which I cannot acquaint you with the merits of, because I am a stranger to the language.... After his harangue, he usually took off two dozen of his little bottles, which he filled from the bucket, and a moment afterwards returned the liquor through his mouth. But what is most extraordinary is that this water, which he threw out with violence, appeared red like wine. And when he had discharged it into two different bottles, it was red in one and russet like beer in the other; as soon as he shifted the bottles to the contrary sides, they changed their complexion respectively to that of wine or beer, and so successively so long as he continued vomiting; in the mean time, I observed that the water grew less discolored in proportion as he continued to discharge. This was the first act. Then he ranged his two dozen of bottles opposite to him on a table, and exposed to everybody's view. Then he took an equal number of bottles, plunged them anew into the bucket, swallowed them too, and returned them in water very transparent, rose-water, orange-flower-water, and brandy.

"I have smelt the several odours of his liquors; nay, I have seen him set fire to a handkerchief dipt in that which smelt like brandy, and it burnt blue like spirituous liquors.... Nay, he frequently promised at Venice to give the water back again in milk and oil. But I think he did not keep his word. In short, he concluded this scene with swallowing successfully thirty or forty glasses of water, always from the same bucket, and after having given notice to the company by his man (who served as an interpreter) that he was going to disembogue, he threw his head back, and spouting out the fair water, he made it spring up with an impetuosity like that of the strongest *jet d'eau*. This last feat delighted the people infinitely more than all the rest, and during the month he was at Francfort numbers from all parts came to see this slovenly exercise. Though he repeated it more than once a day he had more than four hundred spectators at a time. Some threw their handkerchiefs, and some their gloves upon the stage, that he might wet them with the water he had cast up, and he returned them differently perfumed, sometimes with rose-water, sometimes with orange-flower-water, and sometimes with brandy."

Another famous juggler and water-spouter was Floram Marchand, whose picture is herewith reproduced. Judging from his dress, he antedated Manfrede.

Bell's *Messenger* of July 16th, 1816, tells of a sword-swallower whose work is extremely pertinent to this discussion, and the clipping is quoted verbatim:

FLORAM MARCHAND.

Floram Marchand. From an old, undated English publication in the Harry Houdini Collection.

"The French papers give a curious account of one James de Falaise, a Norman, about fifty years of age, living in the Rue St. Honoré. It is said that this extraordinary man will swallow whole walnuts, shell and all, a tobacco pipe, three cards rolled together, a rose with all its leaves, long stalk, and thorns, a living bird, and a living mouse, and, lastly, a live eel. Like to the Indian jugglers, he swallows the blade of a sabre about thirteen inches long of polished steel. This operation he performs very slowly, and with some precaution; though he evinces no symptom of pain. After every solid body that he swallows, he always takes a small dose of wine expressly prepared for him. He does not seem to make any effort to kill the living animals that he takes in his mouth, but boasts that he feels them moving in his stomach."

Position taken by the subject in the Indian basket trick before he is covered by the sheet.

In my collection is the handbill of a stone-swallower who exhibited at No. 10 Cockspur Street, London, charging an admission fee of half-a-crown.

Indian fakir seated in the basket after the subject has been "vanished."

These performers actually swallowed the water, stones, pebbles, etc., and retched them up again so cleverly and at such carefully selected instants that the audience did not know that the disgorging had been accomplished.

Swallowing glass was a different matter, and the modern human ostriches have all wound up at city hospitals where surgeons have removed broken glass, knife blades, and other foreign matter by means of an operation.

I quote the above instances simply to prove that the stones were actually swallowed and then disgorged, and not hidden, as Robert-Houdin claims, in the folds of the Mokadem's burnous.

In this one chapter alone Robert-Houdin quotes six authorities in explaining the tricks he witnessed, which fact only strengthens my belief that he borrowed his tricks, as well as his explanations, from able and graphic writers on the art of magic.

The next work descriptive of the conjurer's art offered by Robert-Houdin was "Les Secrets de la Prestidigitation et de la Magie." Under the title of "The Secrets of Conjuring and Magic; or, How to Become a Wizard," it was translated and edited by Professor Hoffmann and published in 1878 by George Routledge & Co., London and New York.

Absolutely no originality is displayed in this book, and the majority of the tricks explained can be found in French books of a similar character which appeared before Robert-Houdin turned author. The proof of this statement can be found by reading any of the following works upon which Robert-Houdin patently drew for his material:

"Nouvelle Magie Blanche Dévoilée et Cours Complet de Prestidigitation," in two volumes, by J. N. Ponsin, published in Paris in 1853; "Grande Initiation au vraie Pratique des Célèbres Physiciens-Prestidigitateurs," Paris, 1855; "Nouveau Manuel Complet Sorciers, les scènes de Ventriloquie exécutées et communiquées par M. Conte, Physicien du Roi," Paris, 1837; "Anciens et Nouvaux Tours d'Escamotage," of which there are innumerable editions; "Le Manuel des Sorciers. Recréations Physiques, Mathématiques, Tours de Cartes et de Gibecière; suivre, des Jeux de Société," Paris, 1802.

Position of the "vanished" Hindoo while concealed in the basket. From the Harry Houdini Collection.

His third work, "Magie et Physique Amusante," translated by Professor Hoffmann under the title of "The Secrets of Stage Conjuring," and published in English in 1881, is marred by an almost continuous strain of mis-statements, incorrect explanations, and downright falsification.

On page 17 of the American edition Robert-Houdin starts his dramatic tale of inventing a detector lock by which he protected a rich neighbor, M. de l'Escalopier, from robbery, and incidentally in return secured funds with which to open his theatre in the Palais Royal. In his "Mémoirs" Robert-Houdin states that the opening of the theatre was made possible by the invention of the writing and drawing automaton whose history has been traced in chapter III. The reader can choose between the two stories. One is as plausible as the other.

But to return to the detector lock. Count or M. De l'Escalopier having complained grievously to his humble neighbor, the watchmaker Robert-Houdin, that he and his family were being robbed, begged that the latter suggest some means of catching the thief. Robert-Houdin then recalled a childish device by which he had caught his school-fellows in the act of pilfering his desk, etc., and he proposed to the Count that the same device, elaborated to meet the strength of a full-grown man, be attached to his wealthy patron's desk. As first planned, the detector lock was to shoot off a pistol on being tampered with, and then brand the hand of the thief with nitrate of silver. Count de l'Escalopier objected to branding a man for life, so Robert-Houdin substituted for the nitrate of silver a sort of cat's claw which would clamp down on the robber's hand and draw blood. The Count deposited ten thousand francs in his desk and caught the robber, his confidential servant, red-handed. The ten thousand francs he presented to Robert-Houdin as a reward for stopping the thefts.

A charming tale this makes, but, unfortunately for Robert-Houdin's claims to originality, the detector lock was not a novelty in his day. The lock which would first alarm the household by setting off a pistol and then brand the thief's hand, is described by the Marquis of Worcester in his book "Centurie of Inventions." As locks and locksmithing form my hobby, while in England I purchased the entire set of patent-books, to add to a collection of locks and fastenings from every known country of the world. In the introduction of the first book of patents for inventions relating to locks, latches, bolts, etc., from A.D. 1774 to 1866, the following quotation will be found:

"The Marquis of Worcester in his 'Centurie of Inventions' thus describes the first detector lock invented, A.D. 1640, by some mechanical genius of that day: 'This lock is so constructed that, if a stranger attempts to open it, it catches his hand as a trap catches a fox, though not as far as maiming him for life, yet so far marketh him that if suspected he might easily be detected.'"

It appears that to this lock was fitted a steel barb which, if a certain tumbler was overlifted in the act of picking or otherwise, was projected against the hand of the operator by a spring. I have seen such a lock as this in the collection of Hobbs, Hart & Co., London, who have had it in their possession many years. In every respect, it answers the description of the invention claimed by Robert-Houdin as his own.

Chapter VII. of "Secrets of Stage Conjuring" is devoted to Robert-Houdin's very incorrect explanation of the famous Indian Basket Trick. Even his own translator, Professor Hoffmann, takes issue with Robert-Houdin, as will be seen by reading his foot-note on page 104: "We will not venture to question the fact vouched for by so high an authority as Robert-Houdin, that the Indian Basket Trick may sometimes be performed after the manner above described, but we doubt very much whether such is the usual or customary method."

Handbill used by the original Indian jugglers in England during 1818, in which the sword-swallowing trick is featured.

From the Harry Houdini Collection.

Robert-Houdin states that the child is placed in the basket, and the Indian fastens down the lid with leather straps. To facilitate this operation, he rests his knees against the basket, and the bottom of the latter thus being turned toward the audience, the boy slips out through a cunningly contrived trap and quickly conceals himself under the robe of the magician, whose attitude favors this concealment.

As the basket trick is the Hindoo magician's most wonderful offering, a truthful account of his methods of performing the same may be interesting. In the first place, Robert-Houdin's explanation is impossible and unreasonable because the Hindoo magician does not wear flowing robes in which the child could be concealed. Every Hindoo performer I have ever seen wore short trousers and was barefooted.

The correct method of performing the trick, which has been handed down through generations of Hindoos, is as follows: The boy subject is placed in a net in which he is firmly tied, after having had his big toes and thumbs fastened down with bandages. Then, with many a grunt and a groan, he is lifted into the basket. The subject, however, pretends that the basket is too small, so he is really seated on one side and keeps his back in the air. This is done to give the appearance eventually that it was impossible for him to crouch down or around the basket. The lid of the basket is now placed on his back, and a large sheet is thrown over the entire apparatus, which conceals from the audience every movement made by the subject.

Now commences the Hindoo "patter," in reality yells, groans, and incantations, while the magician and his assistant strike the basket with swords or canes, stamp on the ground, gnash their teeth, etc. Gradually the cover of the basket sinks until the basket seems empty, to the spectators at least. The fakir now takes off the cover of the basket, leaving the sheet over it, however. Then he jumps into the presumably empty basket, stamps all around, and takes out the net in which are found the turban worn by the subject and the thumb tie. To prove further that the basket is still empty, the fakir seats himself in the basket, as shown in the illustration. The lid of the basket is now replaced, and under this friendly cover the sheet is taken off and the basket tied up.

Now commences the true Hindoo magic. The magician is a real actor. He apparently adjures Mahomet. He gets very angry and with fierce looks, ejaculations, and muttered curses he grabs up a sword or cane and jabs it through different parts of the basket. During all this time the subject, who is something of a contortionist, is wriggling about on the bottom of the basket, keeping out of reach of the sword, and in fact often guiding its thrusts between his legs, as every movement on the part of the fakir has been carefully thought out and rehearsed in advance.

By this time the fakir has convinced his audience that the basket is empty. To be sure he has not allowed any spectators to come too near him or the basket, nor has any hand save his touched it, but his clever acting almost persuades even an intelligent or sceptical onlooker that the basket is empty.

With the lid of the basket replaced, this time above the friendly sheet, and the basket tied, he resumes his weird incantations. He screams and runs back and forth, playing on a small instrument with a hideous tone which is a cross between the whistle of a locomotive with a cold, and a sawed-off and hammered-down flute in which has been inserted a tin whistle. As this nerve-racking music holds the spectators under its awful spell, the basket begins to rock, the contortionist-subject gradually raises himself inside the basket, and when the noise is at its height he straightens up in the basket and raises it with his back as far as it will go. To the uninitiated, it actually appears as if he had returned to an empty basket in his original position. The trick is a marvellous deception, but only a Hindoo can exhibit it with success, for no white person would ever indulge in the screechings, imbecilities, and contortions which are the spectacular and convincing features of the trick.

Sometimes the trick is varied. Instead of the subject being found in his original position he is seen running toward the crowd as from a distance. This is accomplished by having two subjects, one in the basket and one hidden on the outskirts of the crowd, who are "doubles" or at least who show a marked resemblance and are dressed exactly alike.

The earliest programmes of Hindoo jugglers in my collection are dated 1818. The "Mr. Ramosamee" featured on this bill later split his name thus, "Ramo Samee," and was engaged to perform alone between the acts of "The Broken Heart" at the Garrick Theatre, London. From Ramo Samee, Continental and British magicians learned the trick of juggling brass balls.

On page 135 Professor Hoffmann, in a foot-note, commends Robert-Houdin for the very impartial manner in which he approaches the question of spiritualism and spiritualistic manifestations, in his day a comparative novelty: "In default of absolute certainty, he wisely reserves his opinion. Where, however, as in the case of the Davenport Brothers, he had an opportunity of personally observing the alleged 'phenomena,' he has neither difficulty in penetrating nor hesitation in denouncing the imposture. We venture to believe that any of the so-called spiritualistic manifestations which had come under the test of Robert-Houdin's examination would have met a similar fate."

With this commendation, I cannot agree. Robert-Houdin once had all the leeway he wished at a most remarkable manifestation and made no attempt to hide the fact that he was baffled by the "phenomena." The "Memoirs of Marquis de Mirville" contain a Robert-Houdin letter in which he admits that he could find no explanation of tests just witnessed. The letter, translated from "Die Magie des XIX. Jahrhunderts von Uriarte," 1896, published in Berlin, Germany, by Heusers Verlag, is herewith quoted: "I returned from the séance as greatly astonished as it was possible for me to be, and I am thoroughly convinced that it was entirely out of the possibility, and no chance whatever, that it was either by accident or practised trickery to produce such wonderful materializations. Robert-Houdin, May 18th, 1847."

He further shows his ignorance of séances as offered in his times, by his attempt to describe the methods employed by the Davenport Brothers, to whom he devotes chapter XIII., which might be described as a chapter of errors.

These picturesque American entertainers, the Davenport Brothers, hailed from Buffalo, N. Y., U.S.A. Ira Erastus was born September 17th, 1839, and William Henry, February 1st, 1841. They fairly startled the world by their so-called manifestations of spiritualism during the 60's, and were alternately lauded and reviled for their performances.

The Davenport Brothers in their prime, from photographs furnished by them to the contemporary press, now in the Harry Houdini Collection.

Both were below medium height, rather handsome men, and, as will be seen from the accompanying engraving, looked much alike. Their career, which started in America, ran from about 1853 to the early 70's. They made a trip to Europe in 1864, remaining until August, 1869. Both married abroad; Ira a daughter of France, Mlle. Louise Toulet, and William Henry a Polish girl, Miss Matilda Mag. On the whole, their foreign tour was most profitable, though in some cities they paid a high price for their notoriety. In England, they waged bitter warfare with John Henry Anderson, Tolmaque, and Professor Redmond.

On the occasion of their Paris opening at the Salle Herz they claimed that the hoodlum element mobbed the theatre and broke up their performance at the instigation of Henri Robin, who was playing in opposition. Hamilton, who had succeeded to the management of Robert-Houdin's theatre, in a letter published after witnessing their initial performance announced that he shared this belief; but as Robert-Houdin and Henri Robin were bitter rivals, I believe Hamilton's letter was the result of two things: first the intense ill-will he harbored against Robin, and second, as he had Robert-Houdin as his mentor, he was really ignorant of the Davenport methods and therefore not in a position to defend them. The letter, which is given in full, appeared in *Gazette des Étrangers*, Paris, September 27th, 1865:

"Messrs. Davenport: Yesterday I had the pleasure of being present at the séance you gave, and I came away from it convinced that jealousy alone was the cause of the outcry raised against you. The phenomena produced surpassed my expectations, and your experiments were full of interest to me. I consider it my duty to add that these phenomena are inexplicable; and the more so by such persons as have thought themselves able to guess your supposed secret, and who are, in fact, far indeed from having discovered the truth. Hamilton."

The cabinet trick offered by the Davenport Brothers. From an old print in the Harry Houdini Collection.

After their return to America the Davenport Brothers retired from public life, purchased a farm, and rested on their laurels and a corpulent bank account. One of them is said to have admitted that all their work was skilful manipulation and not spiritualistic manifestations. Nevertheless, their names will live so long as spiritualism is talked of or cabinet effects tolerated by the public.

The trick as offered by the Davenport Brothers consisted of their being tied hand and foot at opposite ends of the cabinet, which was hung with musical instruments, bells, etc. The two men slipped in and out of the ropes without delay or apparent damage to the ropes, and musical instruments were played with arms presumably in bondage.

Robert-Houdin, in attempting to expose the trick, makes two flagrant errors. First, he claims that "by dint of special practice on the part of our mediums, the thumb is made to lie flat in the hand, when the whole assumes a cylindrical form of scarcely greater diameter than the wrist"; and second that the Davenport Brothers had trained themselves to see in the dark.

ST. GEORGE'S HALL,
LANGHAM PLACE.

RETURN
OF THE
BROTHERS DAVENPORT
AND
MR. FAY.

THE BROTHERS DAVENPORT and Mr. FAY have the honour to announce that, after a tour of three years over the greater part of the Continent of Europe, they have returned once more, and probably for the last time, to this Metropolis, where they will give a few Séances previous to their departure for the United States.

During their European tour they have given Séances in Paris, Berlin, Vienna, Moscow, St. Petersburgh, and nearly every great Continental Capital; and have had the honour of appearing before their Majesties the Emperors of France and Russia, the Royal Family of Prussia, and great numbers of the most distinguished Personages in Europe. Many thousands of persons of the highest rank and intelligence have witnessed the astonishing experiments given in their presence.

Throughout the Northern American States, from their first visit to England in 1864, they were seen by hundreds of thousands of persons.

In England, their first Séance was given in private, to a most distinguished party of men of science and letters, who gave their most unequivocal testimony to the excellence and perfection of their experiments.

Two Séances of the Brothers Davenport and Mr. Fay will be given at

ST. GEORGE'S HALL, LANGHAM PLACE,

On THURSDAY EVENING, APRIL 23rd,

And SATURDAY EVENING, APRIL 25th, 1868.
At Eight o'clock.

STALLS, - 3s.   BALCONY, - 2s.
ADMISSION,   ONE SHILLING.

Announcement used by the Davenport Brothers on their return to London, England, after their tour of the Continent in April, 1868. From the Harry Houdini Collection.

As releasing myself from fastenings of all sorts, from ropes to strait-jackets, has been my profession for twenty years, I am in a position to contradict Robert-Houdin's first claim positively. I have met thousands of persons who claimed that the rope, as well as the handcuff trick, was accomplished by folding the hand together or making the wrist larger than the hand, but never have I met men or women who could make their hands smaller than their wrists. I have even gone so far as to have iron bands made and press my hands together, hoping eventually to make my hands smaller than my wrists, but this has failed, too. Even if the entire thumb were cut away, I believe it would still be impossible to slip a rope that was properly bound around the wrist. You may take any cuff of the adjustable make, or a ratchet cuff, place it about a small woman's wrist, and you will find that even she will be unable to slip her wrists. I do not mean by this any hand-cuff that will not come to any size, or the common cuffs which when locked will lock only to a certain size, but I mean a cuff that can be locked and adjusted to any size of wrist.

In rope-tying, the principal trick is to allow yourself to be tied according to certain methods of crossing your hands or wrists, so that by eventually straightening your hands you have made enough room to allow them to slip out very easily. It is not always the size of the wrist that counts. It is the manner of holding your hands when the knots are being tied.

The gift of seeing in the dark, with which Robert-Houdin endowed the Davenports, is equally preposterous. Professor Hoffmann defends Robert-Houdin by citing instances of prisoners who had been confined in cells for an indefinite period and who had learned to see in the dark. This is quite true, but they did not alternate daylight and darkness. Eminent opticians and oculists inform me that the faculty of seeing in the dark cannot be acquired by parties like the Davenports, who spent most of their time in the light.

While the Davenports were pioneers in rope-tying and cabinet séances, had Robert-Houdin been the clever sleight-of-hand performer and inventor he claims to have been, these tricks would have been clear and solvable to him. But as he obviously joined the ranks of the amazed and bewildered masses, making only a futile attempt to explain the performances, he convicts himself of ignorance regarding his own art.

A man who has made a fortune in the world of magic and who desires to hand down to posterity a clean record of his attainments will be clever enough and manly enough to avoid any attempt to explain that which he does not understand. By his flagrant mis-statements regarding the tricks of his predecessors and contemporaries, Robert-Houdin, however, convicts himself of ignorance regarding the fundamental principles of magic, and arouses in the minds of broad, intelligent readers doubts regarding his claims to the invention of the various tricks and automata which he declares to have been the output of his brain, the production of his own deft hands.

CHAPTER XI

THE NARROWNESS OF ROBERT-HOUDIN'S "MEMOIRS"

THE charm of true memoirs lies far beyond the printed pages, in the depth and breadth of the writer's soul. The greatest of all autobiographies are those which detail not only the lives of the men who penned them, but which abound in diverting anecdotes and character studies of the men and women among whom the writer moved. They are not autobiographies alone, but vivid, broad-minded pen-pictures of the period in which the writer was a vigorous, respect-compelling figure. Memoirs written with a view to settling old scores seldom live to accomplish their ends. The narrowness and pettiness of the writer, which intelligent reading of history is bound to disclose, destroy all other charms which the book may possess.

At personal exploitation Robert-Houdin is a brilliant success. As a writer of memoirs he is a wretched failure. Whenever he writes of himself, his pen seems fairly to scintillate. Whenever he refers to other magicians of his times, his pen lags and drops on the pages blots which can emanate only from a narrow, petty, jealous nature.

Even when he writes of his own family, this peculiar trait of petty egotism may be read between the lines. He mentions the name of his son Émile, apparently because the lad shared his stage triumphs. His other children he never mentions by name. The second wife, who, he grudgingly admits, stood valiantly by him in his days of poverty and disappointment, he does not honor by so much as stating her name before marriage. Rather, he refers to her as a person whom he was constrained to place in charge of his household in order that he might continue his experiments and his work on automata. A less gracious tribute to wifely devotion was never penned.

But it is in dealing with contemporary magicians or those whose handiwork in bygone years he cleverly purloined and proclaimed as his original inventions, that the petty jealousy of the man comes to the surface. Whenever he desires to claim for himself credit due a predecessor in the world of magic, he either ignores the man's very existence or writes of his competitor in such a manner that the latter's standing as man and magician is lowered. Not that he makes broad, sweeping statements. Rather, he indulges in the innuendo which is far more dangerous to the party attacked. He never strikes a pen-blow which, because of its brutality, might arouse the sympathy of his readers for the object of his attack. Here, in the gentle art of innuendo and belittling, if not in the conjurer's art, Robert-Houdin is a master.

Wiljalba Frikell in his youth, showing the peculiar costume worn by conjurers at that time. The author secured this portrait a few weeks before Frikell's death and sent it to the veteran conjurer, who was amazed to learn that this print was in existence. Now in the Harry Houdini Collection.

In writing his "Memoirs" he deliberately ignores Compars Herrmann, Henri Robin, Wiljalba Frikell, M. Jacobs, and P. T. Barnum, all of whom he knew personally. He might have written most entertainingly of these men, but in each case, he had an object in avoiding reference to the acquaintance. P. T. Barnum knew the true history of the writing and drawing figure, as reference to chapter III. of this book will show. Frikell was the pioneer in dispensing with cumbersome stage draperies. Robert-Houdin claimed this innovation as the product of his own ingenuity. Compars Herrmann was playing in London when Robert-Houdin made his English début under Mitchell's direction, and was presenting, trick for trick, the répertoire claimed by Robert-Houdin as original with him. Henri Robin disputed Robert-Houdin's claim to having invented the inexhaustible bottle, and proved his case, as will be seen by reference to chapter VIII. Jacobs was one of Anderson's cleverest imitators and a rival of Robert-Houdin in the English provinces.

The adroit manner in which Robert-Houdin flays Pinetti, Anderson, and Bosco would arouse admiration were his pen-lashings devoted to men who deserved such treatment. Under existing circumstances—his debt to Bosco and Pinetti, whose tricks he filched remorselessly, and the fact that Anderson's popularity outlived his own in England—his efforts to belittle these men are unworthy of one who called himself a man and a master magician. The truly great and successful man rises above petty jealousy and personalities. This, Robert-Houdin could not do, even when he sat pen in hand, in retirement, with the fear of competition removed.

It seems almost incredible that Robert-Houdin should ignore Henri Robin in his "Memoirs," for Robin was one of the most interesting characters of that day. He still stands in magic's history as the Chesterfield of conjuring, a man of many gifts, charming address, and broad education. Even in his dispute with Robert-Houdin regarding the invention of the inexhaustible bottle, he never forgot his dignity, but proved his case by that most potent of arguments, a well-edited magazine published under his direction, in which an illustration showed him actually performing the trick in 1844, or a full three years before it appeared on Robert-Houdin's programme.

Robert-Houdin was indebted to Robin for another trick, the Garde Française, introduced by Robert-Houdin in October, 1847. Henri Robin had precisely the same figure, doing precisely the same feats, in the garb of an Arab. An illustration from Robin's magazine, *L'Almanach Cagliostro*, shows Robin offering this figure in March, 1846, or a year and seven months before it was presented by Robert-Houdin. Yet the only reference made by Robert-Houdin to this popular and gifted contemporary is in "The Secrets of Stage Conjuring" where he remarks slightingly that Robin spoiled Mr. Pepper's business by giving a poor imitation of the latter's ghost show.

Again, in ignoring Herrmann, he proves his narrowness of mind, his utter unwillingness to admit any ability in his rivals. Compars Herrmann was no ordinary trickster or mountebank, but a conjurer who remained in London almost a year, playing the very best houses, and later scoring equal popularity in the provinces. He was decorated by various monarchs and was famous for his large gifts to charities. Even the present generation, including theatre-goers and students of magic, remembers the name of Herrmann, when Robert-Houdin is forgotten or would be but for his cleverly written autobiography.

Wiljalba Frikell, to whom should go the credit of cutting out heavy stage draperies, never claimed the innovation as a carefully planned conceit, but as an accident. His paraphernalia were destroyed in a fire, but he desired to live up to his contract and give a performance as announced. He therefore offered sleight-of-hand, pure and simple, with the aid of a few tables, chairs, and other common properties which were absolutely undraped. He was also compelled to don regulation, severely plain, evening clothes. The absence of draperies, which naturally aid a conjurer in attaining results, created so pleasing a sensation that Frikell never again draped his stage nor wore fancy raiment. Had Robert-Houdin told the truth about his so-called innovation, he must have given Frikell credit, wherefore he conveniently ignores Frikell completely.

It is entirely characteristic of Robert-Houdin that he did not openly assail Pinetti in the pages of his "Memoirs." With cleverness worthy of a better cause, he quotes the bitter verbal attack as issuing from the lips of the friend and mentor of his youth, Signor Torrini.

The major portion of chapter VI., pages 92 to 104 inclusive, American edition of his autobiography, is devoted to assailing Pinetti's abilities as a conjurer and his reputation as a man. Granted that Pinetti did put Torrini to shame on the Neapolitan stage, such revenge for a wholesale duplication of the magician's tricks might be termed almost human and natural. Had a minor magician, amateur or professional, dogged the footsteps of Robert-Houdin, copying his tricks, the entire répertoire upon which he depended for a livelihood, thus endangering his future, I doubt that even the author of "Confidences d'un Prestidigitateur" would have hesitated to unmask and undo his rival.

In fact, by reference to the editorial note, foot of page 421, American edition of Robert-Houdin's "Memoirs," it will be seen that in 1850 Robert-Houdin appealed to the law for protection in just such a case. An employee was sent to prison for two years, as judgment for selling to an amateur some of his master's secrets.

Bartolomeo Bosco in his prime. From an engraving in the Harry Houdini Collection.

But in attacking Pinetti, Robert-Houdin goes a step too far and falsifies, not directly but by innuendo, when he permits the impression to go forth that Pinetti was hounded and ruined both financially and professionally by Torrini, as is set forth on page 104. He pictures Torrini as dogging the footsteps of Pinetti through all Italy and finally driving him in a state of abject misery to Russia, where he died in the home of a nobleman, who sheltered him through sheer compassion. Robert-Houdin must have known this was absolutely untrue, for he quotes Robertson, who published Pinetti's true experiences in Russia. Pinetti took a fortune with him to Russia, acquired more wealth there, and then lost his entire financial holdings through his passion for balloon experiments, as is set forth in chapter II. of this book.

Then, to show his own inconsistency, after picturing Pinetti in his "Memoirs" as a charlatan, a conjurer of vulgar, uncouth pretensions rather than as a good showman of real ability, Robert-Houdin is forced to admit on page 25 of "Secrets of Magic" that later conjurers employed Pinetti programmes as a foundation upon which their performances were built! Even here, however, Robert-Houdin fails to acknowledge an iota of the heavy debt which he personally owed the despised Chevalier Pinetti.

Robert-Houdin devotes the greater part of chapter X., American edition of his autobiography, to belittling Bosco, a conjurer whose popularity all over Europe was long-lived. First, he pictures Bosco as a most cruel creature who literally tortured to death the birds used in his performances. Here, as in his attack on Pinetti, Robert-Houdin throws the responsibility for criticism on the shoulders of another. His old friend Antonio accompanies him to watch Bosco's performance, and it is Antonio throughout the narrative who inveighs against Bosco's cruelty and Antonio who insists upon leaving before the performance closes, because the cruelty of the conjurer nauseates him.

At that time, no society for the protection of animals existed, and, even if it had, I doubt whether Bosco's performance would have come under the ban. Certain magicians of to-day employ many of Bosco's tricks in which birds and even small animals are used, but the conjuring is so deftly done that the public of 1907, like that of 1838, thinks it is all sleight-of-hand work and that the birds are neither hurt nor killed. Even in Bosco's time the bird trick was not in his répertoire exclusively. All English magicians employed it. Apparently, the head of the fowl was amputated, but often in reality it was tucked under the wing, and the head and neck of another fowl was shown by sleight-of-hand. Quite probably the Parisian public did not consider Bosco cruel. Robert-Houdin and his friend Antonio, being versed in sleight-of-hand and conjuring methods, read cruelty between the deft movements. Certain it is that the name of Bosco has not been handed down to posterity by other writers as a synonym of cruelty.

The animus of Robert-Houdin's attack on Bosco is evident at every point of the narrative. Now he accuses him of bad taste in appearing in the box-office. Again, he suggests that the somewhat impressive opening of Bosco's act savors of both charlatanism and burlesque, when in reality the secret of showmanship consists not of what you really do, but what the mystery-loving public thinks you do. Bosco undoubtedly secured precisely the effect he desired, because Robert-Houdin devotes more than a page to a most unnecessary attempt to explain away what he considered Bosco's undeserved popularity.

Bosco was not only a clever magician, but a man of many adventures, so that his life reads like a romance. This soldier of fortune, Bartolomeo Bosco, was born of a noble Piedmont family, on January 11th, 1793, in Turin, Italy. From boyhood, he showed great ability as a necromancer, but at the age of nineteen he was forced to serve under Napoleon I. in the Russian campaign. He was a fusilier in the Eleventh Infantry, and at the battle of Borodino was injured in an engagement with Cossacks. Pierced by a lance, he lay upon the ground apparently dead. A Cossack callously roamed among the dead and dying, rifling pockets and belts. When he came to the form of Bosco, that youth feigned death, knowing that resistance to the ghoul meant a death wound. But while the Cossack robbed the Italian soldier, the latter stealthily raised his unwounded arm and by sleight-of-hand rifled the well-filled pockets of the ghoul, which fact was not discovered by the Cossack until he was far from the field of the dead and dying, where he had left one of the enemy considerably better off, thanks to Bosco's conjuring gifts.

Later Bosco was sent captive to Siberia, where he perfected his sleight-of-hand while amusing fellow-prisoners and jailers. In 1814, he was released and returned to his native land, where he studied medicine, but eventually decided to become a public entertainer. He was not only a clever entertainer, but a good business man, and he planned each year on saving enough money to insure a life of ease in his old age. But events intervened to ruin all his well-laid plans. The sins of his youth brought their penalty. An illegitimate son, Eugene, became a heavy drag upon the retired magician, who was compelled to pay large sums to the young man in order to prevent his playing in either France or Germany or assuming the name of Bosco. In a German antiquary's shop at Bonn on the Rhine I found an agreement in which Bosco agreed to pay this youth five thousand francs for not using the name of Bosco. This agreement is too long for reproduction in this volume, but unquestionably it is genuine and tells all too eloquently the troubles which beset Bosco in his old age.

Eugene was said to be the superior of his famous father in sleight-of-hand, but he was wild and given to excesses. Women and wine checked what might have been a brilliant professional career. Disabled, poverty-stricken, and respected by none, he soon disappeared from the conjuring world, and according to Carl Willman in the "Zauberwelt" he died miserably in Hungary in 1891.

Only photograph of Madame Bosco, given to the author by Mrs. Mueller, Madame Bosco's niece, at the funeral of Wiljalba Frikell.

The author at the grave of Bosco. From a photograph in the Harry Houdini Collection.

In the mean time, Bosco and his wife lived in poverty in Dresden, where the once brilliant conjurer died March 2nd, 1863. His wife died three years later and was interred in the grave with her husband in a cemetery on Friedrichstrasse. There was nothing on the tombstone to indicate the double interment, and I discovered the fact only by investigating the municipal and cemetery records. Here I also learned that the grave had merely been leased, and as the lease was about to expire the bones of the great conjurer and his faithful wife might soon be disinterred and reburied in a neglected corner of the graveyard devoted to the poor and unclaimed dead. To prevent this, I purchased the lot and tombstone, and presented the same to the Society of American Magicians, of which organization, at the present writing, I am a member.

A man of noble birth and brilliant attainments was the original Bosco, and his name became a by-word all over the Continent as the synonym, not of cruelty, but of clever deception, yet never has posterity put the name of a great performer to such ignoble uses. For who has not heard the cry of the modern Bosco, "Eat-'em-alive"?

To-day I can close my eyes and summon two visions. First I see myself standing bareheaded before a neglected grave in the quiet cemetery on Friedrichstrasse, Dresden, the sunlight pouring down upon the tombstone which bears not only the cup-and-balls and wand, insignia of Bosco's most famous trick, but this inscription: "Ici repose le célèbre Bartolomeo

Bosco.—Né à Turin le 11 Janvier, 1793; décédé à Dresden le 2 Mars, 1863." The history of this clever conjurer, with all its lights and shadows, sweeps before me like a mental panorama.

The second vision carries me into the country, to the fairs of England and the side-shows of America:

"Bosco! Bosco! Eat-'em-alive Bosco. You can't afford to miss this marvel. Bosco! Bosco!"

Follow me into the enclosure and gaze down into a den. There lies a half-naked human being. His hair is long and matted, a loin cloth does wretched duty as clothing. Torn sandals are on his feet. The eulogistic lecturer dilates upon the powers of this twentieth-century Bosco, but you do not listen. Your fascinated gaze is fixed on various hideous, wriggling, writhing forms on the floor of the den. Snakes—scores of them! Now the creature, half-animal, half-human, glances up to make sure that attention is riveted upon him, then grasps one of the serpents in his hideous hands and in a flash bites off its head. The writhing body falls back to the ground.

You grip the railing in a sudden faintness. Has your brain deceived your eyes, or your eyes your brain? If you are a conjurer you try to convince yourself that it is all a clever sleight-of-hand exhibition, but in your heart, you know it is not true. This creature, so near a beast, has debauched his manhood for a few paltry dollars, and in dragging himself down has dragged down the name of a worthy, a brilliant, a world-famous performer.

Of the twentieth-century Boscos there are, alas, many. You will find them all over the world, in street carnivals, side-shows, fair-booths, and museums, and why the public supports such debasing exhibitions I have never yet been able to understand. I have seen half-starved Russians pick food from refuse-barrels. I have seen besotted Americans creep out from low dives to draw the dregs of beer-barrels into tomato cans. I have seen absinthe fiends in Paris trade body and soul to obtain their beloved stimulant. I have heard morphine fiends in Russia promise to exhibit the effect of the needle in return for the price of an injection. But never has my soul so risen in revolt as at sight of this bestial exhibition with which the name of Bosco, a nobleman and a conjurer of merit, has been linked.

Even more despicable than his attack upon Bosco is Robert-Houdin's flaying of John Henry Anderson. In this he is both unmanly and untruthful. Hinging his attack on his surprise at the press methods and advertising adopted in England as opposed to the less spectacular means employed in France, he insinuates that Anderson's entire success was built not upon merit, ability, originality, or diversified programmes, but solely upon sensational advertising. On page 325 of the American edition of his "Memoirs" Robert-Houdin writes thus of his competitor:

"On my arrival in England a conjurer of the name of Anderson, who assumed the title of Great Wizard of the North, had been performing for a long period at the little Strand Theatre.

"This artist, fearing, doubtlessly, that public attention might be divided, tried to crush the publicity of my performances; hence he sent out on London streets a cavalcade thus organized:

"Four enormous carriages, covered with posters and pictures representing all sorts of witchcraft, opened the procession. Then followed four-and-twenty merry men, each bearing a banner on which was painted a letter a yard in height.

"At each cross-road the four carriages stopped side by side and presented a bill some twenty-five yards in length, while all the men (I should say letters), on receiving the word of command, drew themselves up in a line, like the vehicles.

"Seen in front the letters formed this phrase:

THE CELEBRATED ANDERSON ! ! !

While on the other side of the banners could be read:

THE GREAT WIZARD OF THE NORTH.

Handbill used by Anderson in Germany. January, 1848, when Robert-Houdin claimed that he was playing in the English provinces. From the Harry Houdini Collection.

"Unfortunately for the Wizard, his performances were attacked by a mortal disease; too long a stay in London had ended by producing satiety. Besides, his repertory was out-of-date, and could not contend against the new tricks which I was offering. What could he present to the public in opposition to the second sight, the suspension, and the inexhaustible bottle? Hence he was obliged to close his theatre and start for the provinces, where he managed, as usual, to make excellent receipts, owing to his powerful means of notoriety."

In the first place, Robert Houdin insinuates that when they played in opposition John Henry Anderson's répertoire was stale and uninteresting. Is it possible that Robert-Houdin could not read Anderson's bills, or were his statements deliberate falsehoods, emanating from a malicious, wilful desire to injure Anderson?

What did Anderson have to offer in opposition to Robert-Houdin's much-vaunted Suspension, Second Sight, and Inexhaustible Bottle? Consult the Anderson programme, reproduced, and you will find that the great Wizard of the North duplicated the French conjurer's répertoire. "The Ethereal Suspension" of Robert-Houdin's programme was "Suspension Chloroforeene" on Anderson's. Second Sight appeared on both bills. "The Inexhaustible Bottle" had wisely been dropped by Anderson because he had been using it in one form or another for ten years preceding the date of Robert-Houdin's appearance in London, as is proven in chapter IX. of this book.

Therefore, if Anderson's programme was passé and uninteresting, so also must have been the one offered by Robert-Houdin!

Poster used by Anderson during his closing week at the Strand Theatre, London, January 11th, 1848. From the Harry Houdini Collection.

Second, John Henry Anderson was not in London when Robert-Houdin arrived there in May, 1848. He was on the Continent, and a bill reproduced will show that he was in Germany in January, 1848, and did not open at the Strand Theatre until December 26th, 1848. Then it was Robert-Houdin who had just returned from the provinces, not Anderson. Anderson had been playing the capitals of Europe. Robert-Houdin had been in Manchester, England.

Robert-Houdin again skilfully twists the truth to suit his own ends. He actually states that Anderson, returning from a tour of the provinces, used a new poster, a caricature of the famous painting, "Napoleon's Return from Elba":

"In the foreground, Anderson was seen affecting the attitude of the great man; above his head fluttered an enormous banner bearing the words 'The Wonder of the World'; while, behind him and somewhat lost in the shade, the Emperor of Russia and several other monarchs stood in a respectful posture. As in the original picture, the fanatic admirers of the Wizard embraced his knees, while an immense crowd received him triumphantly. In the distance could be seen the equestrian statue of the Iron Duke, who, hat in hand, bowed before him, the Great Wizard; and lastly, the very dome of St. Paul's bent towards him most humbly.

"At the bottom was the inscription,

RETURN OF THE NAPOLEON OF NECROMANCY.

"Regarded seriously, this picture would be found a puff in very bad taste; but as a caricature it is excessively comic. Besides, it had the double result of making the London public laugh and bringing a great number of shillings into the skilful puffer's pockets."

Eugene Bosco, son of the original Bosco. From the Harry Houdini Collection.

Reference to my collection of Anderson programmes and press clippings proves that while on the Continent his performances had created such a sensation that, according to the ethics and etiquette of his profession, Anderson was quite justified in assuming the title of "The Napoleon of Necromancy" and in depicting even kings and noblemen admiring his abilities as a conjurer. But, alas, Robert-Houdin had played only before English and French monarchs, not before the other crowned heads of Europe, including the Czar of Russia and the German Kaiser!

It required weeks and months of browsing in old book- and print-shops, national libraries, and rare collections on my part to prove that Anderson had really played these engagements, when his bitter rival, Robert-Houdin, his heart eaten with jealousy until his sense of honor and truth was hopelessly blunted, was claiming that Anderson had just returned from a trip in the English provinces.

It will be noted by reference to the Anderson programme that he had been engaged only for the Christmas holidays, but despite Robert-Houdin's claim that he was a failure and was obliged to close and seek new fields of conquest in the provinces, Anderson's engagement was extended. He remained at the Strand until January 11th, 1848, then after a brief provincial tour he actually returned to London and played to big receipts. Again, and again, he appeared in London. Far from being the unpopular, forgotten ex-magician pictured by Robert-Houdin, he performed with great success at the St. James Theatre, London, in 1851. Robert-Houdin appeared in London for the last time in 1853, but in 1865 "the despised and forgotten Anderson" was there again, creating a furor in his exposure of the Davenport Brothers.

John Henry Anderson as he appeared in his later years. From a cut in the Harry Houdini Collection.

Robert-Houdin might have been justified in criticising Anderson's sensational advertising methods, for these were entirely opposed to the more elegant and conservative methods employed by the French conjurer. But certainly, he was not justified in picturing his rival as one who had passed his prime, whose popularity had waned, whose répertoire no longer attracted the public. For, in addition to duplicating Robert-Houdin's entire répertoire, Anderson offered tricks of which Robert-Houdin knew nothing, and for years to come he constantly reconstructed his programmes, keeping them strictly up-to-date.

Anderson did die a poor man, but this was not because the amusement-loving public had wearied of him. A popular performer, like so many of his class he did not know how to invest his huge earnings. It is known that he gave $20,000 to various charities, while no record of Robert-Houdin's charities exists. He was burned out several times. He lost money through a bad contract made for his Australian tour. Certain investments dropped in value because of the Civil War in the United States, during which England sympathized with the South. Finally, during his American tour after the Civil War, Anderson played the Southern States, then steeped in bitterness toward the North, and was unfortunate enough to bill himself as "The Great Wizard of the North." This roused the Southern prejudice to white heat, he was almost mobbed, and was finally driven from that section of the country. He went into bankruptcy, November 19th, 1866, and died at Darlington, County Durham, England, Feb. 3rd, 1874. His remains were interred, in accordance with his dying request, at Aberdeen, Scotland.

So ends the true history of Robert-Houdin. The master-magician, unmasked, stands forth in all the hideous nakedness of historical proof, the prince of pilferers. That he might bask for a few hours in public adulation, he purloined the ideas of magicians long dead and buried, and proclaimed these as the fruits of his own inventive genius. That he might be known to posterity as the king of conjurers, he sold his birthright of manhood and honor for a mere mess of pottage, his "Memoirs," written by the hand of another man, who at his instigation belittled his contemporaries, and juggled facts and truth to further his egotistical, jealous ambitions.

But the day of reckoning is come. Upon the history of magic as promulgated by Robert-Houdin the searchlight of modern investigation has been turned. Credit has been given where it belongs, to those magicians who preceded Robert-Houdin and upon whose abilities and achievements Robert-Houdin built his unearned, unmerited fame. The dust of years has been swept from names long forgotten, which should forever shine in the annals of magic.

Thus end, also, my researches, covering almost two decades of time, researches in which my veneration for old-time magicians grew with each newly discovered bit of history; researches during which my respect for the profession of magic has grown by leaps and bounds. And the fruits of these researches I now lay before the only true jury, the great reading public. My task is finished.

BOOK III

MIRACLE MONGERS AND THEIR METHODS

A COMPLETE EXPOSE' OF THE MODUS
OPERANDI OF FIRE EATERS, HEAT
RESISTERS, POISON EATERS, VENOMOUS
REPTILE DEFIERS, SWORD SWALLOWERS,
HUMAN OSTRICHES, STRONG MEN, ETC.

BY

HOUDINI

AUTHOR OF "THE UNMASKING OF ROBERT HOUDIN," ETC.

**AFFECTIONATELY DEDICATED
TO MY LIFE'S HELPMATE,
WHO STARVED AND STARRED WITH ME
DURING THE YEARS WE SPENT
AMONG "MIRACLE MONGERS"
My Wife**

PREFACE

"All wonder," said Samuel Johnson, "is the effect of novelty on ignorance." Yet we are so created that without something to wonder at we should find life scarcely worth living. That fact does not make ignorance bliss, or make it "folly to be wise." For the wisest man never gets beyond the reach of novelty, nor can ever make it his boast that there is nothing he is ignorant of; on the contrary, the wiser he becomes the more clearly he sees how much there is of which he remains in ignorance. The more he knows, the more he will find to wonder at.

My professional life has been a constant record of disillusion, and many things that seem wonderful to most men are the every-day commonplaces of my business. But I have never been without some seeming marvel to pique my curiosity and challenge my investigation. In this book I have set down some of the stories of strange folk and unusual performers that I have gathered in many years of such research.

Much has been written about the feats of miracle-mongers, and not a little in the way of explaining them. Chaucer was by no means the first to turn shrewd eyes upon wonder-workers and show the clay feet of these popular idols. And since his time innumerable marvels, held to be supernatural, have been exposed for the tricks they were. Yet to-day, if a mystifier lack the ingenuity to invent a new and startling stunt, he can safely fall back upon a trick that has been the favorite of pressagents the world over in all ages. He can imitate the Hindoo fakir who, having thrown a rope high into the air, has a boy climb it until he is lost to view. He can even have the feat photographed. The camera will click; nothing will appear on the developed film; and this, the performer will glibly explain, "proves" that the whole company of onlookers was hypnotized! And he can be certain of a very profitable following to defend and advertise him.

So I do not feel that I need to apologize for adding another volume to the shelves of works dealing with the marvels of the miracle-mongers. My business has given me an intimate knowledge of stage illusions, together with many years of experience among show people of all types. My familiarity with the former, and what I have learned of the psychology of the latter, has placed me at a certain advantage in uncovering the natural explanation of feats that to the ignorant have seemed supernatural. And even if my readers are too well informed to be interested in my descriptions of the methods of the various performers who have seemed to me worthy of attention in these pages, I hope they will find some amusement in following the fortunes and misfortunes of all manner of strange folk who once bewildered the wise men of their day. If I have accomplished that much, I shall feel amply repaid for my labor.

HOUDINI.

CONTENTS

CHAPTERS

CHAPTER ONE

FIRE WORSHIP.--FIRE EATING AND HEAT RESISTANCE.--IN THE MIDDLE AGES.--AMONG THE NAVAJO INDIANS.--FIRE-WALKERS OF JAPAN.--THE FIERY ORDEAL OF FIJI.

Fire has always been and, seemingly, will always remain, the most terrible of the elements. To the early tribes, it must also have been the most mysterious; for, while earth and air and water were always in evidence, fire came and went in a manner which must have been quite unaccountable to them. Thus, it naturally followed that the custom of deifying all things which the primitive mind was unable to grasp, led in direct line to the fire-worship of later days.

That fire could be produced through friction finally came into the knowledge of man, but the early methods entailed much labor. Consequently, our ease-loving forebears cast about for a method to "keep the home fires burning" and hit upon the plan of appointing a person in each community who should at all times carry a burning brand. This arrangement had many faults, however, and after a while it was superseded by the expedient of a fire kept continually burning in a building erected for the purpose.

The Greeks worshiped at an altar of this kind which they called the Altar of Hestia and which the Romans called the Altar of Vesta. The sacred fire itself was known as Vesta, and its burning was considered a proof of the presence of the goddess. The Persians had such a building in each town and village; and the Egyptians, such a fire in every temple; while the Mexicans, Natches, Peruvians and Mayas kept their "national fires" burning upon great pyramids. Eventually the keeping of such fires became a sacred rite, and the "Eternal Lamps" kept burning in synagogues and in Byzantine and Catholic churches may be a survival of these customs.

There is a theory that all architecture, public and private, sacred and profane, began with the erection of sheds to protect the sacred fire. This naturally led men to build for their own protection as well, and thus the family hearth had its genesis.

Another theory holds that the keepers of the sacred fires were the first public servants, and that from this small beginning sprang the intricate public service of the present.

The worship of the fire itself had been a legacy from the earliest tribes; but it remained for the Rosicrucians and the fire philosophers of the Sixteenth Century under the lead of Paracelsus to establish a concrete religious belief on that basis, finding in the Scriptures what seemed to them ample proof that fire was the symbol of the actual presence of God, as in all cases where He is said to have visited this earth. He came either in a flame of fire, or surrounded with glory, which they conceived to mean the same thing.

For example: when God appeared on Mount Sinai (Exod. xix, 18) "The Lord descended upon it in fire." Moses, repeating this history, said: "The Lord spake unto you out of the midst of fire" (Deut. iv, 12). Again, when the angel of the Lord appeared to Moses out of the flaming bush, "the bush burned with fire and the bush was not consumed" (Exod. iii, 3). Fire from the Lord consumed the burnt offering of Aaron (Lev. ix, 24), the sacrifice of Gideon (Judg. vi, 21), the burnt offering of David (1 Chron. xxxi, 26), and that at the dedication of King Solomon's temple (Chron. vii, 1). And when Elijah made his sacrifice to prove that Baal was not God, "the fire of the Lord fell and consumed the burnt sacrifice, and the wood, and the stones, and the dust and the water that was in the trench." (1 Kings, xviii, 38.)

Since sacrifice had from the earliest days been considered as food offered to the gods, it was quite logical to argue that when fire from Heaven fell upon the offering, God himself was present and consumed His own. Thus, the Paracelsists and other fire believers sought, and as they believed found, high authority for continuing a part of the fire worship of the early tribes.

The Theosophists, according to Hargrave Jennings in "The Rosicrucians," called the soul a fire taken from the eternal ocean of light, and in common with other Fire-Philosophers believed that all knowable things, both of the soul and the body, were evolved out of fire and finally resolvable into it; and that fire was the last and only-to-be-known God.

In passing I might call attention to the fact that the Devil is supposed to dwell in the same element.

Some of the secrets of heat resistance as practiced by the dime-museum and sideshow performers of our time, secrets grouped under the general title of "Fire-eating," must have been known in very early times. To quote from Chambers' "Book of Days": "In ancient history we find several examples of people who possessed the art of touching fire without being burned. The Priestesses of Diana, at Castabala, in Cappadocia, commanded public veneration by walking over red-hot iron. The Herpi, a people of Etruria, walked among glowing embers at an annual festival held on Mount Soracte, and thus proved their sacred character, receiving certain privileges, among others, exemption from military service, from the Roman Senate. One of the most astounding stories of antiquity is related in the 'Zenda-Vesta,' to the effect

that Zoroaster, to confute his calumniators, allowed fluid lead to be

poured over his body, without receiving any injury."

To me the "astounding" part of this story is not in the feat itself,

for that is extremely easy to accomplish, but in the fact that the

secret was known at such an early date, which the best authorities

place at 500 to 1000 B.C.

It is said that the earliest recorded instance, in our era, of ordeal

by fire was in the fourth century. Simplicius, Bishop of Autun, who

had been married before his promotion, continued to live with his wife,

and in order to demonstrate the Platonic purity of their intercourse

placed burning coals upon their flesh without injury.

That the clergy of the Middle Ages, who caused accused persons to walk

blindfold among red-hot plowshares, or hold heated irons in their

hands, were in possession of the secret of the trick, is shown by the

fact that after trial by ordeal had been abolished the secret of their

methods were published by Albert, Count of Bollstadt, usually called

Albertus Magnus but sometimes Albertus Teutonicus, a man distinguished

by the range of his inquiries and his efforts for the spread of

knowledge.

These secrets will be fully explained in the section of this history devoted to the Arcana of the Fire-Eaters (Chapter Six).

I take the following from the New York Clipper-Annual of 1885:

The famous fire dance of the Navajo Indians, often described as though it involved some sort of genuine necromancy, is explained by a matter-of-fact spectator. It is true, he says, that the naked worshipers cavort round a big bonfire, with blazing torches in their hands, and dash the flames over their own and their fellows' bodies, all in a most picturesque and maniacal fashion; but their skins are first so thickly coated with a clay paint that they cannot easily be burned.

An illustrated article entitled Rites of the Firewalking Fanatics of Japan, by W. C. Jameson Reid, in the Chicago Sunday Inter-Ocean of September 27th, 1903, reveals so splendid an example of the gullibility of the well-informed when the most ordinary trick is cleverly presented and surrounded with the atmosphere of the occult, that I am impelled to place before my readers a few illuminating excerpts from Mr. Reid's narrative. This man would, in all probability, scorn to spend a dime to witness the performance of a fire-eater in a circus sideshow; but after traveling half round the world he pays a dollar and spends an hour's time watching the fanatical incantations of the solemn little Japanese priests for the sake of seeing the "Hi-Wattarai"--which is merely the stunt of walking over hot coals--and he then writes it down as the "eighth wonder of the world," while if he had taken the trouble to give the matter even the most superficial investigation, he could have discovered that the secret of the trick had been made public centuries before.

Mr. Reid is authority for the statement that the Shintoist priests' fire-walking rites have "long been one of the puzzling mysteries of the scientific world," and adds "If you ever are in Tokio, and can find a few minutes to spare, by all means do not neglect witnessing at least one performance of 'Hi-Wattarai' (fire walking, and that is really what takes place), for, if you are of that incredulous nature which laughs with scorn at so-called Eastern mysticism, you will come away, as has many a visitor before you, with an impression sufficient to last through an ordinary lifetime." Further on he says "If you do not come away convinced that you have been witness of a spectacle which makes you disbelieve the evidence of your own eyes and your most matter-of-fact judgment, then you are a man of stone." All of which proves nothing more than that Mr. Reid was inclined to make positive statements about subjects in which he knew little or nothing.

He tells us further that formerly this rite was performed only in the spring and fall, when, beside the gratuities of the foreigners, the native worshipers brought "gifts of wine, large trays of fish, fruit, rice cakes, loaves, vegetables, and candies." Evidently the combination of box-office receipts with donation parties proved extremely tempting to the thrifty priests, for they now give what might be termed a "continuous performance."

Those who have read the foregoing pages will apply a liberal sprinkling of salt to the solemn assurance of Mr. Reid, advanced on the authority of Jinrikisha boys, that "for days beforehand the priests connected with the temple devote themselves to fasting and prayer to prepare for the ordeal. . . . The performance itself usually takes place in the late afternoon during twilight in the temple court, the preceding three hours being spent by the priests in final outbursts of prayer before the unveiled altar in the inner sanctuary of the little matted temple, and during these invocations no visitors are allowed to enter the sacred precincts."

Mr. Reid's description of the fire walking itself may not be out of place; it will show that the Japs had nothing new to offer aside from the ritualistic ceremonials with which they camouflaged the hocus-pocus of the performance, which is merely a survival of the ordeal by fire of earlier religions.

"Shortly before 5 o'clock the priests filed from before the altar into some interior apartments, where they were to change their beautiful robes for the coarser dress worn during the fire walking. In the meantime coolies had been set to work in the courtyard to ignite the great bed of charcoal, which had already been laid. The dimensions of this bed were about twelve feet by four, and, perhaps, a foot deep. On the top was a quantity of straw and kindling wood, which was lighted, and soon burst into a roaring blaze. The charcoal became more and more thoroughly ignited until the whole mass glowed in the uncertain gloom, like some gigantic and demoniacal eye of a modern Prometheus. As soon as the mass of charcoal was thoroughly ignited from top to bottom, a small gong in the temple gave notice that the wonderful spectacle of 'Hi-Wattarai' was about to begin.

"Soon two of the priests came out, said prayers of almost interminable length at a tiny shrine in the corner of the enclosure, and turned their attention to the fire. Taking long poles and fans from the coolies, they poked and encouraged the blaze till it could plainly be seen that the coal was ignited throughout. The whole bed was a glowing mass, and the heat which rose from it was so intense that we found it uncomfortable to sit fifteen feet away from it without screening our faces with fans. Then they began to pound it down more solidly along the middle; as far as possible inequalities in its surface were beaten down, and the coals which protruded were brushed aside."

There follows a long and detailed description of further ceremonies, the receiving of gifts, etc., which need not be repeated here. Now for the trick itself.

"One of the priests held a pile of white powder on a small wooden stand. This was said to be salt--which in Japan is credited with great cleansing properties--but as far as could be ascertained by superficial examination it was a mixture of alum and salt. He stood at one end of the fire-bed and poised the wooden tray over his head, and then sprinkled a handful of it on the ground before the glowing bed of coals. At the same time, another priest who stood by him chanted a weird recitative of invocation and struck sparks from flint and steel which he held in his hands. This same process was repeated by both the priests at the other end, at the two sides, and at the corners.

"Ten minutes, more or less, was spent in various movements and incantations about the bed of coals. At the end of that time two small pieces of wet matting were brought out and placed at either end and a quantity of the white mixture was placed upon them. At a signal from the head priest, who acted as master of ceremonies during the curious succeeding function, the ascetics who were to perform the first exhibition of fire-walking gathered at one end of the bed of coals, which by this time was a fierce and glowing furnace.

"Having raised both his hands and prostrated himself to render thanks to the god who had taken out the 'soul' of the fire, the priest about to undergo the ordeal stood upon the wet matting, wiped his feet lightly in the white mixture, and while we held our breaths, and our eyes almost leaped from their sockets in awe-struck astonishment, he walked over the glowing mass as unconcernedly as if treading on a carpet in a drawing-room, his feet coming in contact with the white hot coals at every step. He did not hurry or take long steps, but sauntered along with almost incredible sang-froid, and before he reached the opposite side he turned around and sauntered as carelessly back to the mat from which he had started."

The story goes on to tell how the performance was repeated by the other priests, and then by many of the native audience; but none of the Europeans tried it, although invited to do so. Mr. Reid's closing statement is that "no solution of the mystery can be gleaned, even from high scientific authorities who have witnessed and closely studied the physical features of these remarkable Shinto fire-walking rites." Many who are confronted with something that they cannot explain take refuge in the claim that it puzzles the scientists too. As a matter of fact, at the time Mr. Reid wrote, such scientists as had given the subject serious study were pretty well posted on the methods involved.

An article under the title The Fiery Ordeal of Fiji, by Maurice Delcasse, appeared in the Wide World Magazine for May, 1898. From Mr. Delcasse's account it appears that the Fijian ordeal is practically the same as that of the Japanese, as described by Mr. Reid, except that there is very little ceremony surrounding it. The people of Fiji until a comparatively recent date were cannibals; but their islands are now British possessions, most of the natives are Christians, and most of their ancient customs have become obsolete, from which I deduce that the fire-walking rites described in this article must have been performed by natives who had retained their old religious beliefs.

The ordeal takes place on the Island of Benga, which is near Suva, the capital of Fiji, and which, Mr. Delcasse says, "was the supposed residence of some of the old gods of Fiji, and was, therefore, considered a sacred land." Instead of walking on the live coals, as the

Japanese priests do, the Fijians walk on stones that have been brought to a white heat in a great fire of logs.

The familiar claim is made that the performance puzzles scientists, and that no satisfactory solution has yet been discovered. We are about to see that for two or three hundred years the same claims have been made by a long line of more or less clever public performers in Europe and America.

CHAPTER TWO

WATTON'S SHIP-SWABBER "FROM THE INDIES."--RICHARDSON, 1667--DE

HEITERKEIT, 1713.--ROBERT POWELL, 1718-1780.--DUFOUR,

1783.--QUACKENSALBER, 1794.

The earliest mention I have found of a public fire-eater in England is

in the correspondence of Sir Henry Watton, under date of June 3rd,

1633. He speaks of an Englishman "like some swabber of a ship, come

from the Indies, where he has learned to eat fire as familiarly as ever

I saw any eat cakes, even whole glowing brands, which he will crush

with his teeth and swallow." This was shown in London for two pence.

The first to attract the attention of the upper classes, however, was

one Richardson, who appeared in France in the year 1667 and enjoyed a

vogue sufficient to justify the record of his promise in the Journal

des Savants. Later on he came to London, and John Evelyn, in his diary,

mentions him under date of October 8th, 1672, as follows:

I took leave of my Lady Sunderland, who was going to Paris to my Lord,

now Ambassador there. She made me stay dinner at Leicester House, and afterwards sent for Richardson, the famous fire-eater. He devoured

brimstone on glowing coals before us, chewing and swallowing them; he

melted a beere-glass and eate it quite up; then taking a live coale on

his tongue he put on it a raw oyster; the coal was blown on with

bellows till it flamed and sparkled in his mouthe, and so remained

until the oyster gaped and was quite boil'd.

Then he melted pitch and wax with sulphur, which he drank down as it

flamed: I saw it flaming in his mouthe a good while; he also took up a

thick piece of iron, such as laundresses use to put in their

smoothing-boxes, when it was fiery hot, held it between his teeth, then

in his hand, and threw it about like a stone; but this I observ'd he

cared not to hold very long. Then he stoode on a small pot, and,

bending his body, tooke a glowing iron with his mouthe from betweene

his feete, without touching the pot or ground with his hands, with

divers other prodigious feats.

The secret methods employed by Richardson were disclosed by his

servant, and this publicity seems to have brought his career to a

sudden close; at least I have found no record of his subsequent

movements.

About 1713 a fire-eater named De Heiterkeit, a native of Annivi, in Savoy, flourished for a time in London. He performed five times a day at the Duke of Marlborough's Head, in Fleet Street, the prices being half-a-crown, eighteen pence and one shilling.

According to London Tit-Bits, "De Heiterkeit had the honor of exhibiting before Louis XIV., the Emperor of Austria, the King of Sicily and the Doge of Venice, and his name having reached the Inquisition, that holy office proposed experimenting on him to find out whether he was fireproof externally as well as internally. He was preserved from this unwelcome ordeal, however, by the interference of the Duchess Royal, Regent of Savoy."

His programme did not differ materially from that of his predecessor, Richardson, who had antedated him by nearly fifty years.

By far the most famous of the early fire-eaters was Robert Powell, whose public career extended over a period of nearly sixty years, and who was patronized by the English peerage. It was mainly through the instrumentality of Sir Hans Sloane that, in 1751, the Royal Society presented Powell a purse of gold and a large silver medal.

Lounger's Commonplace Book says of Powell: "Such is his passion for this terrible element, that if he were to come hungry into your kitchen, while a sirloin was roasting, he would eat up the fire and leave the beef. It is somewhat surprising that the friends of REAL MERIT have not yet promoted him, living as we do in an age favorable to men of genius. Obliged to wander from place to place, instead of indulging himself in private with his favorite dish, he is under the uncomfortable necessity of eating in public, and helping himself from the kitchen fire of some paltry ale-house in the country."

His advertisements show that he was before the public from 1718 to 1780. One of his later advertisements runs as follows:

SUM SOLUS

Please observe that there are two different performances the same evening, which will be performed by the famous

MR. POWELL, FIRE-EATER, FROM LONDON:

who has had the honor to exhibit, with universal applause, the most surprising performances that were ever attempted by mankind, before His Royal Highness William, late Duke of Cumberland, at Windsor Lodge, May

7th, 1752; before His Royal Highness the Duke of Gloucester, at Gloucester House, January 30th, 1769; before His Royal Highness the present Duke of Cumberland, at Windsor Lodge, September 25th, 1769; before Sir Hans Sloane and several of the Royal Society, March 4th, 1751, who made Mr. Powell a compliment of a purse of gold, and a fine large silver medal, which the curious may view by applying to him; and before most of the Nobility and Quality in the Kingdom.

He intends to sup on the following articles: 1. He eats red-hot coals out of the fire as natural as bread. 2. He licks with his naked tongue red-hot tobacco pipes, flaming with brimstone. 3. He takes a large bunch of deal matches, lights them altogether; and holds them in his mouth till the flame is extinguished. 4. He takes a red-hot heater out of the fire, licks it with his naked tongue several times, and carries it around the room between his teeth. 5. He fills his mouth with red-hot charcoal, and broils a slice of beef or mutton upon his tongue, and any person may blow the fire with a pair of bellows at the same time. 6. He takes a quantity of resin, pitch, bees'-wax, sealing-wax, brimstone, alum, and lead, melts them all together over a chafing-dish of coals, and eats the same combustibles with a spoon, as if it were a porringer of broth (which he calls his dish of soup), to the great and agreeable surprise of the spectators; with various other extraordinary performances never attempted by any other person of this age, and there is scarce a possibility ever will; so that those who neglect this opportunity of seeing the wonders performed by this artist, will lose the sight of the most amazing exhibition ever done by man.

The doors to be opened by six and he sups precisely at seven o'clock, without any notice given by sound of trumpet.

If gentry do not choose to come at seven o'clock, no performance.

Prices of admission to ladies and gentlemen, one shilling. Back Seats for Children and Servants, six pence.

Ladies and children may have a private performance any hour of the day, by giving previous notice.

N. B.--He displaces teeth or stumps so easily as to scarce be felt. He sells a chemical liquid which discharges inflammation, scalds, and burns, in a short time, and is necessary to be kept in all families.

His stay in this place will be but short, not exceeding above two or three nights.

Good fire to keep the gentry warm.

This shows how little advance had been made in the art in a century. Richardson had presented practically the same programme a hundred years before. Perhaps the exposure of Richardson's method by his servant put an end to fire-eating as a form of amusement for a long time, or until the exposure had been forgotten by the public. Powell himself, though not proof against exposure, seems to have been proof against its effects, for he kept on the even tenor of his way for sixty years, and at the end of his life was still exhibiting.

Whatever the reason, the eighteenth-century fire-eaters, like too many magicians of the present day, kept to the stereotyped programmes of their predecessors. A very few did, however, step out of the beaten track and, by adding new tricks and giving a new dress to old ones, succeeded in securing a following that was financially satisfactory.

In this class, a Frenchman by the name of Dufour deserves special mention, from the fact that he was the first to introduce comedy into an act of this nature. He made his bow in Paris in 1783, and is said to have created quite a sensation by his unusual performance. I am indebted to Martin's Naturliche Magie, 1792, for a very complete description of the work of this artist.

Dufour made use of a portable building, which was specially adapted to

his purposes, and his table was spread as if for a banquet, except that

the edibles were such as his performance demanded. He employed a

trumpeter and a tambour player to furnish music for his repast--as well

as to attract public attention. In addition to fire-eating, Dufour

gave exhibitions of his ability to consume immense quantities of solid

food, and he displayed an appetite for live animals, reptiles, and

insects that probably proved highly entertaining to the not overrefined

taste of the audiences of his day. He even advertised a banquet of

which the public was invited to partake at a small fee per plate, but

since the menu consisted of the delicacies just described, his

audiences declined to join him at table.

His usual bill-of-fare was as follows:

Soup--boiling tar torches, glowing coals and small, round, super-heated

stones.

The roast, when Dufour was really hungry, consisted of twenty pounds of

beef or a whole calf. His hearth was either the flat of his hand or

his tongue. The butter in which the roast was served was melted

brimstone or burning wax. When the roast was cooked to suit him he ate coals and roast together.

As a dessert, he would swallow the knives and forks, glasses, and the earthenware dishes.

He kept his audience in good humor by presenting all this in a spirit of crude comedy and, to increase the comedy element, he introduced a number of trained cats. Although the thieving proclivities of cats are well known, Dufour's pets showed no desire to share his repast, and he had them trained to obey his commands during mealtime. At the close of the meal he would become violently angry with one of them, seize the unlucky offender, tear it limb from limb and eat the carcass. One of his musicians would then beg him to produce the cat, dead or alive. In order to do this he would go to a nearby horse-trough and drink it dry; would eat a number of pounds of soap, or other nauseating substance, clowning it in a manner to provoke amusement instead of disgust; and, further to mask the disagreeable features--and also, no doubt, to conceal the trick--would take the cloth from the table and cover his face; whereupon he would bring forth the swallowed cat, or one that looked like it, which would howl piteously and seem to struggle wildly while being disgorged. When freed, the poor cat would rush away among the spectators.

Dufour gave his best performances in the evening, as he could then show his hocus-pocus to best advantage. At these times he appeared with a halo of fire about his head.

His last appearance in Paris was most remarkable. The dinner began with a soup of asps in simmering oil. On each side was a dish of vegetables, one containing thistles and burdocks, and the other fuming acid. Other side dishes, of turtles, rats, bats and moles, were garnished with live coals. For the fish course, he ate a dish of snakes in boiling tar and pitch. His roast was a screech owl in a sauce of glowing brimstone. The salad proved to be spider webs full of small explosive squibs, a plate of butterfly wings and manna worms, a dish of toads surrounded with flies, crickets, grasshoppers, church beetles, spiders, and caterpillars. He washed all this down with flaming brandy, and for dessert ate the four large candles standing on the table, both of the hanging side lamps with their contents, and finally the large center lamp, oil, wick and all. This leaving the room in darkness, Dufour's face shone out in a mask of living flames.

A dog had come in with a farmer, who was probably a confederate, and now began to bark. Since Dufour could not quiet him, he seized him, bit off his head and swallowed it, throwing the body aside. Then ensued a comic scene between Dufour and the farmer, the latter demanding that his dog be brought to life, which threw the audience into paroxysms of laughter. Then suddenly candles reappeared and seemed to light themselves. Dufour made a series of hocus-pocus passes over the dog's body; then the head suddenly appeared in its proper place, and the dog, with a joyous yelp, ran to his master.

Notwithstanding the fact that Dufour must have been by all odds the best performer of his time, I do not find reference to him in any other authority. But something of his originality appeared in the work of a much humbler practitioner, contemporary or very nearly contemporary with him.

We have seen that Richardson, Powell, Dufour, and generally the better class of fire-eaters were able to secure select audiences and even to attract the attention of scientists in England and on the Continent. But many of their effects had been employed by mountebanks and street fakirs since the earliest days of the art, and this has continued until comparatively recent times.

In Naturliche Magie, in 1794, Vol. VI, page 111, I find an account of one Quackensalber, who gave a new twist to the fire-eating industry by making a "High Pitch" at the fairs and on street corners and exhibiting feats of fire-resistance, washing his hands and face in melted tar, pitch and brimstone, in order to attract a crowd. He then strove to sell them a compound--composed of fish glue, alum and brandy--which he claimed would cure burns in two or three hours. He demonstrated that this mixture was used by him in his heat resistance: and then, doubtless, some "capper" started the ball rolling, and Herr Quackensalber (his name indicates a seller of salves) reaped a good harvest.

I have no doubt but that even to-day a clever performer with this "High Pitch" could do a thriving business in that overgrown country village, New York. At any rate there is the so-called, "King of Bees," a gentleman from Pennsylvania, who exhibits himself in a cage of netting filled with bees, and then sells the admiring throng a specific for bee-stings and the wounds of angry wasps. Unfortunately, the only time I ever saw his majesty, some of his bee actors must have forgotten their lines, for he was thoroughly stung.

CHAPTER THREE

THE NINETEENTH CENTURY.--A "WONDERFUL PHENOMENON."--"THE INCOMBUSTIBLE

SPANIARD, SENOR LIONETTO," 1803.--JOSEPHINE GIRARDELLI, 1814.--JOHN

BROOKS, 1817.--W. C. HOUGHTON, 1832.--J. A. B. CHYLINSKI,

1841.--CHAMOUNI, THE RUSSIAN SALAMANDER, 1869.--PROFESSOR REL MAEUB,

1876.--RIVALLI (died 1900).

In the nineteenth century by far the most distinguished heat-resister

was Chabert, who deserves and shall have a chapter to himself. He

commenced exhibiting about 1818, but even earlier in the century

certain obscurer performers had anticipated some of his best effects.

Among my clippings, for instance, I find the following. I regret that

I cannot give the date, but it is evident from the long form of the

letters that it was quite early. This is the first mention I have

found of the hot-oven effect afterwards made famous by Chabert.

WONDERFUL PHENOMENON

A correspondent in France writes as follows: "Paris has, for some days, rung with relations of the wonderful exploits of a Spaniard in that city, who is endowed with qualities by which he resists the action of very high degrees of heat, as well as the influence of strong chemical reagents. Many histories of the trials to which he has been submitted before a Commission of the Institute and Medical School, have appeared in the public papers; but the public waits with impatience for the report to be made in the name of the Commission by Professor Pinel.

The subject of these trials is a young man, a native of Toledo, in Spain, 23 years of age, and free of any apparent peculiarities which can announce anything remarkable in the organization of his skin; after examination, one would be rather disposed to conclude a peculiar softness than that any hardness or thickness of the cuticle existed, either naturally or from mechanical causes. Nor was there any circumstance to indicate that the person had been previously rubbed with any matter capable of resisting the operation of the agents with which he was brought in contact.

This man bathed for the space of five minutes, and without any injury to his sensibility or the surface of the skin, his legs in oil, heated at 97 degrees of Reaumur (250 degrees of Fahrenheit) and with the same

oil, at the same degree of heat, he washed his face and superior

extremities. He held, for the same space of time, and with as little

inconvenience, his legs in a solution of muriate of soda, heated to 102

of the same scale, (261 1/2 degrees Fahr.) He stood on and rubbed the

soles of his feet with a bar of hot iron heated to a white heat; in

this state he held the iron in his hands and rubbed the surface of his

tongue.

He gargled his mouth with concentrated sulphuric and nitric acids,

without the smallest injury or discoloration; the nitric acid changed

the cuticle to a yellow color; with the acids in this state he rubbed

his hands and arms. All these experiments were continued long enough

to prove their inefficiency to produce any impression. It is said, on

unquestionable authority, that he remained a considerable time in an

oven heated to 65 degrees or 70 degrees, (178-189 degrees Fahr.) and

from which he was with difficulty induced to retire, so comfortable did

he feel at that high temperature.

It may be proper to remark, that this man seems totally uninfluenced by

any motive to mislead, and, it is said, he has refused flattering

offers from some religious sectaries of turning to emolument his

singular qualities; yet on the whole it seems to be the opinion of most philosophical men, that this person must possess some matter which counteracts the operation of these agents. To suppose that nature has organized him differently, would be unphilosophic: by habit he might have blunted his sensibilities against those impressions that create pain under ordinary circumstances; but how to explain the power by which he resists the action of those agents which are known to have the strongest affinity for animal matter, is a circumstance difficult to comprehend. It has not failed, however, to excite the wonder of the ignorant and the inquiry of the learned at Paris."

This "Wonderful Phenomenon" may have been "the incombustible Spaniard, Senor Lionetto," whom the London Mirror mentions as performing in Paris in 1803 "where he attracted the particular attention of Dr. Sementeni, Professor of Chemistry, and other scientific gentlemen of that city. It appears that a considerable vapor and smell rose from parts of his body when the fire and heated substances were applied, and in this he seems to differ from the person now in this country." The person here referred to was M. Chabert.

Dr. Sementeni became so interested in the subject that he made a series of experiments upon himself, and these were finally crowned with success. His experiments will receive further attention in the chapter "The Arcana of the Fire-Eaters."

A veritable sensation was created in England in the year 1814 by Senora Josephine Girardelli, who was heralded as having "just arrived from the Continent, where she had the honor of appearing before most of the crowned heads of Europe." She was first spoken of as German, but afterwards proved to be of Italian birth.

Entering a field of endeavor which had heretofore been exclusively occupied by the sterner sex, this lady displayed a taste for hot meals that would seem to recommend her as a matrimonial venture. Like all the earlier exploiters of the devouring element, she was proclaimed as "The Great Phenomena of Nature"--why the plural form was used does not appear--and, doubtless, her feminine instincts led her to impart a daintiness to her performance which must have appealed to the better class of audience in that day.

The portrait that adorned her first English handbill, which I produce from the Picture Magazine, was engraved by Page and published by Smeeton, St. Martins Lane, London. It is said to be a faithful representation of her stage costume and setting.

Richardson, of Bartholomew Fair fame, who was responsible for the introduction of many novelties, first presented Girardelli to an

English audience at Portsmouth, where her success was so pronounced that a London appearance was arranged for the same year; and at Mr. Laston's rooms, 23 New Bond Street, her performance attracted the most fashionable metropolitan audiences for a considerable time. Following this engagement she appeared at Richardson's Theater, at Bartholomew Fair, and afterwards toured England in the company of Signor Germondi, who exhibited a troupe of wonderful trained dogs. One of the canine actors was billed as the "Russian Moscow Fire Dog, an animal unknown in this country, (and never exhibited before) who now delights in that element, having been trained for the last six months at very great expense and fatigue."

Whether Girardelli accumulated sufficient wealth to retire or became discouraged by the exposure of her methods cannot now be determined, but after she had occupied a prominent position in the public eye and the public prints for a few seasons she dropped out of sight, and I have been unable to find where or how she passed the later years of her life.

I am even more at a loss concerning her contemporary, John Brooks, of whom I have no other record than the following letter, which appears in the autobiography of the famous author-actor-manager, Thomas Dibdin, of the Theaters Royal, Covent Garden, Drury Lane, Haymarket and others.

This one communication, however, absolves of any obligation to dig up proofs of John Brooks' versatility: he admits it himself.

To Mr. T. Dibdin, Esq. Pripetor of the Royal Circus.

May 1st, 1817.

Sir:

I have taken the Liberty of Riting those few lines to ask you the favour if a Greeable for me to Come to your House, as i Can do a great many different things i Can Sing a good Song and i Can Eat Boiling hot Lead and Rub my naked arms With a Red hot Poker and Stand on a Red hot sheet of iron, and do Diferent other things.--Sir i hope you Will Excuse me in Riting I do not Want any thing for my Performing for i have Got a Business that will Sirport me I only want to pass a Way 2 or 3 Hours in the Evening. Sir i hope you Will Send me an Answer Weather Agreeple or not.

I am your Humble Servant,

J. B.

Direct to me No. 4 fox and Knot Court King Street Smithfield.

JOHN BROOKS.

We shall let this versatile John Brooks close the pre-Chabert record

and turn our attention to the fire-eaters of Chabert's day. Imitation

may be the sincerest flattery, but in most cases the victim of the

imitation, it is safe to say, will gladly dispense with that form of

adulation. When Chabert first came to America and gave fresh impetus to

the fire-eating art by the introduction of new and startling material,

he was beset by many imitators, or--as they probably styled

themselves--rivals, who immediately proceeded, so far as in them lay,

to out-Chabert Chabert.

One of the most prominent of these was a man named W. C. Houghton, who

claimed to have challenged Chabert at various times. In a newspaper

advertisement in Philadelphia, where he was scheduled to give a benefit

performance on Saturday evening, February 4th, 1832, he practically

promised to expose the method of poison eating. Like that of all

exposers, however, his vogue was of short duration, and very little can be found about this super-Chabert except his advertisements. The following will serve as a sample of them:

ARCH STREET THEATRE BENEFIT

OF THE AMERICAN FIRE KING

A CARD.--W. C. Houghton, has the honor to announce to the ladies and gentlemen of Philadelphia, that his BENEFIT will take place at the ARCH STREET THEATRE, on Saturday evening next, 4th February, when will be presented a variety of entertainments aided by the whole strength of the company.

Mr. H. in addition to his former experiments will exhibit several fiery feats, pronounced by Mons. Chabert an IMPOSSIBILITY. He will give a COMPLETE explanation by illustrations of the PRINCIPLES of the EUROPEAN and the AMERICAN CHESS PLAYERS. He will also (unless prevented by indisposition) swallow a sufficient quantity of phosphorus, (presented by either chemist or druggist of this city) to destroy THE LIFE OF ANY INDIVIDUAL. Should he not feel disposed to take the poison, he will satisfactorily explain to the audience the manner it may be taken without injury.

In our next chapter we shall see how it went with others who challenged Chabert.

A Polish athlete, J. A. B. Chylinski by name, toured Great Britain and Ireland in 1841, and presented a more than usually diversified entertainment. Being gifted by nature with exceptional bodily strength, and trained in gymnastics, he was enabled to present a mixed programme, combining his athletics with feats of strength, fire-eating, poison-swallowing, and fire-resistance.

In The Book of Wonderful Characters, published in 1869 by John Camden Hotten, London, I find an account of Chamouni, the Russian Salamander: "He was insensible, for a given time, to the effects of heat. He was remarkable for the simplicity and singleness of his character, as well as for that idiosyncrasy in his constitution, which enabled him for so many years, not merely to brave the effects of fire, but to take a delight in an element where other men find destruction. He was above all artifice, and would often entreat his visitors to melt their own lead, or boil their own mercury, that they might be perfectly satisfied of the gratification he derived from drinking these preparations. He would also present his tongue in the most obliging manner to all who

wished, to pour melted lead upon it and stamp an impression of their
seals."

A fire-proof billed as Professor Rel Maeub, was on the programme at the
opening of the New National Theater, in Philadelphia, Pa., in the
spring of 1876. If I am not mistaken the date was April 25th. He
called himself "The Great Inferno Fire-King," and his novelty consisted
in having a strip of wet carpeting running parallel to the hot iron
plates on which he walked barefoot, and stepping on it occasionally and
back onto the hot iron, when a loud hissing and a cloud of steam bore
ample proof of the high temperature of the metal.

One of the more recent fireproofs was Eugene Rivalli, whose act
included, besides the usual effects, a cage of fire in which he stood
completely surrounded by flames. Rivalli, whose right name was John
Watkins, died in 1900, in England. He had appeared in Great Britain
and Ireland as well as on the Continent during the later years of the
19th century.

The cage of fire has been used by a number of Rivalli's followers also,
and the reader will find a full explanation of the methods employed for
it in the chapter devoted to the Arcana of the Fire-eaters, to which we
shall come when we have recorded the work of the master Chabert, the

history of some of the heat-resisters featured on magicians'

programmes, particularly in our own day, and the interest taken in this

art by performers whose chief distinction was won in other fields, as

notably Edwin Forrest and the elder Sothern.

CHAPTER FOUR

THE MASTER--CHABERT, 1792-1859.

Ivan Ivanitz Chabert, the only Really Incombustible Phenomenon, as he was billed abroad, or J. Xavier Chabert, A.M., M.D., etc., as he was afterwards known in this country, was probably the most notable, and certainly, the most interesting, character in the history of fire-eating, fire-resistance, and poison eating. He was the last prominent figure in the long line of this type of artists to appeal to the better classes and to attract the attention of scientists, who for a considerable period treated his achievements more or less seriously. Henry Evanion gave me a valuable collection of Chabert clippings, hand-bills, etc., and related many interesting incidents in connection with this man of wonders.

It seems quite impossible for me to write of any historical character in Magic or its allied arts without recalling my dear old friend Evanion, who introduced me to a throng of fascinating characters, with each of whom he seemed almost as familiar as if they had been daily companions.

Subsequently I discovered an old engraving of Chabert, published in London in 1829, and later still another which bore the change of name, as well as the titles enumerated above. The latter was published in New York, September, 1836, and bore the inscription: "One of the most celebrated Chemists, Philosophers, and Physicians of the present day." These discoveries, together with a clue from Evanion, led to further investigations, which resulted in the interesting discovery that this one-time Bartholomew Fair entertainer spent the last years of his life in New York City. He resided here for twenty-seven years and lies buried in the beautiful Cypress Hills Cemetery, quite forgotten by the man on the street.

Nearby is the grave of good old Signor Blitz, and not far away is the plot that holds all that is mortal of my beloved parents. When I finally break away from earthly chains and restraints, I hope to be placed beside them.

During my search for data regarding Chabert I looked in the telephone book for a possible descendant. By accident I picked up the Suburban instead of the Metropolitan edition, and there I found a Victor E. Chabert living at Allenhurst, N. J. I immediately got into communication with him and found that he was a grandson of the Fire King, but he could give me no more information than I already possessed, which I now spread before my readers.

M. Chabert was a son of Joseph and Therese Julienne Chabert. He was born on May 10th, 1792, at Avignon, France.

Chabert was a soldier in the Napoleonic wars, was exiled to Siberia and escaped to England. His grandson has a bronze Napoleon medal which was presented to Chabert, presumably for valor on the field of battle. Napoleon was exiled in 1815 and again three years later. Chabert first attracted public notice in Paris, at which time his demonstrations of heat-resistance were sufficiently astonishing to merit the attention of no less a body than the National Institute.

To the more familiar feats of his predecessors he added startling novelties in the art of heat-resistance, the most spectacular being that of entering a large iron cabinet, which resembled a common baker's oven, heated to the usual temperature of such ovens. He carried in his hand a leg of mutton and remained until the meat was thoroughly cooked. Another thriller involved standing in a flaming tar-barrel until it was entirely consumed around him.

In 1828, Chabert gave a series of performances at the Argyle Rooms in London, and created a veritable sensation. A correspondent in the

London Mirror has this to say of Chabert's work at that time: "Of M. Chabert's wonderful power of withstanding the operation of the fiery element, it is in the recollection of the writer of witnessing, some few years back, this same individual (in connection with the no-less fire-proof Signora Girardelli) exhibiting 'extraordinary proofs of his supernatural power of resisting the most intense heat of every kind.' Since which an IMPROVEMENT of a more formidable nature has to our astonished fancy been just demonstrated. In the newspapers of the past week it is reported that he, in the first instance, refreshed himself with a hearty meal of phosphorus, which was, at his own request, supplied to him very liberally by several of his visitors, who were previously unacquainted with him. He washed down (they say) this infernal fare with solutions of arsenic and oxalic acid; thus throwing into the background the long-established fame of Mithridates. He next swallowed with great gout, several spoonfuls of boiling oil; and, as a dessert to this delicate repast, helped himself with his naked hands to a considerable quantity of molten lead. The experiment, however, of entering into a hot oven, together with a quantity of meat, sufficient, when cooked, to regale those of his friends who were specially invited to witness his performance, was the chef-d'oeuvre of the day. Having ordered three fagots of wood, which is the quantity generally used by bakers, to be thrown into the oven, and they being set on fire, twelve more fagots of the same size were subsequently added to them, which being all consumed by three o'clock, M. Chabert entered the oven with a

dish of raw meat, and when it was sufficiently done he handed it out,

took in another, and remained therein until the second quantity was

also well cooked; he then came out of the oven, and sat down, continues

the report, to partake, with a respectable assembly of friends, of

those viands he had so closely attended during the culinary process.

Publicly, on a subsequent day, and in an oven 6 feet by 7, and at a

heat of about 220, he remained till a steak was properly done, and

again returned to his fiery den and continued for a period of thirty

minutes, in complete triumph over the power of an element so much

dreaded by humankind, and so destructive to animal nature. It has been

properly observed, that there are preparations which so indurate the

cuticle, as to render it insensible to the heat of either boiling oil

or melted lead; and the fatal qualities of certain poisons may be

destroyed, if the medium through which they are imbibed, as we suppose

to be the case here, is a strong alkali. Many experiments, as to the

extent to which the human frame could bear heat, without the

destruction of the vital powers, have been tried from time to time; but

so far as recollection serves, Monsieur Chabert's fire-resisting

qualities are greater than those professed by individuals who, before

him, have undergone this species of ordeal."

It was announced some time ago, in one of the French journals, that experiments had been tried with a female, whose fire-standing qualities had excited great astonishment. She, it appears, was placed in a heated oven, into which live dogs, cats, and rabbits were conveyed. The poor animals died in a state of convulsion almost immediately, while the Fire-queen bore the heat without complaining. In that instance, however, the heat of the oven was not so great as that which M. Chabert encountered.

Much of the power to resist greater degrees of heat than can other men may be a natural gift, much the result of chemical applications, and much from having the parts indurated by long practice; probably all three are combined in this phenomenon, with some portion of artifice.

In Timbs' Curiosities of London, published in 1867, I find the following:

At the Argyle Rooms, London, in 1829, Mons. Chabert, the Fire-King, exhibited his powers of resisting poisons, and withstanding extreme heat. He swallowed forty grains of phosphorus, sipped oil at 333 degrees with impunity, and rubbed a red-hot fire-shovel over his tongue, hair, and face, unharmed.

On September 23d, on a challenge of L50, Chabert repeated these feats and won the wager; he next swallowed a piece of burning torch; and then, dressed in coarse woolen, entered an oven heated to 380 degrees, sang a song, and cooked two dishes of beef steaks.

Still, the performances were suspected, and in fact, proved to be a chemical juggle.

Another challenge in the same year is recorded under the heading, "Sights of London," as follows:

We were tempted on Wednesday to the Argyle Rooms by the challenge of a person of the uncommon name of J. Smith to M. Chabert, our old friend the Fire King, whom this individual dared to invite to a trial of powers in swallowing poison and being baked! The audacity of such a step quite amazed us; and expecting to see in the competitor at least a Vulcan, the God of all Smiths, was hastened to the scene of strife. Alas, our disappointment was complete! Smith had not even the courage of a blacksmith for standing fire, and yielded a stake of L50, as was stated, without a contest, to M. Chabert, on the latter coming out of his oven with his own two steaks perfectly cooked. On this occasion

Chabert took 20 grains of phosphorus, swallowed oil heated to nearly 100 degrees above boiling water, took molten lead out of a ladle with his fingers and cooled it on his tongue; and, besides performing other remarkable feats, remained five minutes in the oven at a temperature of between 300 and 400 degrees by the thermometer. There was about 150 persons present, many of them medical men; and being convinced that these things were fairly done, without trickery, much astonishment was expressed.

The following detailed account of the latter challenge appeared in the Chronicle, London, September, 1829.

THE FIRE KING AND HIS CHALLENGER.--An advertisement appeared lately in one of the papers, in which a Mr. J. Smith after insinuating that M. Chabert practised some juggle when he appeared to enter an oven heated to five hundred degrees, and to swallow twenty grains of phosphorus, challenged him to perform the exploits which he professed to be performing daily. In consequence M. Chabert publicly accepted Mr. J. Smith's challenge for L50, requesting him to provide the poison himself. A day was fixed upon which the challenge was to be determined, and at two o'clock on that day, a number of gentlemen assembled in the Argyle-rooms, where the exhibition was to take place.

At a little before three the fire-king made his appearance near his oven, and as some impatience had been exhibited, owing to the non-arrival of Mr. J. Smith, he offered to amuse the company with a few trifling experiments. He made a shovel red-hot and rubbed it over his tongue, a trick for which no credit, he said, was due, as the moisture of the tongue was sufficient to prevent any injury arising from it. He next rubbed it over his hair and face, declaring that anybody might perform the same feat by first washing themselves in a mixture of spirits of sulphur and alum, which, by cauterising the epidermis, hardened the skin to resist the fire.

He put his hand into some melted lead, took a small portion of it out, placed it in his mouth, and then gave it in a solid state to some of the company. This performance, according to his account, was also very easy; for he seized only a very small particle, which, by a tight compression between the forefinger and the thumb, became cool before it reached the mouth. At this time, Mr. Smith made his appearance, and M. Chabert forthwith prepared himself for mightier undertakings. A cruse of oil was brought forward and poured into a saucepan, which was previously turned upside down, to show that there was no water in it. The alleged reason for this step was, that the vulgar conjurors, who profess to drink boiling oil, place the oil in water, and drink it when the water boils, at which time the oil is not warmer than an ordinary cup of tea. He intended to drink the oil when any person might see it bubbling in the saucepan, and when the thermometer would prove that it was heated to three hundred and sixty degrees. The saucepan was accordingly placed on the fire, and as it was acquiring the requisite heat, the fire-king challenged any man living to drink a spoonful of the oil at the same temperature as that at which he was going to drink it. In a few minutes afterwards, he sipped off a spoonful with greatest apparent ease, although the spoon, from contact with the boiling fluid, had become too hot for ordinary fingers to handle.

"And now, Monsieur Smith," said the fire-king, "now for your challenge. Have you prepared yourself with phosphorus, or will you take some of mine, which is laid on that table?" Mr. Smith, walked up to the table, and pulling a vial bottle out of his pocket, offered it to the poison-swallower.

Fire-king--"I ask you, on your honor as a gentleman, is this genuine unmixed poison?"

Mr. Smith--"It is, upon my honor."

Fire-king--"Is there any medical gentleman here who will examine it?"

A person in the room requested that Dr. Gordon Smith, one of the

medical professors in the London University, would examine the vial,

and decide whether it contained genuine phosphorus.

The professor went to the table, on which the formidable collection of

poisons--such as red and white arsenic, hydrocyanic acid, morphine and

phosphorus--was placed, and, examining the vial, declared, that, to the

best of his judgment, it was genuine phosphorus.

M. Chabert asked Mr. Smith, how many grains he wished to commence his

first draught with. Mr. Smith--"Twenty grains will do as a

commencement."

A medical gentleman then came forward and cut off two parcels of

phosphorus, containing twenty grains each. He was placing them in the

water, when the fire-king requested that his phosphorus might be cut

into small pieces, as he did not wish the pieces to stop on their way

to his stomach. The poisons were now prepared. A wine-glass contained

the portion set aside for the fire-king--a tumbler the portion reserved

for Mr. Smith.

The Fire-king--"I suppose, gentlemen, I must begin, and to convince you

that I do not juggle, I will first take off my coat, and then I will trouble you, doctor (speaking to Dr. Gordon Smith), to tie my hands together behind me. After he had been bandaged in this manner, he planted himself on one knee in the middle of the room, and requested some gentleman to place the phosphorus on his tongue and pour the water down his throat. This was accordingly done, and the water and phosphorus were swallowed together. He then opened his mouth and requested the company to look whether any portion of the phosphorus remained in his mouth. Several gentlemen examined his mouth, and declared that there was no phosphorus perceptible either upon or under his tongue. He was then by his own desire unbandaged. The fire-king forthwith turned to Mr. Smith and offered him the other glass of phosphorus. Mr. Smith started back in infinite alarm--'Not for worlds, Sir, not for worlds; I beg to decline it.'

The Fire-king--"Then wherefore did you send me a challenge? You pledged your honor to drink it, if I did; I have done it; and if you are a gentleman, you must drink it too."

Mr. Smith--"No, no, I must be excused: I am quite satisfied without it."

Here several voices exclaimed that the bet was lost. Some said there must be a confederacy between the challenger and the challenged, and others asked whether any money had been deposited? The fire-king called a Mr. White forward, who deposed that he held the stakes, which had been regularly placed in his hands, by both parties, before twelve o'clock that morning.

The fire-king here turned round with great exultation to the company, and pulling a bottle out of his pocket, exclaimed, "I did never see this gentleman before this morning, and I did not know but that he might be bold enough to venture to take this quantity of poison. I was determined not to let him lose his life by his foolish wager, and therefore, I did bring an antidote in my pocket, which would have prevented him from suffering any harm." Mr. Smith said his object was answered by seeing twenty grains of genuine phosphorus swallowed. He had conceived it impossible, as three grains were quite sufficient to destroy life. The fire-king then withdrew into another room for the professed purpose of putting on his usual dress for entering the oven, but in all probability for the purpose of getting the phosphorus out of his stomach.

After an absence of twenty minutes, he returned, dressed in a coarse woolen coat, to enter the heated oven. Before he entered it, a medical gentleman ascertained that his pulse was vibrating ninety-eight times a minute. He remained in the oven five minutes, during which time he sung Le Vaillant Troubadour, and superintended the cooking of two dishes of beef steaks. At the end of that time he came out, perspiring profusely, and with a pulse making one hundred and sixty-eight vibrations in a minute. The thermometer, when brought out of the oven, stood at three hundred and eighty degrees; within the oven he said it was above six hundred.

Although he was suspected of trickery by many, was often challenged, and had an army of rivals and imitators, all available records show that Chabert was beyond a doubt the greatest fire and poison resister that ever appeared in London.

Seeking new laurels, he came to America in 1832, and although he was successful in New York, his subsequent tour of the States was financially disastrous. He evidently saved enough from the wreck, however, to start in business, and the declining years of his eventful life were passed in the comparative obscurity of a little drug store in Grand Street.

As his biographer I regret to be obliged to chronicle the fact that he made and sold an alleged specific for the White Plague, thus enabling his detractors to couple with his name the word Quack. The following article, which appeared in the New York Herald of September 1st, 1859, three days after Chabert's death, gives further details of his

activities in this country:

We published among the obituary notices in yesterday's Herald the death

of Dr. Julian Xavier Chabert, the "Fire King," aged 67 years, of

pulmonary consumption. Dr. C. was a native of France, and came to this

country in 1832, and was first introduced to the public at the lecture

room of the old Clinton Hall, in Nassau Street, where he gave

exhibitions by entering a hot oven of his own construction, and while

there gave evidence of his salamander qualities by cooking beef steaks,

to the surprise and astonishment of his audiences.

It was a question to many whether the Doctor's oven was red-hot or not,

as he never allowed any person to approach him during the exhibition or

take part in the proceedings. He made a tour of the United States in

giving these exhibitions, which resulted in financial bankruptcy. At

the breaking out of the cholera in 1832 he turned Doctor, and appended

M.D., to his name, and suddenly his newspaper advertisements claimed

for him the title of the celebrated Fire King, the curer of

consumption, the maker of Chinese Lotion, etc.

While the Doctor was at the height of his popularity, some wag perpetrated the following joke in a newspaper paragraph: "During some experiments he was making in chemistry last week, an explosion took place which entirely bewildered his faculties and left him in a condition bordering on the grave. He was blown into a thousand atoms. It took place on Wednesday of last week and some accounts state that it grew out of an experiment with phosphoric ether, others that it was by a too liberal indulgence in Prussic acid, an article which, from its resemblance to the peach, he was remarkably fond of having about him."

The Doctor was extensively accused of quackery, and on one occasion when the Herald touched on the same subject, it brought him to our office and he exhibited diplomas, certificates and medical honors without number.

The Doctor was remarkable for his prolific display of jewelry and medals of honor, and by his extensive display of beard. He found a rival in this city in the person of another French "chemist," who gave the Doctor considerable opposition and consequently much trouble.

The Doctor was famous, also, for his four-horse turnouts in Broadway, alternating, when he saw proper, to a change to the "tandem" style. He married an Irish lady whom he at first supposed to be immensely rich, but after the nuptials it was discovered that she merely had a life interest in a large estate in common with several others.

The Doctor, it appears, was formerly a soldier in the French Army, and quite recently he received from thence a medal of the order of St. Helena, an account of which appeared in the Herald. Prior to his death he was engaged in writing his biography (in French) and had it nearly ready for publication.

Here follows a supposedly humorous speech in broken English, quoted from the London Lancet, in which the Doctor is satirized. Continuing, the articles says:

"The Doctor was what was termed a 'fast liver,' and at the time of his death he kept a drug store in Grand Street, and had very little of this world's goods. He leaves three children to mourn his loss, one of them an educated physician, residing in Hoboken, N. J.

Dr. C. has 'gone to that bourne whence no traveller returns,' and we fervently trust and hope that the disembodied spirits of the tens of thousands whom he has treated in this sphere will treat him with the same science with which he treated them while in this wicked world."

CHAPTER FIVE

FIRE-EATING MAGICIANS: CHING LING FOO AND CHUNG LING SOO.--FIRE-EATERS

EMPLOYED BY MAGICIANS: THE MAN-SALAMANDER, 1816; MR. CARLTON,

PROFESSOR OF CHEMISTRY, 1818; MISS CASSILLIS, AGED NINE, 1820; THE

AFRICAN WONDER, 1843; LING LOOK AND YAMADEVA DIE IN CHINA DURING

KELLAR'S WORLD TOUR, 1872; LING LOOK'S DOUBLE, 1879.--ELECTRICAL

EFFECTS, THE SALAMBOS.--BUENO CORE.--DEL KANO.--BARNELLO.--EDWIN

FORREST AS A HEAT-REGISTER.--THE ELDER SOTHERN AS A FIRE-EATER.--THE

TWILIGHT OF THE ART.

Many of our most noted magicians have considered it not beneath their

dignity to introduce fire-eating into their programmes, either in their

own work or by the employment of a "Fire Artist." Although seldom

presenting it in his recent performances, Ching Ling Foo is a

fire-eater of the highest type, refining the effect with the same

subtle artistry that marks all the work of this super-magician.

Of Foo's thousand imitators the only positively successful one was

William E. Robinson, whose tragic death while in the performance of the bullet-catching trick is the latest addition to the long list of casualties chargeable to that ill-omened juggle. He carried the imitation even as far as the name, calling himself Chung Ling Soo. Robinson was very successful in the classic trick of apparently eating large quantities of cotton and blowing smoke and sparks from the mouth. His teeth were finally quite destroyed by the continued performance of this trick, the method of which may be found in Chapter Six.

The employment of fire-eaters by magicians began a century ago; for in 1816 the magician Sieur Boaz, K. C., featured a performer who was billed as the "Man-Salamander." The fact that Boaz gave him a place on his programme is proof that this man was clever, but the effects there listed show nothing original.

In 1818 a Mr. Carlton, Professor of Chemistry, toured England in company with Rae, the Bartholomew Fair magician. As will be seen by the handbill reproduced here, Carlton promised to explain the "Deceptive Part" of the performance, "when there is a sufficient company."

In 1820, a Mr. Cassillis toured England with a juvenile company, one of the features of which was Miss Cassillis, aged nine years, whose act was a complete reproduction of the programme of Boaz, concluding her performance with the "Chinese Fire Trick."

A Negro, Carlo Alberto, appeared in a benefit performance given by Herr Julian, who styled himself the "Wizard of the South," in London, on November 28th, 1843. Alberto was billed as the "Great African Wonder, the Fire King" and it was promised that he would "go through part of his wonderful performance as given by him in the principal theaters in America, in Boston, New York, Philadelphia, etc."

A later number on the same bill reads: "The African Wonder, Carlo Alberto, will sing several new and popular Negro melodies." Collectors of minstrel data please take notice!

In more recent times there have been a number of Negro fire-eaters, but none seems to have risen to noticeable prominence.

Ling Look, one of the best of contemporary fire performers, was with Dean Harry Kellar when the latter made his famous trip around the world in 1877. Look combined fire-eating and sword-swallowing in a rather startling manner. His best effect was the swallowing of a red-hot sword.[1] Another thriller consisted in fastening a long sword to the stock of a musket; when he had swallowed about half the length of the blade, he discharged the gun and the recoil drove the sword suddenly down his throat to the very hilt. Although Look always appeared in a Chinese make-up, Dean Kellar told me that he thought his right name was Dave Gueter, and that he was born in Buda Pesth.

Yamadeva, a brother of Ling Look, was also with the Kellar Company, doing cabinet manifestations and rope escapes. Both brothers died in China during this engagement, and a strange incident occurred in connection with their deaths. Just before they were to sail from Shanghai on the P. & O. steamer Khiva for Hong Kong, Yamadeva and Kellar visited the bowling alley of The Hermitage, a pleasure resort on the Bubbling Well Road. They were watching a husky sea captain, who was using a huge ball and making a "double spare" at every roll, when Yamadeva suddenly remarked, "I can handle one as heavy as that big loafer can." Suiting the action to the word, he seized one of the largest balls and drove it down the alley with all his might; but he had misjudged his own strength, and he paid for the foolhardy act with his life, for he had no sooner delivered the ball than he grasped his side and moaned with pain. He had hardly sufficient strength to get back to the ship, where he went immediately to bed and died shortly afterward. An examination showed that he had ruptured an artery.

Kellar and Ling Look had much difficulty in persuading the captain to take the body to Hong Kong, but he finally consented. On the way down

the Yang Tse Kiang River, Look was greatly depressed; but all at once

he became strangely excited, and said that his brother was not dead,

for he had just heard the peculiar whistle with which they had always

called each other. The whistle was several times repeated, and was

heard by all on board. Finally the captain, convinced that something

was wrong, had the lid removed from the coffin, but the body of

Yamadeva gave no indication of life, and all save Ling Look decided

that they must have been mistaken.

Poor Ling Look, however, sobbingly said to Kellar, "I shall never leave

Hong Kong alive. My brother has called me to join him." This

prediction was fulfilled, for shortly after their arrival in Hong Kong

he underwent an operation for a liver trouble, and died under the

knife. The brothers were buried in Happy Valley, Hong Kong, in the

year 1877.

All this was related to me at the Marlborough-Blenheim, Atlantic City,

in June, 1908, by Kellar himself, and portions of it were repeated in

1917 when Dean Kellar sat by me at the Society of American Magicians'

dinner.

In 1879, there appeared in England a performer who claimed to be the original Ling Look. He wore his make-up both on and off the stage, and copied, so far as he could, Ling's style of work. His fame reached this country and the New York Clipper published, in its Letter Columns, an article stating that Ling Look was not dead, but was alive and working in England. His imitator had the nerve to stick to his story even when confronted by Kellar, but when the latter assured him that he had personally attended the burial of Ling, in Hong Kong, he broke down and confessed that he was a younger brother of the original Ling Look.

Kellar later informed me that the resemblance was so strong that had he not seen the original Ling Look consigned to the earth, he himself would have been duped into believing that this was the man who had been with him in Hong Kong.

The Salambos were among the first to use electrical effects in a fire act, combining these with the natural gas and "human volcano" stunts of their predecessors, so that they were able to present an extremely spectacular performance without having recourse to such unpleasant features as had marred the effect of earlier fire acts. Bueno Core, too, deserves honorable mention for the cleanness and snap of his act; and Del Kano should also be named among the cleverer performers.

One of the best known of the modern fire-eaters was Barnello, who was a good business man as well, and kept steadily employed at a better salary than the rank and file of his contemporaries. He did a thriving business in the sale of the various concoctions used in his art, and published and sold a most complete book of formulas and general instructions for those interested in the craft. He had, indeed, many irons in the fire, and he kept them all hot.

It will perhaps surprise the present generation to learn that the well-known circus man Jacob Showles was once a fire-eater, and that Del Fugo, well-known in his day as a dancer in the music halls, began as a fire-resister, and did his dance on hot iron plates. But the reader has two keener surprises in store for him before I close the long history of the heat-resisters. The first concerns our great American tragedian Edwin Forrest (1806-1872) who, according to James Rees (Colley Cibber), once essayed a fire-resisting act. Forrest was always fond of athletics and at one time made an engagement with the manager of a circus to appear as a tumbler and rider. The engagement was not fulfilled, however, as his friend Sol Smith induced him to break it and return to the legitimate stage. Smith afterwards admitted to Cibber that if Forrest had remained with the circus he would have become one of the most daring riders and vaulters that ever appeared in the ring.

His adventure in fire-resistance was on the occasion of the benefit to

"Charley Young," on which eventful night, as the last of his acrobatic feats, he made a flying leap through a barrel of red fire, singeing his hair and eyebrows terribly. This particular leap through fire was the big sensation of those days, and Forrest evidently had a hankering to show his friends that he could accomplish it--and he did.

The second concerns an equally popular actor, a comedian this time, the elder Sothern (1826-1881). On March 20, 1878, a writer in the Chicago Inter-Ocean communicated to that paper the following curiously descriptive article:

Is Mr. Sothern a medium?

This is the question that fifteen puzzled investigators are asking themselves this morning, after witnessing a number of astounding manifestations at a private seance given by Mr. Sothern last night.

It lacked a few minutes of 12 when a number of Mr. Sothern's friends, who had been given to understand that something remarkable was to be performed, assembled in the former's room at the Sherman House and took seats around a marble-top table, which was placed in the center of the apartment. On the table were a number of glasses, two very large bottles, and five lemons. A sprightly young gentleman attempted to crack a joke about spirits being confined in bottles, but the company frowned him down, and for once Mr. Sothern had a sober audience to begin with.

There was a good deal of curiosity regarding the object of the gathering, but no one was able to explain. Each gentleman testified to the fact Mr. Sothern's agent had waited upon him, and solicited his presence at a little exhibition to be given by the actor, NOT of a comical nature.

Mr. Sothern himself soon after appeared, and, after shaking hands with the party, thus addressed them:

"Gentlemen, I have invited you here this evening to witness a few manifestations, demonstrations, tests, or whatever you choose to call them, which I have accidentally discovered that I am able to perform.

"I am a fire-eater, as it were. (Applause).

"I used to DREAD the fire, having been scorched once when an innocent child. (A laugh.)

Mr. Sothern (severely)--"I HOPE there will be no levity here, and I wish to say now that demonstrations of any kind are liable to upset me, while demonstrations of a particular kind may upset the audience."

Silence and decorum being restored, Mr. Sothern thus continued:

"Thirteen weeks ago, while walking up Greenwich Street, in New York, I stepped into a store to buy a cigar. To show you there is no trick about it, here are cigars out of the same box from which I selected the one I that day lighted." (Here Mr. Sothern passed around a box of tolerable cigars.)

"Well, I stepped to the little hanging gas-jet to light it, and, having done so, stood contemplatively holding the gas-jet and the cigar in either hand, thinking what a saving it would be to smoke a pipe, when, in my absent-mindedness, I dropped the cigar and put the gas-jet into my mouth. Strange as it may appear, I felt no pain, and stood there holding the thing in my mouth and puffing till the man in charge yelled out to me that I was swallowing his gas. Then I looked up, and, sure enough, there I was pulling away at the slender flame that came from the glass tube.

"I dropped it instantly, and felt of my mouth, but noticed no inconvenience or unpleasant sensation whatever.

"'What do you mean by it?' said the proprietor.

"As I didn't know what I meant by it I couldn't answer, so I picked up my cigar and went home. Once there I tried the experiment again, and in doing so I found that not only my mouth, but my hands and face, indeed, all of my body, was proof against fire. I called on a physician, and he examined me, and reported nothing wrong with my flesh, which appeared to be in normal condition. I said nothing about it publicly, but the fact greatly surprised me, and I have invited you here to-night to witness a few experiments."

Saying this, Mr. Sothern, who had lit a cigar while pausing in his speech, turned the fire end into his mouth and sat down, smoking unconcernedly.

"I suppose you wish to give us the fire-test," remarked one of the company.

Mr. Sothern nodded.

There was probably never a gathering more dumbfounded than that present in the room. A few questions were asked, and then five gentlemen were

appointed to examine Mr. Sothern's hands, etc., before he began his

experiments. Having thoroughly washed the parts that he proposed to

subject to the flames, Mr. Sothern began by burning his arm, and

passing it through the gas-jet very slowly, twice stopping the motion

and holding it still in the flames. He then picked up a poker with a

sort of hook on the end, and proceeded to fish a small coil of wire

from the grate. The wire came out fairly white with the heat. Mr.

Sothern took the coil in his hands and cooly proceeded to wrap it round

his left leg to the knee. Having done so, he stood on the table in the

center of the circle and requested the committee to examine the

wrappings and the leg and report if both were there. The committee did

so and reported in the affirmative.

While this was going on, there was a smile, almost seraphic in its

beauty, on Mr. Sothern's face.

After this an enormous hot iron, in the shape of a horseshoe, was

placed on Mr. Sothern's body, where it cooled, without leaving a sign

of a burn.

As a final test, a tailor's goose was put on the coals, and, after

being thoroughly heated, was placed on Mr. Sothern's chair. The latter lighted a fresh cigar, and then coolly took a seat on the goose without the least seeming inconvenience. During the last experiment Mr. Sothern sang in an excellent tone and voice, "I'm Sitting on the Stile, Mary."

The question now is, were the fifteen auditors of Mr. Sothern fooled and deceived, or was this a genuine manifestation of extraordinary power? Sothern is such an inveterate joker that he may have put the thing upon the boys for his own amusement; but if so, it was one of the nicest tricks ever witnessed by yours truly,

ONE OF THE COMMITTEE.

P. S.--What is equally marvellous to me is that the fire didn't burn his clothes where it touched them, any more than his flesh.

P. C.

(There is nothing new in this. Mr. Sothern has long been known as one of the most expert jugglers in the profession. Some years ago he gained the soubriquet of the "Fire King!" He frequently amuses his friends by eating fire, though he long ago ceased to give public exhibitions. Probably the success of the experiments last night were largely owing to the lemons present. There is a good deal of trickery in those same lemons.--Editor Inter-Ocean.)

Which suggests that the editor of the Inter-Ocean was either pretty well acquainted with the comedian's addiction to spoofing, or else less susceptible to superstition than certain scientists of our generation.

The great day of the Fire-eater--or, should I say, the day of the great Fire-eater--has passed. No longer does fashion flock to his doors, nor science study his wonders, and he must now seek a following in the gaping loiterers of the circus side-show, the pumpkin-and-prize-pig country fair, or the tawdry booth at Coney Island. The credulous, wonder-loving scientist, however, still abides with us and, while his serious-minded brothers are wringing from Nature her jealously guarded secrets, the knowledge of which benefits all mankind, he gravely follows that perennial Will-of-the-wisp, spiritism, and lays the flattering unction to his soul that he is investigating "psychic phenomena," when in reality he is merely gazing with unseeing eyes on the flimsy juggling of pseudo-mediums.

[1] I never saw Ling Look's work, but I know that some of the sword swallowers have made use of a sheath which was swallowed before the performance, and the swords were simply pushed into it. A sheath of

this kind lined with asbestos might easily have served as a protection

against the red-hot blade.

CHAPTER SIX

THE ARCANA OF THE FIRE-EATERS: THE FORMULA OF ALBERTUS MAGNUS.--OF

HOCUS   POCUS.--RICHARDSON'S   METHOD.--PHILOPYRAPHAGUS ASHBURNIENSIS.--TO

BREATHE FORTH SPARKS, SMOKE, AND FLAMES.--TO SPOUT NATURAL

GAS.--PROFESSOR SEMENTINI'S DISCOVERIES.--TO BITE OFF RED-HOT IRON.--TO

COOK IN A BURNING CAGE.--CHABERT'S OVEN. TO EAT COALS OF FIRE.--TO

DRINK BURNING OIL.--TO CHEW MOLTEN LEAD.--TO CHEW BURNING

BRIMSTONE.--TO WREATHE THE FACE IN FLAMES.--TO IGNITE PAPER WITH THE

BREATH.--TO DRINK BOILING LIQUOR AND EAT FLAMING WAX.

The yellow thread of exposure seems to be inextricably woven into all

fabrics whose strength is secrecy, and experience proves that it is

much easier to become fireproof than to become exposure proof. It is

still an open question, however, as to what extent exposure really

injures a performer. Exposure of the secrets of the fire-eaters, for

instance, dates back almost to the beginning of the art itself. The

priests were exposed, Richardson was exposed, Powell was exposed and so

on down the line; but the business continued to prosper, the really clever performers drew quite fashionable audiences for a long time, and it was probably the demand for a higher form of entertainment, resulting from a refinement of the public taste, rather than the result of the many exposures, that finally relegated the Fire-eaters to the haunts of the proletariat.

How the early priests came into possession of these secrets does not appear, and if there were ever any records of this kind the Church would hardly allow them to become public. That they used practically the same system which has been adopted by all their followers is amply proved by the fact that after trial by ordeal had been abolished Albertus Magnus, in his work De Mirabilibus Mundi, at the end of his book De Secretis Mulierum, Amstelod, 1702, made public the underlying principles of heat-resistance; namely, the use of certain compounds which render the exposed parts to a more or less extent impervious to heat. Many different formulas have been discovered which accomplish the purpose, but the principle remains unchanged. The formula set down by Albertus Magnus was probably the first ever made public: the following translation of it is from the London Mirror:

Take juice of marshmallow, and white of egg, flea-bane seeds, and lime; powder them and mix juice of radish with the white of egg; mix all thoroughly and with this composition annoint your body or hand and allow it to dry and afterwards annoint it again, and after this you may boldly take up hot iron without hurt.

"Such a paste," says the correspondent to the Mirror, "would indeed be very visible."

Another early formula is given in the 1763 edition of Hocus Pocus. Examination of the different editions of this book in my library discloses the fact that there are no fire formulas in the second edition, 1635, which is the earliest I have (first editions are very rare and there is only one record of a sale of that edition at auction). From the fact that this formula was published during the time that Powell was appearing in England I gather that that circumstance may account for its addition to the book. It does not appear in the German or Dutch editions.

The following is an exact copy:

HOW TO WALK ON A HOT IRON BAR WITHOUT ANY DANGER OF SCALDING OR BURNING.

Take half an ounce of samphire, dissolve it in two ounces of aquaevitae, add to it one ounce of quicksilver, one ounce of liquid storax, which is the droppings of Myrrh and hinders the camphire from firing; take also two ounces of hematitus, a red stone to be had at the druggist's, and when you buy it let them beat it to powder in their great mortar, for it is so very hard that it cannot be done in a small one; put this to the afore-mentioned composition, and when you intend to walk on the bar you must annoint your feet well therewith, and you may walk over without danger: by this you may wash your hands in boiling lead.

This was the secret modus operandi made use of by Richardson, the first notably successful fire artist to appear in Europe, and it was disclosed by his servant.[1]

Hone's Table Book, London, 1827, page 315, gives Richardson's method as follows:

It consisted only in rubbing the hands and thoroughly washing the mouth, lips, tongue, teeth and other parts which were to touch the fire, with pure spirits of sulphur. This burns and cauterizes the

epidermis or upper skin, till it becomes as hard and thick as leather,

and each time the experiment is tried it becomes still easier. But if,

after it has been very often repeated the upper skin should grow so

callous and hard as to become troublesome, washing the parts affected

with very warm water, or hot wine, will bring away all the shrivelled

or parched epidermis. The flesh, however, will continue tender and

unfit for such business till it has been frequently rubbed over with

the same spirit.

This preparation may be rendered much stronger and more efficacious by

mixing equal quantities of spirit of sulphur, sal ammoniac, essence of

rosemary and juice of onions. The bad effects which frequently

swallowing red-hot coals, melted sealing wax, rosin, brimstone and

other calcined and inflammable matter, might have had upon his stomach

were prevented by drinking plentifully of warm water and oil, as soon

as he left the company, till he had vomited it all up again.

This anecdote was communicated to the author of the Journal des Savants

by Mr. Panthot, Doctor of Physics and Member of the College at Lyons.

It appeared at the time Powell was showing his fire-eating stunts in

London, and the correspondent naively added:

Whether Mr. Powell will take it kindly of me thus to have published his

secret I cannot tell; but as he now begins to drop into years, has no

children that I know of and may die suddenly, or without making a will,

I think it a great pity so genteel an occupation should become one of

the artes perditae, as possibly it may, if proper care is not taken,

and therefore hope, after this information, some true-hearted

ENGLISHMAN will take it up again, for the honor of his country, when he

reads in the newspapers, "Yesterday, died, much lamented, the famous

Mr. Powell. He was the best, if not the only, fire-eater in the world,

and it is greatly to be feared that his art is dead with him."

After a couple of columns more in a similar strain, the correspondent

signs himself Philopyraphagus Ashburniensis. In his History of

Inventions, Vol. III, page 272, 1817 edition, Beckmann thus describes

the process:

The deception of breathing out flames, which at present excites, in a

particular manner, the astonishment of the ignorant, is very ancient.

When the slaves in Sicily, about a century and a half before our era,

made a formidable insurrection, and avenged themselves in a cruel manner, for the severities which they had suffered, there was amongst them a Syrian named Eunus--a man of great craft and courage; who having passed through many scenes of life, had become acquainted with a variety of arts. He pretended to have immediate communication with the gods; was the oracle and leader of his fellow-slaves; and, as is usual on such occasions confirmed his divine mission by miracles. When heated by enthusiasm and desirous of inspiring his followers with courage, he breathed flames or sparks among them from his mouth while he was addressing them. We are told by historians that for this purpose he pierced a nut shell at both ends, and, having filled it with some burning substance, put it into his mouth and breathed through it. This deception, at present, is performed much better. The juggler rolls together some flax or hemp, so as to form a ball about the size of a walnut; sets it on fire; and suffers it to burn until it is nearly consumed; he then rolls round it, while burning, some more flax; and by these means the fire may be retained in it for a long time. When he wishes to exhibit he slips the ball unperceived into his mouth, and breathes through it; which again revives the fire, so that a number of weak sparks proceed from it; and the performer sustains no hurt, provided he inspire the air not through the mouth, but the nostrils. By this art the Rabbi Bar-Cocheba, in the reign of the Emperor Hadrian, made the credulous Jews believe that he was the hoped-for Messiah; and two centuries after, the Emperor Constantius was thrown into great terror when Valentinian informed him that he had seen one of the

body-guards breathing out fire and flames in the evening.

Since Beckmann wrote, the method of producing smoke and sparks from the

mouth has been still further improved. The fire can now be produced in

various ways. One way is by the use of a piece of thick cotton string

which has been soaked in a solution of nitre and then thoroughly dried.

This string, when once lighted, burns very slowly and a piece one inch

long is sufficient for the purpose. Some performers prefer a small

piece of punk, as it requires no preparation. Still others use tinder

made by burning linen rags, as our forefathers used to do. This will

not flame, but merely smoulders until the breath blows it into a glow.

The tinder is made by charring linen rags, that is, burning them to a

crisp, but stopping the combustion before they are reduced to ashes.

Flames from the lips may be produced by holding in the mouth a sponge

saturated with the purest gasoline. When the breath is exhaled sharply

it can be lighted from a torch or a candle. Closing the lips firmly

will extinguish the flame. A wad of oakum will give better results

than the sponge.

Natural gas is produced as simply. A T-shaped gas pipe has three or four gas tips on the cross-piece. The long end is placed in the mouth, which already holds concealed a sponge, or preferably a ball of oakum, saturated with pure gasoline. Blowing through the pipe will force the gas through the tips, where it can be ignited with a match. It will burn as long as the breath lasts.

In a London periodical, The Terrific Record, appears a reprint from the Mercure de France, giving an account of experiments in Naples which led to the discovery of the means by which jugglers have appeared to be incombustible. They first gradually habituate the skin, the mouth, throat and stomach to great degrees of heat, then they rub the skin with hard soap. The tongue is also covered with hard soap and over that a layer of powdered sugar. By this means an investigating professor was enabled to reproduce the wonders which had puzzled many scientists.

The investigating professor in all probability, was Professor Sementini, who experimented with Lionetto. I find an account of Sementini's discoveries in an old newspaper clipping, the name and date of which have unfortunately been lost:

Sementini's efforts, after performing several experiments upon himself, were finally crowned with success. He found that by friction with sulphuric acid deluted with water, the skin might be made insensible to the action of the heat of red-hot iron; a solution of alum, evaporated till it became spongy, appeared to be more effectual in these frictions. After having rubbed the parts which were thus rendered in some degree insensible, with hard soap, he discovered, on the application of hot iron, that their insensibility was increased. He then determined on again rubbing the parts with soap, and after that found that the hot iron not only occasioned no pain but that it actually did not burn the hair.

Being thus far satisfied, the Professor applied hard soap to his tongue until it became insensible to the heat of the iron; and having placed an ointment composed of soap mixed with a solution of alum upon it, burning oil did not burn it; while the oil remained on the tongue a slight hissing was heard, similar to that of hot iron when thrust into water; the oil soon cooled and might then be swallowed without danger.

Several scientific men have since repeated the experiments of Professor Sementini, but we would not recommend any except professionals to try the experiments.

Liquid storax is now used to anoint the tongue when red-hot irons are to be placed in the mouth. It is claimed that with this alone a red-hot poker can be licked until it is cold.

Another formula is given by Griffin, as follows: 1 bar ivory soap, cut fine, 1 pound of brown sugar, 2 ounces liquid storax (not the gum). Dissolve in hot water and add a wine-glassful of carbolic acid. This is rubbed on all parts liable to come in contact with the hot articles. After anointing the mouth with this solution rinse with strong vinegar.

No performer should attempt to bite off red-hot iron unless he has a good set of teeth. A piece of hoop iron may be prepared by bending it back and forth at a point about one inch from the end, until the fragment is nearly broken off, or by cutting nearly through it with a cold chisel. When the iron has been heated red-hot, the prepared end is taken between the teeth, a couple of bends will complete the break. The piece which drops from the teeth into a dish of water will make a puff of steam and a hissing sound, which will demonstrate that it is still very hot.

The mystery of the burning cage, in which the Fire King remains while a steak is thoroughly cooked, is explained by Barnello as follows:

Have a large iron cage constructed about 4 x 6 feet, the bottom made of heavy sheet iron. The cage should stand on iron legs or horses. Wrap each of the bars of the cage with cotton batting saturated with oil. Now take a raw beefsteak in your hand and enter the cage, which is now set on fire. Remain in the cage until the fire has burned out, then issue from the cage with the steak burned to a crisp.

Explanation: On entering the cage the performer places the steak on a large iron hook which is fastened in one of the upper corners. The dress worn is of asbestos cloth with a hood that completely covers the head and neck. There is a small hole over the mouth through which he breathes.

As soon as the fire starts the smoke and flames completely hide the performer from the spectators, and he immediately lies down on the bottom of the cage, placing the mouth over one of the small air holes in the floor of the same.

Heat always goes up and will soon cook the steak.

I deduce from the above that the performer arises and recovers the steak when the fire slackens but while there is still sufficient flame and smoke to mask his action.

It is obvious that the above explanation covers the baker's oven mystery as well. In the case of the oven, however, the inmate is concealed from start to finish, and this gives him much greater latitude for his actions. M. Chabert made the oven the big feature of his programme and succeeded in puzzling many of the best informed scientists of his day.

Eating coals of fire has always been one of the sensational feats of the Fire Kings, as it is quite generally known that charcoal burns with an extremely intense heat. This fervent lunch, however, like many of the feasts of the Fire Kings, is produced by trick methods. Mixed with the charcoal in the brazier are a few coals of soft white pine, which when burnt look exactly like charcoal. These will not burn the mouth as charcoal will. They should be picked up with a fork which will penetrate the pine coals, but not the charcoal, the latter being brittle.

Another method of eating burning coals employs small balls of burned cotton in a dish of burning alcohol. When lifted on the fork these have the appearance of charcoal, but are harmless if the mouth be immediately closed, so that the flame is extinguished.

In all feats of fire-eating it should be noted that the head is thrown well back, so that the flame may pass out of the open mouth instead of up into the roof, as it would if the head were held naturally.

To drink burning oil set fire to a small quantity of kerosene in a ladle. Into this dip an iron spoon and bring it up to all appearance, filled with burning oil, though in reality the spoon is merely wet with the oil. It is carried blazing to the mouth, where it is tipped, as if to pour the oil into the mouth, just as a puff of breath blows out all the flame. The process is continued until all the oil in the ladle has been consumed; then the ladle is turned bottom up, in order to show that all the oil has been drunk. A method of drinking what seems to be molten lead is given in the Chambers' Book of Days, 1863, Vol. II, page 278:

The performer taking an iron spoon, holds it up to the spectators, to show that it is empty; then, dipping it into a pot containing melted lead, he again shows it to the spectators full of the molten metal; then, after putting the spoon in his mouth, he once more shows it to be empty; and after compressing his lips, with a look expressive of pain, he, in a few moments, ejects from his mouth a piece of lead impressed with the exact form of his teeth. Ask a spectator what he saw, and he will say that the performer took a spoonful of molten lead, placed it in his mouth, and soon afterwards showed it in a solid state, bearing the exact form and impression of his teeth. If deception be insinuated, the spectator will say. "No! Having the evidence of my senses, I cannot be deceived; if it had been a matter of opinion I might, but seeing, you know, is believing." Now the piece of lead, cast from a plaster mould of the performer's teeth, has probably officiated in a thousand previous performances, and is placed in the mouth between the gum and the cheek, just before the trick commences. The spoon is made with a hollow handle containing quicksilver, which, by a simple motion, can be let run into the bowl, or back again into the handle at will.

The spoon is first shown with the quicksilver concealed in the handle, the bowl is then dipped just within the rim of the pot containing the molten lead, but not into the lead itself, and, at the same instant the quicksilver is allowed to run into the bowl. The spoon is then shown with the quicksilver (which the audience takes to be the melted lead) in the bowl, and when placed in the mouth, the quicksilver is again allowed to run into the handle.

The performer, in fact, takes a spoonful of nothing, and soon after exhibits the lead bearing the impression of the teeth.

Molten lead, for fire-eating purposes, is made as follows:

Bismuth . . . . 5 oz.

Lead. . . . . 3 oz.

Block tin . . . . 2 oz.

Melt these together. When the metal has cooled, a piece the size of a silver quarter can be melted and taken into the mouth and held there until it hardens. This alloy will melt in boiling water. Robert-Houdin calls it Arcet's metal, but I cannot find the name elsewhere.

The eating of burning brimstone is an entirely fake performance. A number of small pieces of brimstone are shown, and then wrapped in cotton which has been saturated with a half-and-half mixture of kerosene and gasoline, the surplus oil having been squeezed out so there shall be NO DRIP. When these are lighted they may be held in the palm of any hand which has been anointed with one of the fire mixtures described in this chapter. Then throw back the head, place the burning ball in the mouth, and a freshly extinguished candle can be lighted from the flame. Close the lips firmly, which will extinguish the flame, then chew and pretend to swallow the brimstone, which can afterwards be removed under cover of a handkerchief.

Observe that the brimstone has not been burned at all, and that the cotton protects the teeth. To add to the effect, a small piece of brimstone may be dropped into the furnace, a very small piece will suffice to convince all that it is the genuine article that is being eaten.

To cause the face to appear in a mass of flame make use of the following: mix together thoroughly petroleum, lard, mutton tallow and quick lime. Distill this over a charcoal fire, and the liquid which results can be burned on the face without harm.[2]

To set paper on fire by blowing upon it, small pieces of wet phosphorus are taken into the mouth, and a sheet of tissue paper is held about a foot from the lips. While the paper is being blown upon the phosphorus is ejected on it, although this passes unnoticed by the spectators, and as soon as the continued blowing has dried the phosphorus it will ignite the paper.

Drinking boiling liquor is accomplished by using a cup with a false bottom, under which the liquor is retained.

A solution of spermaceti in sulphuric ether tinged with alkanet root, which solidifies at 50 degrees F., and melts and boils with the heat of the hand, is described in Beckmann's History of Inventions, Vol. II., page 121.

Dennison's No. 2 sealing wax may be melted in the flame of a candle and, while still blazing, dropped upon the tongue without causing a burn, as the moisture of the tongue instantly cools it. Care must be used, however, that none touches the hands or lips. It can be chewed, and apparently swallowed, but removed in the handkerchief while wiping the lips.

The above is the method practiced by all the Fire-Eaters, and absolutely no preparation is necessary except that the tongue must be well moistened with saliva.

Barnello once said, "A person wishing to become a Fire-Eater must make up his or her mind to suffer a little at first from burns, as there is no one who works at the business but that gets burns either from carelessness or from accident."

This is verified by the following, which I clip from the London Globe of August 11th, 1880:

Accident to a Fire-Eater. A correspondent telegraphs: A terrible

scene was witnessed in the market place, Leighton Buzzard, yesterday.

A travelling Negro fire eater was performing on a stand, licking

red-hot iron, bending heated pokers with his naked foot, burning tow in

his mouth, and the like. At last he filled his mouth with benzolene,

saying that he would burn it as he allowed it to escape. He had no

sooner applied a lighted match to his lips than the whole mouthful of

spirit took fire and before it was consumed the man was burned in a

frightful manner, the blazing spirit running all over his face, neck

and chest as he dashed from his stand and raced about like a madman

among the assembled crowd, tearing his clothing from him and howling in

most intense agony. A portion of the spirit was swallowed and the

inside of his mouth was also terribly burnt. He was taken into a

chemist's shop and oils were administered and applied, but afterwards

in agonizing frenzy he escaped in a state almost of nudity from a

lodging house and was captured by the police and taken to the

work-house infirmary, where he remains in a dreadful condition.

REMEMBER! Always have a large blanket at hand to smother flames in burning clothing--also a bucket of water and a quantity of sand. A

siphon of carbonic water is an excellent fire extinguisher.

The gas of gasoline is heavier than air, so a container should never be

held ABOVE a flame. Keep kerosene and gasoline containers well corked

and at a distance from fire.

Never inhale breath while performing with fire. FLAME DRAWN INTO THE

LUNGS IS FATAL TO LIFE.

So much for the entertaining side of the art. There are, however, some

further scientific principles so interesting that I reserve them for

another chapter.

[1] Such disloyalty in trusted servants is one of the most

disheartening things that can happen to a public performer. But it must

not be thought that I say this out of personal experience: for in the

many years that I have been before the public my secret methods have

been steadily shielded by the strict integrity of my assistants, most

of whom have been with me for years. Only one man ever betrayed my

confidence, and that only in a minor matter. But then, so far as I

know, I am the only performer who ever pledged his assistants to secrecy, honor and allegiance under a notarial oath.

[3] Barnello's Red Demon.

CHAPTER SEVEN

THE SPHEROIDAL CONDITION OF LIQUIDS.--WHY THE HAND MAY BE DIPPED IN

MOLTEN METALS.--PRINCIPLES OF HEAT-RESISTANCE PUT TO PRACTICAL USES:

ALDINI, 1829.--IN EARLY FIRE-FIGHTING. TEMPERATURES THE BODY CAN

ENDURE.

The spheroidal condition of liquids was discovered by Leidenfrost, but

M. Boutigny was the first to give this singular subject careful

investigation. From time out of mind the test of letting a drop of

water fall on the face of a hot flat-iron has been employed to discover

whether it may safely be used. Everybody knows that if it is not too

hot the water will spread over the surface and evaporate; but if it is

too hot, the water will glance off without wetting the iron, and if

this drop be allowed to fall on the hand it will be found that it is

still cool. The fact is that the water never touches the hot iron at

all, provided the heat is sufficiently intense, but assumes a slightly

elliptical shape and is supported by a cushion of vapor. If, instead

of a flat-iron, we use a concave metal disk about the size and shape of

a watch crystal, some very interesting results may be obtained. If the temperature of the disk is at, or slightly above, the boiling point,

water dropped on it from a medicine dropper will boil; but if the disk

is heated to 340 degrees F., the drop practically retains its

roundness--becoming only slightly oblate--and does not boil. In fact

the temperature never rises above 206 degrees F., since the vapor is so

rapidly evaporated from the surface of the drop that it forms the

cushion just mentioned. By a careful manipulation of the dropper, the

disk may be filled with water which, notwithstanding the intense heat,

never reaches the boiling point. On the other hand, if boiling water

be dropped on the superheated disk its temperature will immediately be

REDUCED to six degrees below the boiling point; thus the hot metal

really cools the water.

By taking advantage of the fact that different liquids assume a

spheroidal form at widely different temperatures, one may obtain some

startling results. For example, liquid sulphurous acid is so volatile

as to have a temperature of only 13 degrees F. when in that state, or

19 degrees below the freezing point of water, so that if a little water

be dropped into the acid, it will immediately freeze and the pellet of

ice may be dropped into the hand from the still red-hot disk. Even

mercury can be frozen in this way by a combination of chemicals.

Through the action of this principle it is possible to dip the hand for a short time into melted lead, or even into melted copper, the moisture

of the skin supplying a vapor which prevents direct contact with the

molten metal; no more than an endurable degree of heat reaches the hand

while the moisture lasts, although the temperature of the fusing copper

is 1996 degrees. The natural moisture of the hand is usually

sufficient for this result, but it is better to wipe the hand with a

damp towel.

In David A. Wells' Things not Generally Known, New York, 1857, I find a

translation of an article by M. Boutigny in The Comptes Rendus, in

which he notes that "the portion of the hands which are not immersed in

the fused metal, but are exposed to the action of the heat radiated

from its surface, experience a painful sensation of heat." He adds

that when the hand was dampened with ether "there was no sensation of

heat, but, on the contrary, an agreeable feeling of coolness."

Beckmann, in his History of Inventions, Vol. II., page 122, says:

In the month of September, 1765, when I visited the copper works at

Awested, one of the workmen, for a little drink money, took some of the

melted copper in his hand, and after showing it to us, threw it against

the wall. He then squeezed the fingers of his horny hand close together, put it for a few minutes under his armpit, to make it sweat, as he said; and, taking it again out, drew it over a ladle filled with melted copper, some of which he skimmed off, and moved his hand backwards and forwards, very quickly, by way of ostentation.

While I was viewing this performance, I remarked a smell like that of singed horn or leather, though his hand was not burnt.

The workmen at the Swedish melting-house showed the same thing to some travellers in the seventeenth century; for Regnard saw it in 1681, at the copper-works in Lapland.

My friend Quincy Kilby, of Brookline, Mass., saw the same stunt performed by workmen at the Meridan Brittania Company's plant. They told him that if the hand had been wet it would have been badly scalded.

Thus, far our interest in heat-resistance has uncovered secrets of no very great practical value, however entertaining the uses to which we have seen them put. But not all the investigation of these principles has been dictated by considerations of curiosity and entertainment. As long ago as 1829, for instance, an English newspaper printed the following:

Proof against Fire--On Tuesday week an experiment was made in presence of a Committee of the Academy of Sciences at Paris, by M. Aldini, for the purpose of showing that he can secure the body against the action of flames so as to enable firemen to carry on their operations with safety. His experiment is stated to have given satisfaction. The pompiers were clothed in asbestos, over which was a network of iron. Some of them, it was stated, who wore double gloves of amianthus, held a red-hot bar during four minutes.

Sir David Brewster, in his Letters on Natural Magic, page 305, gives a more detailed account of Aldini, from which the natural deduction is that the Chevalier was a showman with an intellect fully up to the demands of his art. Sir David says:

In our own times the art of defending the hands and face, and indeed the whole body, from the action of heated iron and intense fire, has been applied to the nobler purpose of saving human life, and rescuing property from the flames. The revival and the improvement of this art we owe to the benevolence and the ingenuity of the Chevalier Aldini of

Milan, who has travelled through all Europe to present this valuable gift to his species. Sir H. Davy had long ago shown that a safety lamp for illuminating mines, containing inflammable air, might be constructed of wire-gauze, alone, which prevented the flame within, however large or intense, from setting fire to the inflammable air without. This valuable property, which has been long in practical use, he ascribed to the conducting and radiating power of the wire-gauze, which carried off the heat of the flame, and deprived it of its power. The Chevalier Aldini conceived the idea of applying the same material, in combination with other badly conducting substances, as a protection against fire. The incombustible pieces of dress which he uses for the body, arms, and legs, are formed out of strong cloth, which has been steeped in a solution of alum, while those for the head, hands, and feet, are made of cloth of asbestos or amianthus. The head dress is a large cap which envelops the whole head down to the neck, having suitable perforations for the eyes, nose, and mouth. The stockings and cap are single, but the gloves are made of double amianthus cloth, to enable the fireman to take into his hand burning or red-hot bodies. The piece of ancient asbestos cloth preserved in the Vatican was formed, we believe, by mixing the asbestos with other fibrous substances; but M. Aldini has executed a piece of nearly the same size, 9 feet 5 inches long, and 5 feet 3 inches wide, which is much stronger than the ancient piece, and possesses superior qualities, in consequence of having been woven without the introduction of any foreign substance. In this manufacture the fibers are prevented from breaking by action of steam, the cloth is made loose in its fabric, and the threads are about the fiftieth of an inch in diameter.

The metallic dress which is superadded to these means of defence consists of five principal pieces, viz., a casque or cap, with a mask large enough to leave a proper space between it and the asbestos cap; a cuirass with its brassets; a piece of armour for the trunk and thighs; a pair of boots of double wire-gauze; and an oval shield 5 feet long by 2 1/2 feet wide, made by stretching the wire-gauze over a slender frame of iron. All these pieces are made of iron wire-gauze, having the interval between its threads the twenty-fifth part of an inch.

In order to prove the efficacy of this apparatus, and inspire the firemen with confidence in its protection, he showed them that a finger first enveloped in asbestos, and then in a double case of wire-gauze, might be held a long time in the flame of a spirit-lamp or candle before the heat became inconvenient. A fireman having his hand within a double asbestos glove, and its palm protected by a piece of asbestos cloth, seized with impunity a large piece of red hot iron, carried it deliberately to the distance of 150 feet, inflamed straw with it, and brought it back again to the furnace. On other occasions the fireman handled blazing wood and burning substances, and walked during five minutes upon an iron grating placed over flaming fagots.

In order to show how the head, eyes, and lungs are protected, the fireman put on the asbestos and wire-gauze cap, and the cuirass, and held the shield before his breast. A fire of shavings was then lighted, and kept burning in a large raised chafing-dish; the fireman plunged his head into the middle of the flames with his face to the fuel, and in that position went several times round the chafing-dish for a period longer than a minute. In a subsequent trial, at Paris, a fireman placed his head in the middle of a large brazier filled with flaming hay and wood, and resisted the action of the fire during five or six minutes and even ten minutes.

In the experiments which were made at Paris in the presence of a committee of the Academy of Sciences, two parallel rows of straw and brushwood supported by iron wires, were formed at the distance of 3 feet from each other, and extended 30 feet in length. When this combustible mass was set on fire, it was necessary to stand at a distance of 8 or 10 yards to avoid the heat. The flames from both the rows seemed to fill up the whole space between them, and rose to the height of 9 or 10 feet. At this moment six firemen, clothed in the incombustible dresses, and marching at a slow pace behind each other, repeatedly passed through the whole length between the two rows of flame, which were constantly fed with additional combustibles. One of the firemen carried on his back a child eight years old, in a wicker-basket covered with metallic gauze, and the child had no other dress than a cap made of amianthine cloth.

In February, 1829, a still more striking experiment was made in the yard of the barracks of St. Gervais. Two towers were erected two stories high, and were surrounded with heaps of inflamed materials consisting of fagots and straw. The firemen braved the danger with impunity. In opposition to the advice of M. Aldini, one of them, with the basket and child, rushed into a narrow place, where the flames were raging 8 yards high. The violence of the fire was so great that he could not be seen, while a thick black smoke spread around, throwing out a heat which was unsupportable by spectators. The fireman remained so long invisible that serious doubts were entertained of his safety. He at length, however, issued from the fiery gulf uninjured, and proud of having succeeded in braving so great a danger.

It is a remarkable result of these experiments, that the firemen are able to breathe without difficulty in the middle of the flames. This effect is owing not only to the heat being intercepted by the wire-gauze as it passes to the lungs, in consequence of which its temperature becomes supportable, but also to the singular power which the body possesses of resisting great heats, and of breathing air of high temperatures.

A series of curious experiments were made on this subject by M. Tillet, in France, and by Dr. Fordyce and Sir Charles Blagden, in England. Sir Joseph Banks, Dr. Solander, and Sir Charles Blagden entered a room in which the air had a temperature of 198 degrees Fahr., and remained ten minutes; but as the thermometer sunk very rapidly, they resolved to enter the room singly. Dr. Solander went in alone and found the heat 210 degrees, and Sir Joseph entered when the heat was 211 degrees. Though exposed to such an elevated temperature, their bodies preserved their natural degree of heat. Whenever they breathed upon a thermometer it sunk several degrees; every expiration, particularly if strongly made, gave a pleasant impression of coolness to their nostrils, and their cold breath cooled their fingers whenever it reached them. On touching his side, Sir Charles Blagden found it cold like a corpse, and yet the heat of his body under his tongue was 98 degrees. Hence, they concluded that the human body possesses the power of destroying a certain degree of heat when communicated with a certain degree of quickness. This power, however, varies greatly in different media. The same person who experienced no inconvenience from air heated to 211 degrees, could just bear rectified spirits of wine at 130 degrees, cooling oil at 129 degrees, cooling water at 123 degrees, and cooling quicksilver at 118 degrees. A familiar instance of this occurred in the heated room. All the pieces of metal there, even their watch-chains, felt so hot that they could scarcely bear to touch them for a moment, while the air from which the metal had derived all its heat was only unpleasant. M. Duhamel and Tillet observed, at Rochefoucault in France, that the girls who were accustomed to attend ovens in a bakehouse, were capable of enduring for ten minutes a temperature of 270 degrees.

The same gentleman who performed the experiments above described ventured to expose themselves to still higher temperatures. Sir Charles Blagden went into a room where the heat was 1 degree or 2 degrees above 260 degrees, and remained eight minutes in this situation, frequently walking about to all the different parts of the room, but standing still most of the time in the coolest spot, where the heat was above 240 degrees. The air, though very hot, gave no pain, and Sir Charles and all the other gentlemen were of opinion that they could support a much greater heat. During seven minutes Sir C. Blagden's breathing continued perfectly good, but after that time he felt an oppression in his lungs, with a sense of anxiety, which induced him to leave the room. His pulse was then 144, double its ordinary quickness. In order to prove that there was no mistake respecting the degree of heat indicated by the thermometer, and that the air which they breathed was capable of producing all the well-known effects of such a heat on inanimate matter, they placed some eggs and a beef-steak upon a tin frame near the thermometer, but more distant from the furnace than from the wall of the room. In the space of twenty minutes the eggs were roasted quite hard, and in forty-seven minutes the steak was not only dressed, but almost dry. Another beef-steak, similarly placed, was rather overdone in thirty-three minutes. In the evening, when the heat was still more elevated, a third beef-steak was laid in the same place, and as they had noticed that the effect of the hot air was greatly increased by putting it in motion, they blew upon the steak with a pair of bellows, and thus hastened the dressing of it to such a degree, that the greatest portion of it was found to be pretty well done in thirteen minutes.

Our distinguished countryman, Sir F. Chantrey, has very recently exposed himself to a temperature still higher than any which we have mentioned. The furnace which he employs for drying his moulds is about 14 feet long, 12 feet high, and 12 feet broad. When it is raised to its highest temperature, with the doors closed, the thermometer stands at 350 degrees, and the iron floor is red hot. The workmen often enter it at a temperature of 340 degrees, walking over the iron floor with wooden clogs, which are of course charred on the surface. On one occasion Sir F. Chantrey, accompanied by five or six of his friends, entered the furnace, and, after remaining two minutes, they brought out a thermometer which stood at 320 degrees. Some of the party experienced sharp pains in the tips of their ears, and in the septum of the nose, while others felt a pain in their eyes.

CHAPTER EIGHT

SWORD-SWALLOWERS: CLIQUOT, DELNO FRITZ, DEODATA, A RAZOR-SWALLOWER, AN

UMBRELLA-SWALLOWER, WILLIAM DEMPSTER, JOHN CUMMING, EDITH CLIFFORD,

VICTORINA.

It has sometimes been noted in the foregoing pages, that fire-eaters, finding it difficult to invent new effects in their own sphere, have strayed into other fields of endeavor in order to amplify their programmes. Thus, we find them resorting to the allied arts of poison-eating, sword-swallowing and the stunts of the so-called Human Ostrich.

In this connection, I consider it not out of place for me to include a description of a number of those who have, either through unusual gifts of nature or through clever artifice, seemingly submitted to tests which we have been taught to believe were far and away beyond the outposts of human endurance. By the introduction of these thrills each notable newcomer has endeavored to go his predecessors one better, and the issue of challenges to all comers to match these startling effects has been by no means infrequent, but I fail to discover a single acceptance of such a challenge.

To accomplish the sword-swallowing feat, it is only necessary to overcome the nausea that results from the metal's touching the mucous membrane of the pharynx, for there is an unobstructed passage, large enough to accommodate several of the thin blades used, from the mouth to the bottom of the stomach. This passage is not straight, but the passing of the sword straightens it. Some throats are more sensitive than others, but practice will soon accustom any throat to the passage of the blade. When a sword with a sharp point is used the performer secretly slips a rubber cap over the point to guard against accident.

It is said that the medical fraternity first learned of the possibility of overcoming the sensitiveness of the pharynx by investigating the methods of the sword-swallowers.

Cliquot, who was one of the most prominent sword-swallowers of his time, finally "reformed" and is now a music hall agent in England. The Strand Magazine (1896) has this to say of Cliquot and his art:

The Chevalier Cliquot (these fellows MUST have titles) in the act of swallowing the major part of a cavalry sword 22 inches long.

Cliquot, whose name suggests the swallowing of something much more grateful and comforting than steel swords, is a French Canadian by birth, and has been the admitted chief in his profession for more than 18 years. He ran away from his home in Quebec at an early age, and joined a travelling circus bound for South America. On seeing an arrant old humbug swallow a small machete, in Buenos Ayres, the boy took a fancy to the performance, and approached the old humbug aforesaid with the view of being taught the business. Not having any money, however, wherewith to pay the necessary premium, the overtures of the would-be apprentice were repulsed; whereupon he set about experimenting with his own aesophagus with a piece of silver wire.

To say the preliminary training for this sort of thing is painful, is to state the fact most moderately; and even when stern purpose has triumphed over the laws of anatomy, terrible danger still remains.

On one occasion having swallowed a sword, and then bent his body in different directions, as an adventurous sensation, Cliquot found that the weapon also had bent to a sharp angle; and quick as thought, realizing his own position as well as that of the sword, he whipped it out, tearing his throat in a dreadful manner. Plainly, had the upper part of the weapon become detached, the sword swallower's career must infallibly have come to an untimely end. Again, in New York, when

swallowing 14 nine-inch bayonet swords at once, Cliquot had the

misfortune to have a too sceptical audience, one of whom, a medical man

who ought to have known better, rushed forward and impulsively dragged

out the whole bunch, inflicting such injuries upon this peculiar

entertainer as to endanger his life, and incapacitate him for months.

In one of his acts Cliquot swallows a real bayonet sword, weighted with

a cross-bar, and two 18-lib. dumb bells. In order to vary this

performance, the sword-swallower allows only a part of the weapon to

pass into his body, the remainder being "kicked" down by the recoil of

a rifle, which is fixed to a spike in the centre of the bar, and fired

by the performer's sister.

The last act in this extraordinary performance is the swallowing of a

gold watch. As a rule, Cliquot borrows one, but as no timepiece was

forthcoming at the private exhibition where I saw him, he proceeded to

lower his own big chronometer into his aesophagus by a slender gold

chain. Many of the most eminent physicians and surgeons in this

country immediately rushed forward with various instruments, and the

privileged few took turns in listening for the ticking of the watch

inside the performer's body. "Poor, outraged nature is biding her

time," remarked one physician, "but mark me, she will have a terrible revenge sooner or later!"

Eaters of glass, tacks, pebbles, and like objects, actually swallow these seemingly impossible things, and disgorge them after the performance is over. That the disgorging is not always successful is evidenced by the hospital records of many surgical operations on performers of this class, when quantities of solid matter are found lodged in the stomach.

Delno Fritz was not only an excellent sword-swallower, but a good showman as well. The last time I saw him he was working the "halls" in England. I hope he saved his money, for he was a clean man with a clean reputation, and, I can truly say, he was a master in his manner of indulging his appetite for the cold steel.

Deodota, an Italian Magician, was also a sword-swallower of more than average ability. He succumbed to the lure of commercialism finally, and is now in the jewelry business in the "down-town district" of New York City.

Sword-swallowing may be harmlessly imitated by the use of a fake sword with a telescopic blade, which slides into the handle. Vosin, the Paris manufacturer of magical apparatus, made swords of this type, but they were generally used in theatrical enchantment scenes, and it is very doubtful if they were ever used by professional swallowers.

It is quite probable that the swords now most generally used by the profession, which are cut from one piece of metal-handle and all--were introduced to show that they were free from any telescoping device. Swords of this type are quite thin, less than one-eighth of an inch thick, and four or five of them can be swallowed at once. Slowly withdrawing them one at a time, and throwing them on the stage in different directions, makes an effective display.

A small, but strong, electric light bulb attached to the end of a cane, is a very effective piece of apparatus for sword swallowers, as, on a darkened stage, the passage of the light down the throat and into the stomach can be plainly seen by the audience. The medical profession now make use of this idea.

By apparently swallowing sharp razors, a dime-museum performer, whose name I do not recall, gave a variation to the sword-swallowing stunt. This was in the later days, and the act was partly fake and partly genuine. That is to say, the swallowing was fair enough, but the sharp razors, after being tested by cutting hairs, etc., were exchanged for dull duplicates, in a manner that, in better hands, might have been effective. This chap belonged to the great army of unconscious exposers, and the "switch" was quite apparent to all save the most careless observers.

His apparatus consisted of a fancy rack on which three sharp razors were displayed, and a large bandanna handkerchief, in which there were several pockets of the size to hold a razor, the three dull razors being loaded in this. After testing the edge of the sharp razors, he pretended to wipe them, one by one, with the handkerchief, and under cover of this he made the "switch" for the dull ones, which he proceeded to swallow in the orthodox fashion. His work was crude, and the crowd was inclined to poke fun at him.

I have seen one of these performers on the street, in London, swallow a borrowed umbrella, after carefully wiping the ferrule, and then return it to its owner only slightly dampened from its unusual journey. A borrowed watch was swallowed by the same performer, and while one end of the chain hung from the lips, the incredulous onlookers were invited to place their ears against his chest and listen to the ticking of the watch, which had passed as far into the aesophagus as the chain would allow.

The following anecdote from the Carlisle Journal, shows that playing with sword-swallowing is about as dangerous as playing with fire.

DISTRESSING OCCURRENCE

On Monday evening last, a man named William Dempster, a juggler of inferior dexterity while exhibiting his tricks in a public house in Botchergate, kept by a person named Purdy, actually accomplished the sad reality of one of those feats, with the semblance only of which he intended to amuse his audience. Having introduced into his throat a common table knife which he was intending to swallow, he accidentally slipped his hold, and the knife passed into his stomach. An alarm was immediately given, and surgical aid procured, but the knife had passed beyond the reach of instruments, and now remains in his stomach. He has since been attended by most of the medical gentlemen of this city; and we understand that no very alarming symptoms have yet appeared, and that it is possible he may exist a considerable time, even in this awkward state. His sufferings at first were very severe, but he is now, when not in motion, comparatively easy. The knife is 9 1/2 inches long, 1 inch broad in the blade, round pointed, and a handle of bone, and may generally be distinctly felt by applying the finger to the unfortunate man's belly; but occasionally, however, from change of its situation it is not perceptible. A brief notice of the analogous case of John Cumming, an American sailor, may not be unacceptable to our readers. About the year 1799 he, in imitation of some jugglers whose exhibition he had then witnessed, in an hour of intoxication, swallowed four clasp knives such as sailors commonly use; all of which passed from him in a few days without much inconvenience. Six years afterward, he swallowed FOURTEEN knives of different sizes; by these, however, he was much disordered, but recovered; and again, in a paroxysm of intoxication, he actually swallowed SEVENTEEN, of the effects of which he died in March, 1809. On dissection, fourteen knife blades were found remaining in his stomach, and the back spring of one penetrating through the bowel, seemed the immediate cause of his death.

Several women have adopted the profession of sword-swallowing, and some have won much more than a passing fame. Notable among these is Mlle. Edith Clifford, who is, perhaps, the most generously endowed. Possessed of more than ordinary personal charms, a refined taste for dressing both herself and her stage, and an unswerving devotion to her art, she has perfected an act that has found favor even in the Royal Courts of Europe.

Mlle. Clifford was born in London in 1884 and began swallowing the blades when only 15 years of age. During the foreign tour of the

Barnum & Bailey show she joined that Organization in Vienna, 1901, and remained with it for five years, and now, after eighteen years of service, she stands well up among the stars. She has swallowed a 26-inch blade, but the physicians advise her not to indulge her appetite for such luxuries often, as it is quite dangerous. Blades of 18 or 20 inches give her no trouble whatever.

In the spring of 1919 I visited the Ringling Bros., and the Barnum & Bailey Show especially to witness Mlle. Clifford's act. In addition to swallowing the customary swords and sabers she introduced such novelties as a specially constructed razor, with a blade five or six times the usual length, a pair of scissors of unusual size, a saw which is 2 1/2 inches wide at the broadest point, with ugly looking teeth, although somewhat rounded at the points, and several other items quite unknown to the bill-of-fare of ordinary mortals. A set of ten thin blades slip easily down her throat and are removed one at a time.

The sensation of her act is reached when the point of a bayonet, 23 1/2 inches long, fastened to the breech of a cannon, is placed in her mouth and the piece discharged; the recoil driving the bayonet suddenly down her throat. The gun is loaded with a 10 gauge cannon shell.

Mlle. Clifford's handsomely arranged stage occupied the place of honor in the section devoted to freaks and specialties.

Cliquot told me that Delno Fritz was his pupil, and Mlle. Clifford claims to be a pupil of Fritz.

Deserving of honorable mention also is a native of Berlin, who bills herself as Victorina. This lady is able to swallow a dozen sharp-bladed swords at once. Of Victorina, the Boston Herald of December 28th, 1902, said:

By long practice she has accustomed herself to swallow swords, daggers, bayonets, walking sticks, rods, and other dangerous articles.

Her throat and food passages have become so expansive that she can swallow three long swords almost up to the hilts, and can accommodate a dozen shorter blades.

This woman is enabled to bend a blade after swallowing it. By moving her head back and forth she may even twist instruments in her throat. To bend the body after one has swallowed a sword is a dangerous feat, even for a professional swallower. There is a possibility of severing some of the ligaments of the throat or else large arteries or veins.

Victorina has already had several narrow escapes.

On one occasion, while sword-swallowing before a Boston audience, a sword pierced a vein in her throat. The blade was half-way down, but instead of immediately drawing it forth, she thrust it farther. She was laid up in a hospital for three months after this performance.

In Chicago she had a still narrower escape. One day while performing at a museum on Clark Street, Victorina passed a long thin dagger down her throat. In withdrawing it, the blade snapped in two, leaving the pointed portion some distance in the passage. The woman nearly fainted when she realized what had occurred, but, by a masterful effort, controlled her feelings. Dropping the hilt of the dagger on the floor, she leaned forward, and placing her finger and thumb down her throat, just succeeded in catching the end of the blade. Had it gone down an eighth of an inch farther her death would have been certain.

CHAPTER NINE

STONE-EATERS: A SILESIAN IN PRAGUE, 1006; FRANCOIS BATTALIA, ca. 1641;

PLATERUS' BEGGAR BOY; FATHER PAULIAN'S LITHOPHAGUS OF AVIGNON, 1760;

"THE ONLY ONE IN THE WORLD," LONDON, 1788; SPANIARDS IN LONDON, 1790; A

SECRET FOR TWO AND SIX; JAPANESE TRAINING.--FROG-SWALLOWERS: NORTON;

ENGLISH JACK; BOSCO, THE SNAKE-EATER; BILLINGTON'S PRESCRIPTION FOR

HANGMEN; CAPTAIN VEITRO.--WATER-SPOUTERS: BLAISE MANFREDE, ca. 1650;

FLORAM MARCHAND, 1650.

That the genesis of stone-eating dates back hundreds of years farther

than is generally supposed, is shown by a statement in Wanley's Wonders

of the Little World, London, 1906, Vol. II, page 58, which reads as

follows:

Anno 1006, there was at Prague a certain Silesian, who, for a small reward in money, did (in the presence of many persons) swallow down white stones to the number of thirty-six; they weighed very near three pounds; the least of them was of the size of a pigeon's egg, so that I could scarce hold them all in my hand at four times: this rash adventure he divers years made for gain, and was sensible of no injury to his health thereby.

The next man of this type of whom I find record lived over six hundred years later. This was an Italian named Francois Battalia. The print shown here is from the Book of Wonderful Characters, and is a reproduction from an etching made by Hollar in 1641.

Doctor Bulwer, in his Artificial Changeling, tells a preposterous story of Battalia's being born with two pebbles in one hand and one in the other; that he refused both the breast and the pap offered him, but ate the pebbles and continued to subsist on stones for the remainder of his life. Doctor Bulwer thus describes his manner of feeding:

His manner is to put three or four stones into a spoon, and so putting them into his mouth together, he swallows them all down, one after another; then (first spitting) he drinks a glass of beer after them.

He devours about half a peck of these stones every day, and when he clinks upon his stomach, or shakes his body, you may hear the stones rattle as if they were in a sack, all of which in twenty-four hours are resolved. Once in three weeks he voids a great quantity of sand, after which he has a fresh appetite for these stones, as we have for our victuals, and by these, with a cup of beer, and a pipe of tobacco, he has his whole subsistence.

From a modern point of view the Doctor "looks easy."

The Book of Wonderful Characters continues:

Platerus speaks of a beggar boy, who for four farthings would suddenly swallow many stones which he met with by chance in any place, though they were big as walnuts, so filling his belly that by the collision of them while they were pressed, the sound was distinctly heard. Father Paulian says that a true lithophagus, or stone-eater, was brought to Avignon in the beginning of May, 1760. He not only swallowed flints an inch and a half long, a full inch broad, and half an inch thick, but such stones as he could reduce to powder, such as marble, pebbles, etc., he made up into paste, which to him was a most agreeable and wholesome food. Father Paulian examined this man with all the attention he possibly could, and found his gullet very large, his teeth exceedingly strong, his saliva very corrosive, and his stomach lower than ordinary.

This stone eater was found on Good Friday, in 1757, in a northern inhabited island, by some of the crew of a Dutch ship. He was made by his keeper to eat raw flesh with his stones; but he never could be got to swallow bread. He would drink water, wine, and brandy, which last liquor gave him infinite pleasure. He slept at least twelve hours a day, sitting on the ground with one knee over the other, and his chin resting on his right knee. He smoked almost all the time he was not asleep or not eating. Some physicians at Paris got him blooded; the blood had little or no serum, and in two hours time it became as fragile as coral.

He was unable to pronounce more than a few words, such as Oui, Non, Caillou, Bon. "He has been taught," adds the pious father, evidently pleased with the docility of his interesting pupil, "to make the sign of the cross, and was baptized some months ago in the church of St. Come, at Paris. THE RESPECT HE SHOWS TO ECCLESIASTICS AND HIS READY

DISPOSITION TO PLEASE THEM, afforded me the opportunity of satisfying myself as to all these particulars; and I AM FULLY CONVINCED THAT HE IS NO CHEAT."

Here is the advertisement of a stone-eater who appeared in England in 1788.

An Extraordinary Stone-Eater

The Original

STONE-EATER

The Only One in the World,

Has arrived, and means to perform this, and every day (Sunday excepted) at Mr. Hatch's, trunk maker, 404 Strand, opposite Adelphi.

STONE-EATING

and

STONE-SWALLOWING

And after the stones are swallowed may

be heard to clink in

the belly, the same as in a pocket.

The present is allowed to be the age of Wonders and Improvements in the Arts. The idea of Man's flying in the Air, twenty years ago, before the discovery of the use of the balloon, would have been laughed at by the most credulous! Nor does the History of Nature afford so extraordinary a relation as that of the man's eating and subsisting on pebbles, flints, tobacco pipes and mineral excrescences; but so it is and the Ladies and Gentlemen of this Metropolis and its vicinity have now an opportunity of witnessing this extraordinary Fact by seeing the Most Wonderful Phenomenon of the Age, who Grinds and Swallows stones, etc., with as much ease as a Person would crack a nut, and masticate the kernel.

This Extraordinary Stone-eater appears not to suffer the least Inconvenience from so ponderous, and to all other persons in the World, so indigestible a Meal, which he repeats from twelve at noon to seven.

Any Lady or Gentleman may bring Black Flints or Pebbles with them. N. B.--His Merit is fully demonstrated by Dr. Monroe, who in his Medical Commentary, 1772, and several other Gentlemen of the Faculty. Likewise Dr. John Hunter and Sir Joseph Banks can witness the Surprising Performance of this most Extraordinary STONE-EATER.

Admittance, Two shillings and Six pence.

A Private Performance for five guineas on short notice.

A Spanish stone-eater exhibited at the Richmond Theater, on August 2nd, 1790, and another at a later date, at the Great Room, late Globe Tavern, corner of Craven Street, Strand.

All of these phenomenal gentry claimed to subsist entirely on stones, but their modern followers hardly dare make such claims, so that the art has fallen into disrepute.

A number of years ago, in London, I watched several performances of one of these chaps who swallowed half a hatful of stones, nearly the size of hen's eggs, and then jumped up and down, to make them rattle in his stomach. I could discover no fake in the performance, and I finally gave him two and six for his secret, which was simple enough. He merely took a dose of powerful physic to clear himself of the stones, and was then ready for the next performance.

During my engagement in 1895 with Welsh Bros. Circus I became quite well acquainted with an aged Jap of the San Kitchy Akimoto troupe and from him I learned the method of swallowing quite large objects and bringing them up again at will. For practice very small potatoes are used at first, to guard against accident; and after one has mastered the art of bringing these up, the size is increased gradually till objects as large as the throat will receive can be swallowed and returned.

I recall a very amusing incident in connection with this old chap.

In one number of the programme he sat down on the ring bank and balanced a bamboo pole, at the top of which little Massay went through the regular routine of posturings. After years spent in this work, my aged friend became so used to his job that he did it automatically, and scarcely gave a thought to the boy at the top. One warm day, however, he carried his indifference a trifle too far, and dropped into a quiet nap, from which he woke only to find that the pole was falling and had already gone too far to be recovered, but the agility of the boy saved him from injury. As my knowledge of Japanese is limited to the more polite forms, I cannot repeat the remarks of the lad.

Until a comparatively recent date, incredible as it may seem, frog-swallowers were far from uncommon on the bills of the Continental theaters. The most prominent, Norton, a Frenchman, was billed as a leading feature in the high-class houses of Europe. I saw him work at the Apollo Theater, Nuremberg, where I was to follow him in; and during my engagement at the Circus Busch, Berlin, we were on the same programme, which gave me an opportunity to watch him closely.

One of his features was to drink thirty or forty large glasses of beer in slow succession. The filled glasses were displayed on shelves at the back of the stage, and had handles so that he could bring forward two or three in each hand. When he had finished these he would return for others and, while gathering another handful, would bring up the beer and eject it into a receptacle arranged between the shelves, just below the line of vision of the audience.

Norton could swallow a number of half-grown frogs and bring them up alive. I remember his anxiety on one occasion when returning to his dressing-room; it seems he had lost a frog--at least he could not account for the entire flock--and he looked very much scared, probably at the uncertainty as to whether or not he had to digest a live frog.

The Muenchen October Fest, is the annual fair at that city, and a most wonderful show it is. I have been there twice; once as the big feature with Circus Carre, in 1901, and again in 1913, with the Circus Corty Althoff. The Continental Circuses are not, like those of this country, under canvas, but show in wooden buildings. At these October Fests I saw a number of frog-swallowers, and to me they were very repulsive indeed. In fact, Norton was the only one I ever saw who presented his act in a dignified manner.

Willie Hammerstein once had Norton booked to appear at the Victoria Theater, New York, but the Society for the Prevention of Cruelty to Animals would not allow him to open; so he returned to Europe without exhibiting his art (?) in America.

In my earlier days in the smaller theaters of America, before the advent of the B. F. Keith and E. F. Albee theaters, I occasionally ran across a sailor calling himself English Jack, who could swallow live frogs and bring them up again with apparent ease.

I also witnessed the disgusting pit act of that degenerate, Bosco, who ate living snakes, and whose act gave rise to the well-known barkers' cry HE EATS 'EM ALIVE! If the reader wishes further description of this creature's work, he must find it in my book, The Unmasking of Robert Houdin, for I cannot bring myself to repeat the nauseating details here.

During an engagement in Bolton, Eng., I met Billington, the official hangman, who was convinced that I could not escape from the restraint he used to secure those he was about to execute.

Much to his astonishment, I succeeded in releasing myself, but he said the time consumed was more than sufficient to spring the trap and launch the doomed soul into eternity. Billington told me that he had hardened himself to the demands of his office by killing rats with his teeth.

During my engagement at the Winter Garten, Berlin, Captain Veitro, a performer that I had known for years in America, where he worked in side shows and museums, came to Berlin and made quite a stir by eating poisons. He appeared only a few times, however, as his act did not appeal to the public, presumably for the reason that he had his stomach pumped out at each performance, to prove that it contained the poison. This may have been instructive, but it possessed little appeal as entertainment, and I rarely heard of the venturesome captain after that.

Years ago, I saw a colored poison-eater at Worth's Museum, New York City, who told me that he escaped the noxious effects of the drugs by eating quantities of oatmeal mush.

Another colored performer took an ordinary bottle, and, after breaking it, would bite off chunks, crunch them with his teeth, and finally swallow them. I have every reason to believe that his performance was genuine.

The beer-drinking of Norton was a more refined version of the so-called water-spouting of previous generations, in which the returning was done openly, a performance that could not fail to disgust a modern audience. To be sure, in the days of the Dime Museum, a Negro who returned the water worked those houses; but his performance met with little approval, and it is years since I have heard of such an exhibition.

The first water-spouter of whom I find a record was Blaise Manfrede or de Manfre, who toured Europe about the middle of the seventeenth century. An interesting account of this man may be found in my book The Unmasking of Robert Houdin.

A pupil of Manfrede's, by the name of Floram Marchand, who seems to have been fully the equal of his master, appeared in England in 1650. The following description of Marchand's performance is from The Book of Wonderful Characters, edition of 1869, page 126:

In the summer of 1650, a Frenchman named Floram Marchand was brought over from Tours to London, who professed to be able to "turn water into wine," and at his vomit render not only the tincture, but the strength and smell of several wines, and several waters. He learnt the rudiments of this art from Bloise, an Italian, who not long before was questioned by Cardinal Mazarin, who threatened him with all the miseries that a tedious imprisonment could bring upon him, unless he would discover to him by what art he did it. Bloise, startled at the sentence, and fearing the event, made a full confession on these terms, that the Cardinal would communicate it to no one else.

From this Bloise, Marchand received all his instruction; and finding his teacher the more sought after in France, he came by the advice of two English friends to England, where the trick was new. Here--the cause of it being utterly unknown--he seems for a time to have gulled and astonished the public to no small extent, and to his great profit.

Before long, however, the whole mystery was cleared up by his two friends, who had probably not received the share of the profits to which they thought themselves entitled. Their somewhat circumstantial account runs as follows.

To prepare his body for so hardy a task, before he makes his appearance on the stage, he takes a pill about the quantity of a hazel nut, confected with the gall of an heifer, and wheat flour baked. After which he drinks privately in his chamber four or five pints of luke-warm water, to take all the foulness and slime from his stomach, and to avoid that loathsome spectacle which otherwise would make thick the water, and offend the eye of the observer.

In the first place, he presents you with a pail of luke-warm water, and sixteen glasses in a basket, but you are to understand that every morning he boils two ounces of Brazil thin-sliced in three pints of running water, so long till the whole strength and color of the Brazil is exhausted: of this he drinks half a pint in his private chamber before he comes on the stage: you are also to understand that he neither eats nor drinks in the morning on those days when he comes on the stage, the cleansing pill and water only excepted; but in the evening will make a very good supper, and eat as much as two or three other men who have not their stomachs so thoroughly purged.

Before he presents himself to the spectators, he washes all his glasses in the best white-wine vinegar he can procure. Coming on the stage, he always washes his first glass, and rinses it two or three times, to take away the strength of the vinegar, that it may in no wise discolour the complexion of what is represented to be wine.

At his first entrance, he drinks four and twenty glasses of luke-warm water, the first vomit he makes the water seems to be a full deep claret: you are to observe that his gall-pill in the morning, and so many glasses of luke-warm water afterwards, will force him into a sudden capacity to vomit, which vomit upon so much warm water, is for the most part so violent on him, that he cannot forbear if he would.

You are again to understand that all that comes from him is red of itself, or has a tincture of it from the first Brazil water; but by degrees, the more water he drinks, as on every new trial he drinks as many glasses of water as his stomach will contain, the water that comes from him will grow paler and paler. Having then made his essay on claret, and proved it to be of the same complexion, he again drinks four or five glasses of luke-warm water, and brings forth claret and beer at once into two several glasses: now you are to observe that the glass which appears to be claret is rinsed as before, but the beer glass not rinsed at all, but is still moist with the white-wine vinegar, and the first strength of the Brazil water being lost, it makes the water which he vomits up to be of a more pale colour, and much like our English beer.

He then brings his rouse again, and drinks up fifteen or sixteen glasses of luke-warm water, which the pail will plentifully afford him: he will not bring you up the pale Burgundian wine, which, though more faint of complexion than the claret, he will tell you is the purest

wine in Christendom. The strength of the Brazil water, which he took

immediately before his appearance on the stage, grows fainter and

fainter. This glass, like the first glass in which he brings forth his

claret, is washed, the better to represent the colour of the wine

therein.

The next he drinks comes forth sack from him, or according to that

complexion. Here he does not wash his glass at all; for the strength of

the vinegar must alter what is left of the complexion of the Brazil

water, which he took in the morning before he appeared on the stage.

You are always to remember, that in the interim, he will commonly drink

up four or five glasses of the luke-warm water, the better to provoke

his stomach to a disgorgement, if the first rouse will not serve turn.

He will now (for on every disgorge he will bring you forth a new

colour), he will now present you with white wine. Here also he will

not wash his glass, which (according to the vinegar in which it was

washed) will give it a colour like it. You are to understand, that

when he gives you the colour of so many wines, he never washes the

glass, but at his first evacuation, the strength of the vinegar being

no wise compatible with the colour of the Brazil water.

Having performed this task, he will then give you a show of rose-water; and this indeed, he does so cunningly, that it is not the show of rose-water, but rose-water itself. If you observe him, you will find that either behind the pail where his luke-warm water is, or behind the basket in which his glasses are, he will have on purpose a glass of rose-water prepared for him. After he has taken it, he will make the spectators believe that he drank nothing but the luke-warm water out of the pail; but he saves the rose-water in the glass, and holding his hand in an indirect way, the people believe, observing the water dropping from his fingers, that it is nothing but the water out of the pail. After this he will drink four or five glasses more out of the pail, and then comes up the rose-water, to the admiration of the beholders. You are to understand, that the heat of his body working with his rose-water gives a full and fragrant smell to all the water that comes from him as if it were the same.

The spectators, confused at the novelty of the sight, and looking and smelling on the water, immediately he takes the opportunity to convey into his hand another glass; and this is a glass of Angelica water, which stood prepared for him behind the pail or basket, which having drunk off, and it being furthered with four or five glasses of luke-warm water, out comes the evacuation, and brings with it a perfect smell of the Angelica, as it was in the rose-water above specified.

To conclude all, and to show you what a man of might he is, he has an instrument made of tin, which he puts between his lips and teeth; this instrument has three several pipes, out of which, his arms a-kimbo, a putting forth himself, he will throw forth water from him in three pipes, the distance of four or five yards. This is all clear water, which he does with so much port and such a flowing grace, as if it were his master-piece.

He has been invited by divers gentlemen and personages of honour to make the like evacuation in milk, as he made a semblance in wine. You are to understand that when he goes into another room, and drinks two or three pints of milk. On his return, which is always speedy, he goes first to his pail, and afterwards to his vomit. The milk which comes from him looks curdled, and shows like curdled milk and drink. If there be no milk ready to be had, he will excuse himself to his spectators, and make a large promise of what he will perform the next day, at which time being sure to have milk enough to serve his turn, he will perform his promise.

His milk he always drinks in a withdrawing room, that it may not be discovered, for that would be too apparent, nor has he any other shift to evade the discerning eye of the observers.

It is also to be considered that he never comes on the stage (as he does sometimes three or four times in a day) but he first drinks the Brazil water, without which he can do nothing at all, for all that comes from him has a tincture of the red, and it only varies and alters according to the abundance of water which he takes, and the strength of the white-wine vinegar, in which all the glasses are washed.

CHAPTER TEN

DEFIERS OF POISONOUS REPTILES: THARDO; MRS. LEARN, DEALER IN
FOR RATTLESNAKES.--SIR ARTHUR THURLOW CUNYNGHAME ON ANTIDOTES

SNAKE-BITE.--JACK THE VIPER.--WILLIAM OLIVER, 1735.--THE ADVICE OF

CORNELIUS HEINRICH AGRIPPA, (1486-1535).--AN AUSTRALIAN SNAKE

STORY.--ANTIDOTES FOR VARIOUS POISONS.

About twenty-two years ago, during one of my many engagements at Kohl

and Middleton's, Chicago, there appeared at the same house a marvelous

"rattle-snake poison defier" named Thardo. I watched her act with deep

interest for a number of weeks, never missing a single performance.

For the simple reason that I worked within twelve feet from her, my

statement that there was absolutely no fake attached to her startling

performance can be taken in all seriousness, as the details are still

fresh in my mind.

Thardo was a woman of exceptional beauty, both of form and feature, a

fluent speaker and a fearless enthusiast in her devotion to her art.

She would allow herself to be repeatedly bitten by rattle-snakes and

received no harm excepting the ordinary pain of the wound. After years of investigation, I have come to the belief that this immunity was the result of an absolutely empty stomach, into which a large quantity of milk was taken shortly after the wound was inflicted, the theory being that the virus acts directly on the contents of the stomach, changing it to a deadly poison.

It was Thardo's custom to give weekly demonstrations of this power, to which the medical profession were invited, and on these occasions she was invariably greeted with a packed house. When the moment of the supreme test came, an awed silence obtained; for the thrill of seeing the serpent flash up and strike possessed a positive fascination for her audiences. Her bare arms and shoulders presented a tempting target for the death-dealing reptile whose anger she had aroused. As soon as he had buried his fangs in her expectant flesh, she would coolly tear him from the wound and allow one of the physicians present to extract a portion of the venom and immediately inject it into a rabbit, with the result that the poor creature would almost instantly go into convulsions and would soon die in great agony.

Another rattle-snake defier is a resident of San Antonio, Texas. Her name is Learn, and she once told me that she was the preceptor of Thardo. This lady deals in live rattle-snakes and their by-products--rattle-snake skin, which is used for fancy bags and purses; rattle-snake oil, which is highly esteemed in some quarters as a specific for rheumatism; and the venom, which has a pharmaceutical value.

She employs a number of men as snake trappers. Their usual technique is to pin the rattler to the ground by means of a forked stick thrust dexterously over his neck, after which he is conveyed into a bag made for the purpose. Probably the cleverest of her trappers is a Mexican who has a faculty of catching these dangerous creatures with his bare hands. The story goes that this chap has been bitten so many times that the virus no longer has any effect on him. Even that most poisonous of all reptiles, the Gila monster, has no terrors for him. He swims along the shore where venomous reptiles most abound, and fearlessly attacks any and all that promise any income to his employer.

In a very rare book by General Sir Arthur Thurlow Cunynghame, entitled, My Command in South Africa, 1880, I find the following:

The subject of snake bites is one of no small interest in this country.

Liquid ammonia is, par excellence, the best antidote. It must be administered immediately after the bite, both internally, diluted with water, and externally, in its concentrated form.

The "Eau de luce" and other nostrums sold for this purpose have ammonia for their main ingredient. But it generally happens in the case of a snake bite that the remedy is not at hand, and hours may elapse before it can be obtained. In this case, the following treatment will work well. Tie a ligature tightly ABOVE the bite, scarify the wound deeply with a knife, and allow it to bleed freely. After having drawn an ounce of blood, remove the ligature and ignite three times successively about two drams of gunpowder right on the wound.

If gunpowder be not at hand, an ordinary fusee will answer the purpose: or, in default of this, the glowing end of a piece of wood from the fire. Having done this, proceed to administer as much brandy as the patient will take. Intoxicate him as rapidly as possible, and, once intoxicated, he is safe. If, however, through delay in treatment, the poison has once got into circulation no amount of brandy will either intoxicate him or save his life.

An odd character, rejoicing in the nick-name of Jack the Viper, is mentioned on page 763 of Hone's Table Book, 1829. In part the writer says:

Jack has traveled, seen the world, and profited by his travels; for he has learned to be contented.

He is not entirely idle, nor wholly industrious. If he can get a crust sufficient for the day, he leaves the evil of it should visit him. The first time I saw him was in the high noon of a scorching day, at an inn in Laytonstone. He came in while a sudden storm descended, and a rainbow of exquisite majesty vaulted the earth. Sitting down at a table, he beckoned the hostess for his beer, and conversed freely with his acquaintance. By his arch replies I found that I was in company with an original--a man that might stretch forth his arms in the wilderness without fear, and like Paul, grasp an adder without harm. He playfully entwined his fingers with their coils and curled crests, and played with their forked tongues. He had unbuttoned his waistcoat, and as cleverly as a fish-woman handles her eels, let out several snakes and adders, warmed by his breast, and spread them on the table. He took off his hat, and others of different sizes and lengths twisted before me; some of them, when he unbosomed his shirt, returned to the genial temperature of his skin; and some curled around the legs of the table, and others rose in a defensive attitude. He irritated and humored them, to express either pleasure or pain at his will. Some were purchased by individuals, and Jack pocketed his gains, observing, "A frog, or a mouse, occasionally, is enough for a snake's satisfaction."

The Naturalist's Cabinet says, that "In presence of the Grand Duke of Tuscany, while the philosophers were making elaborate dissertations on the danger of the poison of vipers, taken inwardly, a viper catcher, who happened to be present, requested that a quantity of it might be put into a vessel; and then, with the utmost confidence, and to the astonishment of the whole company, he drank it off. Everyone expected the man instantly to drop down dead; but they soon perceived their mistake, and found that, taken inwardly, the poison was as harmless as water."

William Oliver, a viper catcher at Bath, was the first who discovered that, by the application of olive oil, the bite of the viper is effectually cured. On the first of June, 1735, he suffered himself to be bitten by an old black viper; and after enduring the agonizing symptoms of approaching death, by using olive oil he perfectly recovered.

Vipers' flesh was formerly esteemed for its medicinal virtues, and its salt was thought to exceed every other animal product in giving vigor to a languid constitution.

According to Cornelius Heinrich Agrippa (called Agrippa of Nettesheim),
a German philosopher, and student of alchemy and magic, who was born in
1486, and died in 1535, "if you would handle adders and snakes without
harm, wash your hands in the juice of radishes, and you may do so
without harm."

Even though it may seem a digression, I yield to the temptation to
include here an extraordinary "snake story" taken from An Actor Abroad,
which Edmund Leathes published in 1880:

I will here relate the story of a sad death--I might feel inclined to
call it suicide--which occurred in Melbourne shortly before my arrival
in the colonies. About a year previous to the time of which I am now
writing, a gentleman of birth and education, a Cambridge B. A., a
barrister by profession and a literary man by choice, with his wife and
three children emigrated to Victoria. He arrived in Melbourne with one
hundred and fifty pounds in his pocket, and hope unlimited in his heart.

Poor man! He, like many another man, quickly discovered that muscles
in Australia are more marketable than brains. His little store of money

began to melt under the necessities of his wife and family. To make matters worse he was visited by a severe illness. He was confined to his bed for some weeks, and during his convalescence his wife presented him with another of those "blessings to the poor man," a son.

It was Christmas time, his health was thoroughly restored, he naturally possessed a vigorous constitution; but his heart was beginning to fail him, and his funds were sinking lower and lower.

At last one day, returning from a long and solitary walk, he sat down with pen and paper and made a calculation by which he found he had sufficient money left to pay the insurance upon his life for one year, which, in the case of his death occurring within that time, would bring to his widow the sum of three thousand pounds. He went to the insurance office, and made his application--was examined by the doctor--the policy was made out, his life was insured. From that day he grew moody and morose, despair had conquered hope.

At this time a snake-charmer came to Melbourne, who advertised a wonderful cure for snake-bites. This charmer took one of the halls in the town, and there displayed his live stock, which consisted of a great number of the most deadly and venomous snakes which were to be found in India and Australia.

This man had certainly some most wonderful antidote to the poison of a snake's fangs. In his exhibitions, he would allow a cobra to bite a dog or a rabbit, and, in a short time after he had applied his nostrum the animal would thoroughly revive; he advertised his desire to perform upon humanity, but, of course, he could find no one would be fool enough to risk his life so unnecessarily.

The advertisement caught the eye of the unfortunate emigrant, who at once proceeded to the hall where the snake charmer was holding his exhibition. He offered himself to be experimented upon; the fanatic snake-charmer was delighted, and an appointment was made for the same evening as soon as the "show" should be over.

The evening came; the unfortunate man kept his appointment, and, in the presence of several witnesses, who tried to dissuade him from the trial, bared his arm and placed it in the cage of an enraged cobra and was quickly bitten. The nostrum was applied apparently in the same manner as it had been to the lower animals which had that evening been experimented upon, but whether it was that the poor fellow wilfully did something to prevent its taking effect--or whatever the reason--he soon became insensible, and in a couple of hours he was taken home to his wife and family--a corpse. The next morning the snake-charmer had flown, and left his snakes behind him.

The insurance company at first refused payment of the policy, asserting that the death was suicide; the case was tried and the company lost it, and the widow received the three thousand pounds. The snake-charmer was sought in vain; he had the good fortune and good sense to be seen no more in the Australian colonies.

As several methods of combating the effects of poisons have been mentioned in the foregoing pages, I feel in duty bound to carry the subject a little farther and present a list of antidotes. I shall not attempt to educate my readers in the art of medicine, but simply to give a list of such ordinary materials as are to be found in practically every household, materials cited as antidotes for the more common poisons. I have taken them from the best authorities obtainable and they are offered in the way of first aid, to keep the patient alive till the doctor arrives; and if they should do no good, they can hardly do harm.

The first great rule to be adopted is SEND FOR THE DOCTOR AT ONCE and give him all possible information about the case without delay. Use every possible means to keep the patient at a normal temperature. When artificial respiration is necessary, always get hold of the tongue and

pull it well forward in order to keep the throat clear, then turn the

patient over on his face and press the abdomen to force out the air,

then turn him over on the back so that the lungs may fill again,

repeating this again and again till the doctor arrives. The best

stimulants are strong tea or coffee; but when these are not sufficient,

a tablespoon of brandy, whisky, or wine may be added.

Vegetable and mineral poisons, with few exceptions, act as efficiently

in the blood as in the stomach. Animal poisons act only through the

blood, and are inert when introduced into the stomach. Therefore there

is absolutely no danger in sucking the virus from a snake bite, except

that the virus should not be allowed to touch any spot where the skin

is broken.

The following list of antidotes is taken largely from Appleton's

Medical Dictionary, and Sollmann's A Manual of Pharmacology,

Philadelphia, 1917, pages 56 and 57, and has been verified by

comparison with various other authorities at the library of the Medical

Society of the County of New York:

Arsenic   Induce vomiting with a dessert-spoonful

of ground mustard in tepid water. Also

put the finger in the throat to induce

retching. When the stomach has been

emptied, give the patient all the milk

he can take.

Aconite   Induce vomiting as above. Also give

active purgative. Stimulate with strong

tea or coffee. Keep the patient roused.

Alcohol   Same as for aconite.

Belladonna   Same as for aconite.

Bitter-sweet   Same as for aconite.

Blue vitriol   Induce vomiting as in arsenic. Then give

milk, or white of egg, or mucilage.

Cantharides   Induce vomiting. Give soothing drinks.

NO OIL. Rub abdomen with camphor,

or camphorated oil.

Chloral   Same as for aconite.

Camphor   Same as for aconite.

Conium (Hemlock)   Same as for aconite.

Carbolic Acid   White of egg in water, or olive oil,

followed by a large quantity of milk.

Calomel   Give white of egg, followed by milk, or flour gruel.

Corrosive Sublimate Same as for calomel.

Croton Oil   Induce vomiting. Also give strong purgative

AS SOON AS POSSIBLE. Stimulate with

strong tea or coffee.

Colocynth   Same as for croton oil.

Ergot   Same as for aconite.

Food cooked in a

  copper vessel Same as for blue vitriol.

Fish poison   Same as for croton oil.

Gases   Plenty of fresh air. Inhale ammonia

(not too strong). Artificial

respiration if necessary. Stimulate

with strong tea or coffee.

Green coloring

    matter   Same as for arsenic.

Hellebore   Same as for aconite.

Hyoscyamus   Same as for aconite.

Iodine   Give starch.

Lobelia   Same as for aconite.

Lead   Same as for calomel.

Matches   Induce vomiting. Give magnesia and

mucilage. NO OIL.

Mercury	Same as for calomel.
Morphine	Spasms may be quieted by inhaling ether.
Nitric Acid	Induce vomiting. Give Carbonate of Magnesia, or lime-water.
Nitrate of Silver	Give common salt in water, or carbonate of soda in solution, followed by milk, or white of egg.
Nux Vomica	Same as for aconite.
Oxalic Acid	Same as for nitric acid.
Opium	Same as for morphine.
Prussic Acid	Not much can be done, as fatal dose kills in from three to five minutes. Dilute ammonia given instantly might save life.
Paris Green	Same as for arsenic.
Phosphorus	Same as for matches.
Rough on Rats	Same as for arsenic.
Strychnin	Same as for morphine.
Sulphuric Acid	Strong soap-suds.
Toadstool	Same as for morphine.
Turpentine	Same as for morphine.
Tin	Same as for nitrate of silver.
Verdigris	Same as for arsenic.
Vermilion	Same as for calomel.

White vitriol   Same as for nitrate of silver.

Zinc   Same as for nitrate of silver.

For Snake-bite   The best general treatment for snake-bite

    is to tie a ligature tightly ABOVE the

    wound, then suck out as much of the

    virus as possible. Give the patient

    large quantities of whisky or brandy,

    to induce intoxication. Incise the

    wound with a red-hot nail, or knitting

    needle. Keep the patient intoxicated

    till the doctor arrives.

For Burns   All burns are more painful when exposed

    to the air. For lesser burns a cloth

    saturated with a strong solution of

    bicarbonate of soda (common cooking

    soda) laid on the burn is probably best.

    This is soothing and keeps out the air.

For burning clothes Do not allow the victim to run about, for

    that increases the flames. Throw her--

    these accidents usually occur to women--on

    the floor and smother the flames

    with a blanket, rug, or large garment.

    Then, if the burns are severe, place

her in a bath at a temperature of 100

degrees or over, keeping her there till

the doctor arrives. Give stimulants.

Do not touch the burns more than is

absolutely unavoidable.

For Burns of Acids   Dash cold water on the burns, then cover

with lime-water and sweet oil, or

linseed oil.

For Burns of

 Caustic Alkalies   Apply vinegar.

Glass, coarse or   Give the patient large quantities of bread

 powdered   crumbs, and then induce vomiting.

Ivy poison   Wash at once with soap and water; using

scrubbing brush. Then lay on cloths

saturated with strong solution bicarbonate

of soda. Give cooling drinks.

Keep the patient quiet and on a low diet.

CHAPTER ELEVEN

STRONG MEN OF THE EIGHTEENTH CENTURY: THOMAS TOPHAM (died, 1749);

JOYCE, 1703; VAN ECKENBERG, 1718; BARSABAS AND HIS SISTER; THE ITALIAN

FEMALE SAMPSON, 1724; THE "LITTLE WOMAN FROM GENEVA," 1751; BELZONI,

1778-1823.

Bodily strength has won the admiration--I might almost say, the

worship--of mankind from the days of Hercules and his ten mythical

labors, to the days of Sandow with his scores of actual achievements.

Each generation has produced its quota of strongmen, but almost all of

them have resorted to some sort of artifice or subterfuge in order to

appear superhumanly strong. That is to say, they added brain to their

brawn, and it is a difficult question whether their efforts deserve to

be called trickery or good showmanship.

Many of the tricks of the profession were laid bare by Dr. Desaguliers

over a hundred and fifty years ago and have been generally discarded by

athletes, only to be taken up and vastly improved by women of the type

of The Georgia Magnet, who gave the world of science a decided start about a generation ago. I shall have more to say of her a little further on.

The jiu jitsu of the Japanese is, in part, a development of the same principles, but here again much new material has been added, so that it deserves to be considered a new art.

The following, from Dr. Desaguliers' Experimental Philosophy, London, 1763, Vol. 1, page 289, contrasts feats of actual strength with the tricks of the old-time performers:

Thomas Topham, born in London, and now about thirty-one years of age, five feet ten inches high, with muscles very hard and prominent, was brought up a carpenter, which trade he practiced till within these six or seven years that he has shewed feats of strength; but he is entirely ignorant of any art to make his strength appear more surprising; Nay, sometimes he does things which become more difficult by his disadvantageous situation; attempting and often doing, what he hears other strong men have done, without making use of the same advantages.

About six years ago he pulled against a horse, sitting on the ground with his feet against two stumps driven into the ground, but without the advantage represented by the first figure, Plate 19; for the horse

pulling against him drew upwards at a considerable angle, such as is

represented in the second figure in that plate, when hN is the line of

traction, which makes the angle of traction to be NhL: and in this case

his strength was no farther employed than to keep his legs and thighs

straight, so as to make them act like the long arm of a bended lever,

represented by Lh, on whose end h the trunk of his body rested as a

weight, against which the horse drew, applying his power at right

angles to the end l of the short arm of said lever, the center of the

motion being a L at the bottom of the stumps l, o (for to draw

obliquely by a rope fastened at h is the same as to draw by an arm of a

lever at l L, because l L is a line drawn perpendicularly from the

center of motion to the line of direction hN) and the horse not being

strong enough to raise the man's weight with such disadvantage, he

thought he was in the right posture for drawing against a horse; but

when in the same posture, he attempted to draw against two horses, he

was pulled out of his place by being lifted up, and had one of his

knees struck against the stumps, which shattered it so, that even to

this day, the patella or knee-pan is so loose, that the ligaments of it

seem either to be broken or quite relaxed, which has taken away most of

the strength of that leg.

But if he had sat upon such a frame as is represented in the first figure, (Plate 19) he might (considering his strength) have kept his situation against the pulling of four strong horses without the least inconvenience.

The feats which I saw him perform, a few days ago, were the following:

1. By the strength of his fingers (only rubbed in coal-ashes to keep them from slipping) he rolled up a very strong and large pewter-dish.

2. He broke seven or eight short and strong pieces of tobacco-pipe with the force of his middle finger, having laid them on the first and third finger.

3. Having thrust under his garter the bowl of a strong tobacco-pipe, his legs being bent, he broke it to pieces by the tendons of his hams, without altering the bending of his leg.

4. He broke such another bowl between his first and second finger, by pressing his fingers together side-ways.

5. He lifted a table six feet long, which had half a hundred weight hanging to the end of it, with his teeth, and held it in a horizontal position for a considerable time. IT IS TRUE THE FEET OF THE TABLE

RESTED AGAINST HIS KNEES; BUT AS THE LENGTH OF THE TABLE WAS MUCH

GREATER THAN ITS HEIGHT, THAT PERFORMANCE REQUIRED A GREAT STRENGTH TO

BE EXERTED BY THE MUSCLES OF HIS LOINS, THOSE OF HIS NECK, THE MASSETER

AND TEMPORAL (MUSCLES OF THE JAWS) BESIDES A GOOD SET OF TEETH.

6. He took an iron kitchen-poker, about a yard long, and three inches

in circumference, and holding it in his right hand, he struck upon his

bare left arm, between the elbow and the wrist till he bent the poker

nearly to a right angle.

7. He took such another poker, and holding the ends in his hands, and

the middle against the back of his neck, he brought both ends of it

together before him; and, what was yet more difficult, he pulled it

almost straight again: because the muscles which separate the arms

horizontally from each other, are not so strong as those that bring

them together.

8. He broke a rope of about two inches in circumference which was in

part wound about a cylinder of four inches' diameter, having fastened

the other end of it to straps that went over his shoulders; but he

exerted more force to do this than any other of his feats, from his awkwardness in going about it: as the rope yielded and stretched as he stood upon the cylinder, so that when the extensors of his legs and thighs had done their office in bringing the legs and thighs straight, he was forced to raise his heels from their bearings, and use other muscles that are weaker. But if the rope had been so fixed, that the part to be broken had been short, it would have been broken with four times less difficulty.

9. I have seen him lift a rolling stone of about 800 lib. with his hand only, standing in a frame above it, and taking hold of a chain that was fastened to it. By this I reckon that he may be almost as strong again as those who are generally reckoned as the strongest men, they generally lifting no more than 400 lib. in that manner. The weakest men who are in health and not too fat, lift about 125 lib. having about half the strength of the strongest. (N.B. This sort of comparison is chiefly in relation to the muscles of the loins; because in doing this one must stoop forward a little. We must also add the weight of the body to the weight lifted. So that if the weakest man's body weighs 150 lib. that added to 125 lib. makes the whole weight lifted by him 275 lib. Then if the stronger man's body weighs also 150 lib. the whole weight lifted by him will be 550 lib. that is, 400 lib. and the 150 lib. which his body weighs. Topham weighs about 200 lib. which added to the 800 lib. that he lifts, makes 1000 lib. But he

ought to lift 900 lib. besides the weight of his body, to be as strong again as a man of 150 lib.-weight who can lift 400 lib.

Now as all men are not proportionably strong in every part, but some are stronger in the arms, some in the legs, and others in the back, according to the work and exercise which they use, we can't judge of a man's strength by lifting only; but a method may be found to compare together the strength of different men in the same parts, and that too without straining the persons who try the experiment.

Here follows a long description of a machine for the above purpose.

Topham was not endowed with a strength of mind equal to the strength of his body. He was married to a wanton who rendered existence so insupportable that he committed suicide before he was forty years of age, on August 10th, 1749.[1]

About the year 1703 there appeared in London a native of Kent, by the name of Joyce, who won the name of a second Samson by a series of feats of strength that to the people of that day seemed little short of superhuman. Dr. Desaguliers, in his Experimental Philosophy, gives the following account of Joyce and his methods.

About thirty years ago one Joyce,[2] a Kentish man, famous for his great strength (tho' not quite so strong as the King of Poland, by the accounts we have of that Prince) shewed several feats in London and the country, which so much surprised the spectators, that he was by most people called the second Sampson.[3] But tho' the postures which he had learned to put his body into, and found out by practice without any mechanical theory, were such as would make a man of common strength do such feats as would appear surprising to everybody that did not know the advantages of those positions of the body; yet nobody then attempted to draw against horses, or raise great weights, or to do anything in imitation of him; because, as he was very strong in the arms, and grasped those that try'd his strength that way so hard, that they were obliged immediately to desire him to desist, his other feats (wherein his manner of acting was chiefly owing to the mechanical advantages gained by the position of his body) were entirely attributed to his extraordinary strength.

But when he had gone out of England, or had ceased to shew his performances, for eight or ten years; men of ordinary strength found out the way of making such advantage of the same postures as Joyce had put himself into, as to pass for men of more than common strength, by

drawing against horses, breaking ropes, lifting vast weights, &c. (tho'
they cou'd in none of the postures really perform so much as Joyce; yet
they did enough to amaze and amuse, and get a great deal of money) so
that every two or three years we have a new SECOND SAMPSON.

Some fifteen years subsequent to Joyce's advent, another so-called
Samson, this time a German named John Charles Van Eckenberg, toured
Europe with a remarkable performance along the same lines as Joyce's.
Dr. Desaguliers saw this man and has this to say of him:

After having seen him once, I guessed at his manner of imposing on the
multitude; and being resolved to be fully satisfied in the matter, I
took four very curious persons with me to see him again, viz. the Lord
Marquis of Tullibardine, Dr. Alexander Stuart, Dr. Pringle, and a
mechanical workman, who used to assist me in my courses of experiments.
We placed ourselves in such a manner round the operator, as to be able
to observe nicely all that he did, and found it so practicable that we
performed several of his feats that evening by ourselves, and
afterwards I did most of the rest as soon as I had a frame made to fit
in to draw, and another to stand in and lift great weights, together
with a proper girdle and hooks.

Dr. Desaguliers illustrates Van Eckenberg's methods in a very exhaustive set of notes and plates, which are too technical and voluminous to repeat here, but I will quote sufficiently from them to make the modus operandi clear. The figures will be found on plate 19.

In breaking the rope one thing is to be observ'd, which will much facilitate the performance; and that is to place the iron eye L, thro' which the rope goes, in such a situation, that a plane going thro' its ring shall be parallel to the two parts of the rope; because then the rope will in a manner be jamm'd in it, and not slipping thro' it, the whole force of the man's action will be exerted on that part of the rope which is in the eye, which will make it break more easily than if more parts of the rope were acted upon. So, the eye, tho' made round and smooth, may be said in some measure to CUT THE ROPE. And it is after this manner that one may break a whip cord, nay, a small jack-line with one's hand without hurting it; only by bringing one part of the rope to cut the other; that is, placing it so round one's left hand, that by a sudden jerk, the whole force exerted shall act on one point of the rope.

B is a feather bed upon which the performer falls.

The posture of where the strong man having an anvil on

his breast or belly, suffers another man to strike with a sledge hammer

and forge a piece of iron, or cut a bar cold with chizzels tho' it

seems surprising to some people, has nothing in it to be really

wondered at; for sustaining the anvil is the whole matter, and the

heavier the anvil is, the less the blows are felt: And if the anvil

was but two or three times heavier than the hammer, the strong man

would be killed by a few blows; for the more matter the anvil has, the

more INERTIA and the less liable it is to be struck out of its place;

because when it has by the blow receiv'd the whole MOMENTUM of the

hammer, its velocity will be so much less than that of the hammer as it

has more matter than the hammer. Neither are we to attribute to the

anvil a velocity less than the hammer in a reciprocal proportion of

their masses or quantities of matter; for that would happen only if the

anvil was to hang freely in the air (for example) by a rope, and it was

struck horizontally by the hammer. Thus, is the velocity given by the

hammer distributed to all parts of a great stone, when it is laid on a

man's breast to be broken; but when the blow is given, the man feels

less of the weight of the stone than he did before, because in the

reaction of the stone, all the parts of it round about the hammer rise

towards the blow; and if the tenacity of the parts of the stone, is not

stronger than the force with which it moves towards the hammer, the stone must break; which it does when the blow is strong, and struck

upon the centre of gravity of the stone.

In the 6th Fig. of Plate 19, the man IHL (the chairs IL, being made

fast) makes so strong an arch with his backbone and the bones of his

legs and thighs, as to be able not only to sustain one man, but three

or four, if they had room to stand; or, in their stead, a great stone

to be broken with one blow.

In the 6th and 7th Fig. of the same plate, a man or two are raised in

the direction CM, by the knees of the strong man IHL lying upon his

back. A trial will suffice to show that this is not a difficult feat

for a man of ordinary strength.

Wanley enumerates thirty men of might, each of whom was famous in

his time. Notable among them was Barsabas, who first made a reputation

in Flanders, where he lifted the coach of Louis XIV, which had sunk to

the nave in the mud, all the oxen and horses yoked to it having exerted

their strength in vain. For this service, the king granted him a

pension, and being soon promoted, he at length rose to be town-major of

Valenciennes.

Barsabas entering one day a farrier's shop in a country village, asked for horse shoes, the farrier showed him some, which Barsabas snapped in pieces as if they had been rotten wood, telling the farrier at the same time that they were too brittle, and good for nothing. The farrier wanted to forge some more, but Barsabas took up the anvil and hid it under his cloak. The farrier, when the iron was hot, could not conceive what had become of his anvil, but his astonishment was still increased when he saw Barsabas deposit it in its place with the utmost ease. Imagining that he had got the devil in his shop, he ran out as fast as he could, and did not venture to return till his unwelcome visitor had disappeared.

Barsabas had a sister as strong as himself, but as he quitted his home very young, and before his sister was born, he had never seen her. He met with her in a small town of Flanders, where she carried on a rope manufactury. The modern Sampson bought some of her largest ropes which he broke like pack-thread, telling her they were very bad.--"I will give some better," replied she, "but will you pay a good price for them?"--"Whatever you choose," returned Barsabas, showing her some crown pieces. His sister took them, and breaking two or three of them said, "Your crowns are as little worth as my ropes, give me better money." Barsabas, astonished at the strength exhibited by this female, then questioned her respecting her country and family, and soon learned that she belonged to the same stock.

The dauphin being desirous to see Barsabas exhibit some of his feats, the latter said, "My horse has carried me so long that I will carry him in my turn." He then placed himself below the animal and raising him up, carried him more than fifty paces, and then placed him on the ground without being the least hurt.

Barsabas' sister was not unique in her century. I quote from a magazine called The Parlor Portfolio or Post-Chaise Companion, published in London in 1724:

To be seen, at Mr. John Syme's, Peruke maker, opposite the Mews, Charing Cross, the surprising and famous Italian Female Sampson, who has been seen in several courts of Europe with great applause. She will absolutely walk, barefoot, on a red-hot bar of iron: a large block of marble of between two and three thousand weight she will permit to lie on her for some time, after which she will throw it off at about six feet distance, without using her hands, and exhibit several other curious performances, equally astonishing, which were never before seen in England. She performs exactly at twelve o'clock, and four, and six in the afternoon. Price half-a-crown, servants and children a shilling.

From the spelling, I judge that the person who selected this lady's title must have been more familiar with the City Directory than with the Scriptures.

In Edward J. Wood's Giants and Dwarfs, London, 1868, I find the following:

A newspaper of December 19th, 1751, announces as follows:

At the new theatre in the Haymarket, this day, will be performed a concert of musick, in two acts. Boxes 3s., pit 2s., gallery 1s. Between the acts of the concert will be given, gratis, several exercises of rope-dancing and tumbling. There is also arrived the little woman from Geneva, who, by her extraordinary strength, performs several curious things, viz. 1st. She beats a red-hot iron that is made crooked straight with her naked feet. 2ndly. She puts her head on one chair, and her feet on another, in an equilibrium, and suffers five or six men to stand on her body, which after some time she flings off. 3rdly. An anvil is put on her body, on which two men strike with large hammers. 4thly. A stone of a hundred pounds weight is put on her body, and beat to pieces with a hammer. 5thly. She lies down on the ground, and suffers a stone of 1500 pounds weight to be laid on her breasts, in which position she speaks to the audience, and drinks a glass of wine, then throws the stone off her body by mere strength, without any assistance. Lastly, she lifts an anvil of 200 pound weight from the ground with her own hair. To begin exactly at six o'clock.

At present the stunt with the two chairs and the six men is being exhibited as a hypnotic test.

Giovanni Battista Belzoni, the famous Egyptian archeologist, who was a man of gigantic stature, began his public career as a strongman at the Bartholomew Fair, under the management of Gyngell, the conjuror, who dubbed him The Young Hercules. Shortly afterward he appeared at Sadler's Wells Theater, where he created a profound sensation, under the name of The Patagonian Samson. The feature of his act was carrying a pyramid of from seven to ten men in a manner never before attempted. He wore a sort of harness with footholds for the men, and when all were in position he moved about the stage with perfect ease, soliciting "kind applause" by waving a flag. He afterwards became a magician, and after various other ventures he finally landed in Egypt, where his discoveries were of such a nature as to secure for him an enviable position in "Who's Who in Archeology."

[1] Interesting accounts of Topham's career may be found in Wonders of Bodily Strength, New York, 1873, a translation from the French of Depping, by Charles Russell; Sir David Brewster's, Letters on Natural Magic; London, 1838; Wanley's Wonders of the Little World, London, 1806; Wilson's Wonderful Characters, London, 1821, (but not in the reprint of 1869).

[2] Or William Joy.

[3] This is the spelling used by Joyce, Eckenberg and others, for the Samson of the Bible.

[4] Wonders of the little World, by Nathaniel Wanley, London, 1806. Vol. I., page 76.

CHAPTER TWELVE

CONTEMPORARY STRONG PEOPLE: CHARLES JEFFERSON; LOUIS CYR; JOHN GRUN

MARX; WILLIAM LE ROY.--THE NAIL KING, THE HUMAN CLAW-HAMMER; ALEXANDER

WEYER; MEXICAN BILLY WELLS; A FOOLHARDY ITALIAN; WILSON; HERMAN;

SAMPSON; SANDOW; YUCCA; LA BLANCHE; LULU HURST.--THE GEORGIA MAGNET,

THE ELECTRIC GIRL, ETC.; ANNIE ABBOTT; MATTIE LEE PRICE.--THE TWILIGHT

OF THE FREAKS. THE DIME MUSEUMS.

Feats of strength have always interested me greatly, so that in my

travels around the world I have made it a point to come in contact with

the most powerful human beings of my generation. The one among these

who deserves first mention is Charles Jefferson, with whose

achievements I became quite familiar while we were working in the same

museum many years ago. I am convinced that he must have been the

strongest man of his time at lifting with the bare hands alone. He had

two feats that he challenged any mortal to duplicate. One was picking

up a heavy blacksmith's anvil by the horn and placing it on a kitchen

table; for the other he had a block of steel, which, as near as I can remember, must have been about 14 inches long, 12 inches wide, and 7 inches thick. This block lay on the floor, and his challenge was for anyone to pick it up with bare hands. I noticed that it required unusually long fingers to grasp it, since one could get only the thumb on one side. Though thousands tried, I never saw, or heard, of anyone else who could juggle his anvil or pick up the weight. True, I saw him surreptitiously rub his fingers with resin, to assist in the gripping, but that could have been only of slight assistance to the marvelous grip the man possessed.

It is generally conceded that Louis Cyr was, in his best days, the strongest man in the known world at all-round straight lifting. Cyr did not give the impression of being an athlete, nor of a man in training, for he appeared to be over-fat and not particularly muscular; but he made records in lifting which, to the best of my knowledge, no other man has been able to duplicate.

John Grun Marx, a Luxemberger, must have been among the strongest men in the world at the time I knew him. We worked on the same bill several times; but it was at the Olympia, in Paris, that he shone supreme as a strongman--and at the same time as a weak one. For, in spite of his sovereign strength, Mars was no match for a pair of bright eyes; all a pretty woman had to do was to smile and John would wilt.

And--Paris was Paris.

Marx's strength was prodigious, and he juggled hundreds, and toyed with thousands, of pounds as a child plays with a rattle. He must have weighed in the neighborhood of three hundred pounds, and he walked like a veritable colossus. In fact, he reminded me of a two-footed baby elephant.

Always good-natured, he made a host of friends both in the profession and out of it. After years of professional work he settled down as landlord of a public house in England, where, finally, he was prostrated by a mortal illness. Wishing to die in his native city, he returned to Luxemberg. He did not realize that he was bereft of his enormous strength, and those about him humored him: the doctor and the nurses would pretend that he hurt them when he grasped their hands. He died almost forgotten except by his brother artists, but they (myself among them) built a monument to this good-natured Hercules, whose only care was to entertain.

Among the strongmen that I met during my days with the museums, one whom I found most interesting was William Le Roy, known as The Nail King and The Human Claw-Hammer, whose act appealed to me for its originality. So far as I could learn, it had never been duplicated.

Le Roy was born in Cincinnati, Ohio, October 3rd, 1873. He was about 5 feet 10 inches in height, and well set up. The inordinate strength of his jaws, teeth, and neck, enabled him to push a nail, held between his teeth, through a one-inch board; or to nail together, with his teeth, two 3/4-inch boards. He could draw with his teeth a large nail that had been driven completely through a two-inch plank. Then he would screw an ordinary two-inch screw into a hardwood plank with his teeth, pull it out with his teeth, and then screw it into the plank again and offer $100 to any man who could pull it out with a large pair of pincers which he proffered for the purpose. When he had performed these stunts in various positions, he would bend his body backward till his head pointed toward the floor, and in that position push a nail through a one-inch board held perpendicularly in a metal frame. I saw no chance for trickery in Le Roy's act.

Another nail act was that of Alexander Weyer, who, either by superior strength or by a peculiar knack, could hold a nail between the middle fingers of his right hand with the head against the palm, and drive it through a one-inch board. But since this act did not get him very far either on the road to fame, or toward the big money--he turned to magic and finally became one of the leading Continental magicians, boasting that he was one of the few really expert sleight-of-hand magicians of the world.

I met Weyer at Liege, Belgium, where we had an all-night match with playing cards. He admitted that there were some tricks he did not know, but he claimed that after once seeing any magician work he could duplicate the tricks. On this occasion, however, he was unable to make the boast good.

Another clever performer of those days was Mexican Billy Wells, who worked on the Curio platform. His act was the old stone-breaking stunt, already explained, except that he had the stones broken on his head instead of on his body. He protected his head with a small blanket, which he passed for examination, and this protection seemed excusable, considering that he had to do at least seven shows a day. A strong man from the audience did the real work of the act by swinging the heavy sledge-hammer on the stone, as shown in the accompanying illustration. Usually the stone would be riven by a single blow; but if it was not, Wells would yell, "Harder! harder! hit harder!" until the stone was broken.

The last I saw of Billy was during one of my engagements at the Palace Theater, New York. He was then soliciting orders for some photograph firm, the halcyon days of his big money having faded to a memory. But he had been a good showman and his was one of the best liked working acts in the Curio, as the dime-museum profession was called.

Of all the acts of this nature that I have ever seen I think the most foolhardy was that of an under-sized Italian who lay on his back on the floor and let fall from his hands, extended upward at arm's length heavy weights upon his chest--the silly fool! I said as much to him--and some other things too. His act had little entertainment to show as compared with the pain and danger involved. I do not know what became of him, but I can guess.

Among the museum attractions of those years was a man named Wilson who had the incredible chest expansion of twenty-one inches. This man would allow a strong leather strap, about the size of a trunk-strap, to be buckled round his chest; and then, inflating his lungs, would break it with very little apparent exertion. An imitator, named Herman, worked the side shows for a long time with a similar act, and was fairly successful, although his expansion was only about sixteen inches. The last time I heard of Wilson, he was working in the shipyards at Newport News, Virginia.

Another "Samson," a German, among other sensational feats, such as breaking coins with his fingers, used to flex his muscles and break a dog-chain that had been fastened round the biceps of his right arm. While he was performing at the Aquarium, in London, he issued a challenge. Sandow, then a youth without reputation, accepted the challenge, went upon the stage, defeated him, and, since Samson's act had been the talk of the town, thus brought himself into instant notice, the beginning of a career in which he rose to the top of his profession. After several successful years on the stage, Sandow settled down in London, where I last heard of him as conducting a school of instruction in health and strength methods.

In the tradition of the "Female Sampsons" noted in Chapter Eleven, I recall two strong-women who were notably good; Yucca, who lifted a horse by means of a harness over the shoulders; and La Blanche, who toyed with heavy articles in a most entertaining way. I remember these ladies particularly because both were remarkably good talkers--and I am referring to conversational quality, not to volume.

Lulu Hurst--known variously as The Georgia Magnet, The Electric Girl, The Georgia Wonder, etc.--created a veritable sensation a generation ago by a series of feats which seemed to set the law of gravitation at defiance. Her methods consisted in utilizing the principles of the lever and fulcrum in a manner so cleverly disguised that it appeared to the audience that some supernatural power must be at work. Although she was exposed many times, her success was so marked that several other muscular ladies entered her province with acts that were, in several instances, superior to the original.

One of the cleverest of these was Annie Abbott, who, if I remember rightly, also called herself The Georgia Magnet. She took the act to England and her opening performance at the Alhambra is recorded as one of the three big sensations of the London vaudeville stage of those days. The second sensation was credited to the Bullet-Proof Man. This chap wore a jacket that rifle bullets, fired point-blank, failed to penetrate. The composition of this jacket was a secret, but after the owner's death the garment was ripped open and found to contain-ground glass! The third sensation I must, with all due modesty, (business of bowing) claim for myself.

The Magnet failed to attract after about forty-eight hours, for a keen-witted reporter discovered her methods and promptly published them. The bullet detainer also lasted only a short time only. When my opening added a third sensational surprise, one of the London dailies asked, "Is this going to be another Georgia Magnet fiasco?"

That they were gunning for me is proved by the fact that the same newspaper investigator who exposed the Magnet, came upon the stage of the Alhambra at my press performance--the same stage where the unhappy

Dixie lode-stone had collapsed--and though he brought along an antique

slave iron, which he seemed to think would put an end to my public

career on the spot, I managed to escape in less than three minutes.

When I passed back his irons, he grinned at me and said, "I don't know

how you did it, but you did!" and he shook me cordially by the hand.

Some twenty-six years ago I was on the bill with Mattie Lee Price, who,

though less well known, was in many ways superior to either Miss Hurst

or Miss Abbott. For a time, she was a sensation of the highest order,

for which thanks were largely due to the management of her husband, a

wonderful lecturer and a thorough showman. I think his name was White.

He "sold" the act as no other man has sold an act before or since.

We worked together at Kohl and Middleton's, Chicago, and the following

week at Burton's Museum, Milwaukee; but when we made the next jump I

found that White was not along. They had had a family squabble, the

other apex of the triangle being a circus grafter who "shibbolethed" at

some of the "brace games," which at that time had police protection, so

far as that could be given. He had interfered between the couple, and

was, I am sorry to say, quite successful as an interferer; but he was a

diabolical failure when he attempted to duplicate White's work as

lecturer, and the act, after playing a date or two, sank out of sight and I have heard nothing more of her professionally. Lately I have learned that she died in London in 1900 and is buried in Clements Cemetery, Fulham.

This was one of the most positive demonstrations I have ever seen of the fact that showmanship is the largest factor in putting an act over. Miss Price was a marvelous performer, but without her husband-lecturer she was no longer a drawing card, and dropped to the level of an ordinary entertainer even lower, for her act was no longer even entertaining.

In Chapter Eleven we read Dr. Desaguliers' analysis of the mechanics of what may be called strongmanship. Similar investigations have attended the appearance of more recent performers.

For instance, reviewing one of Lulu Hurst's performances, the New York Times, of July 13th, 1884, said:

The "Phenomenon of the Nineteenth Century," which may be seen nightly at Wallack's, is not so much the famous Georgia girl, with her mysterious muscle, as is the audience which gathers to wonder at her performance. It is a phenomenon of stupidity, and it only goes to show

how willingly people will be fooled, and with what cheerful asininity they will help on their deceivers.

Then follows a description of her performance, which was far from successful, thanks to the efforts of one of the committee, a man described as "Mr. Thomas Johnson, a powerfully-built engraver connected with the Century magazine." Mr. Johnson had evidently caught her secret, and he got the better of her in all the tests in which he was allowed to take part.

A disclosure of the methods employed in a few of her "tests" will serve to convince the reader of the fact that she possessed no supernormal power, the same general principles shown here being used throughout her performance.

These explanations are taken from the French periodical La Nature, in which Mr. Nelson W. Perry thus sums up the attitude of the public in regard to this class of performance: "Electricity is a mysterious agent; therefore, everything mysterious is electric." Of the performance of the Electric Girl this magazine says:

It is a question of a simple application of the elementary principles of the laws of mechanics, chapter of equilibrium.

We propose to point out here a certain number of such artifices and to describe a few of the experiments, utilizing for this purpose the data furnished by Mr. Perry, as well as those resulting from our own observations.

One of the experiments consists in having a man or several men hold a cane or a billiard cue horizontally above the head, as shown in Fig. 1. On pushing with one hand, the girl forces back two or three men, who, in unstable equilibrium and under the oblique action of the thrust exerted, are obliged to fall back. This first experiment is so elementary and infantile that it is not necessary to dwell upon it. In order to show the relative sizes of the persons, the artist has supposed the little girl to be standing on a platform in the first experiment, but in the experiment that we witnessed this platform was rendered useless by the fact that the girl who performed them was of sufficient height to reach the cue by extending her arms and standing on tiptoes.

Next, we have a second and more complex experiment, less easily explained at first sight.

Two men take a stick about three feet in length, and are asked

to hold it firmly in a vertical position. The girl places her hand

against the lower end of the stick, in the position shown, and the two

men are invited to make the latter slide vertically in the girl's hand,

which they are unable to do, in spite of their conscientious and

oft-repeated attempts.

Mr. Perry explains this exercise as follows: The men are requested to

place themselves parallel to each other, and the girl, who stands

opposite them, places the palm of her hand against the stick and turned

toward her. She takes care to place her hand as far as possible from

the hands of the two men, so as to give herself a certain leverage.

She then begins to slide her hand along the stick, gently at first, and

then with an increasing pressure, as if she wished to better the

contact between the stick and her hand. She thus moves it from the

perpendicular and asks the two men to hold it in a vertical position.

This they do under very disadvantageous conditions, seeing the

difference in the length of the arms of the lever. The stress exerted

by the girl is very feeble, because, on the one hand, she has the lever

arm to herself, and, on the other, the action upon her lever arm is a

simple traction. When she feels that the pressure exerted is great enough, she directs the two men to exert a vertical stress strong

enough to cause the stick to descend. They then imagine that they are

exerting a VERTICAL stress, while in reality their stresses are

HORIZONTAL and tend to keep the stick in a vertical position in order

to react against the pressure exerted at the lower end of the stick.

There is evidently a certain vertical component that tends to cause the

stick to descend, but the lateral pressure produces a sufficient

friction between the hand and the stick to support this vertical force

without difficulty. Mr. Perry performed the experiment by placing

himself upon a spring balance and assuming the role of the girl, with

two very strong men as adversaries. All the efforts made to cause the

stick to slide in the open hand failed, and the excess of weight due to

the vertical force always remained less than twenty-five pounds,

despite the very determined and sincere stresses of the two men, who,

unbeknown to themselves, were exerting their strength in a HORIZONTAL

direction.

In the experiment, which recalls to mind the

first one, the two men are requested to hold the stick firmly

and immovable, but the slightest pressure upon the extremity suffices

to move the arms and body of the subject. Such pressure in the first

place is exerted but slightly, and the stresses are gradually increased. Then, all at once, when the force exerted horizontally is as great as possible, and the men are exerting their strength in the opposite direction in order to resist it, the girl abruptly ceases the pressure WITHOUT WARNING and exerts it in the OPPOSITE DIRECTION. Unprepared for this change, the victims lose their equilibrium and find themselves at the mercy of the girl, and so much the more so in proportion as they are stronger and their efforts are greater. The experiment succeeds still better with three than with two men, or with one man.

The experiment represented, where it concerns the easy lifting of a very heavy person, the trick is no less simple. Out of a hundred persons submitted to the experiment, ninety-nine, knowing that the experimenter wishes to lift them and cause them to fall forward, grasp the seat or arms of the chair, and, in endeavoring to resist, make the whole weight of their body bear upon their feet. If they do not do so at the first instant, they do so when they are conscious of the attempts of the girl to raise the seat, and they help therein unconsciously. The experimenter, therefore, needs only to exert a horizontal thrust, without doing any lifting, and such horizontal thrust is facilitated by taking the knees as points of support for her elbows. As soon as a slight movement is effected, the hardest part of the work is over, for it is only necessary for the girl to cease to exert her stresses in order to have the chair fall back or move laterally in one direction or the other. At all events, the equilibrium is destroyed, and, before it is established again, it requires but little dexterity to move the subject about in all directions without a great expenditure of energy. The difficulty is not increased on seating two men, or three men, upon each other's knees since, in the latter case, the third acts as a true counter-poise to the first, and the whole pretty well resembles an apparatus of unstable equilibrium, whose centre of gravity is very high and, consequently, so much more easily displaced.

All these experiments require some little skill and practice, but are attended with no difficulty, and, upon the whole, do not merit the enthusiastic articles that have given the "electric" or "magnetic" girl her European reputation.

Strong people, whether tricksters or genuine athletes, or both, we shall probably have always with us. But with the gradual refinement of the public taste, the demand for such exhibitions as fire-eating, sword-swallowing, glass-chewing, and the whole repertoire of the so-called Human Ostrich, steadily declined, and I recall only one engagement of a performer of this type at a first-class theater in this country during the present generation, and that date was not played.

There was still a considerable demand for these people in the dime museums, until the enormous increase in the number of such houses created a demand for freaks that was far in excess of the supply, and many houses were obliged to close because no freaks were obtainable, even at the enormous increase in salaries then in vogue. The small price of admission, and the fact that feature curios like Laloo or the Tocci Twins drew down seven or eight hundred dollars a week, show that these houses catered to a multitude of people; and not a few of the leading managers of to-day's vaudeville, owe their start in life to the dime museum.

Among the museums that were veritable gold mines, I might mention Epstein's of Chicago; Brandenberg's of Philadelphia; Moore's of Detroit and Rochester; The Sackett and Wiggins Tour; Kohl and Middleton's; Austin and Stone's of Boston; Robinson of Buffalo; Ans Huber's, Globe, Harlem, Worth's, and the Gayety of New York.

The dime museum is but a memory now, and in three generations it will, in all probability, be utterly forgotten. A few of the acts had sufficient intrinsic worth to follow the managers into vaudeville, but these have no part in this chronicle, which has been written rather to commemorate some forms of entertainment over which oblivion threatens to stretch her darkening wings.

THE END

Thank you for reading The Book of Houdini

PUBLISHED BY GALGALIM PRESS

Made in the USA
Middletown, DE
03 August 2023